MLA Style Manual
and
Guide to Scholarly Publishing

MLA STYLE MANUAL

AND GUIDE TO SCHOLARLY PUBLISHING

THIRD EDITION

THE MODERN LANGUAGE ASSOCIATION OF AMERICA

NEW YORK

2008

© 1985, 1998, 2008 by The Modern Language Association of America

First edition 1985. Second edition 1998. Third edition 2008.

Printed in the United States of America

For information about obtaining permission to reprint material from MLA book publications, send your request by mail (see address below), e-mail (permissions@mla.org), or fax (646 458-0030).

Library of Congress Cataloging-in-Publication Data

MLA style manual and guide to scholarly publishing. — 3rd ed.
    p. cm.
    Rev. ed. of: MLA style manual and guide to scholarly publishing / Joseph Gibaldi. 2nd ed. 1998.
    Includes bibliographical references and index.
    ISBN 978-0-87352-297-7 (cloth : alk. paper) — ISBN 978-0-87352-298-4 (large print : alk. paper)
    1. Authorship—Style manuals.   2. Humanities literature—Authorship—Handbooks, manuals, etc.   3. Scholarly publishing—Handbooks, manuals, etc.   4. Academic writing—Handbooks, manuals, etc.   I. Gibaldi, Joseph, 1942– MLA style manual and guide to scholarly publishing.
PN147.G444 2008
808′.027—dc22   2008002894

Text design by Ellen C. Dawson
Typeset in Dante and Egyptienne
Printed on acid-free paper

Published by The Modern Language Association of America
26 Broadway, 3rd floor, New York, New York 10004-1789

CONTENTS

FOREWORD

Domna C. Stanton

"For me, having a style would be worse than being a murderer," declares Olive, one of the central illustrators in Orhan Pamuk's *My Name Is Red* (457). Set in late-sixteenth-century Istanbul, this murder mystery is a serious reflection on the implications of shifts in style: Sultan Murat III orders the great Osman, master of eighty apprentices, to produce a secret book that incorporates the techniques and sensibilities of European "infidels," who dare to draw, not from God's perspective, but from the level of a mangy street dog (191). Does this radical aim to give an impression of reality rather than create the likeness of a painting that follows traditional rules constitute a heresy prompted by Satan, as the murdering Olive claims? If a collective style is the mark of a civilization, would the shift to Western techniques destroy the Eastern conception of art and reduce the East to being a bad imitation of the West (486–89)? Yet for Stork, one of the suspects, this shift might signal a return to even older Arab masters who perceived the world as the "infidels" now do (83). And if individual style is a flaw inimical to the goals inculcated in—beaten into—apprentices by their demanding masters, how can it be that Black, the protagonist, and Osman painstakingly solve the crime by the clipped nostril of a horse the murderer illustrated?[1] Indeed, how is it that one master and not another can produce the clearly recognizable, "absolutely matchless red" that gives Pamuk's novel its title (278)?

The ambiguities that mark Pamuk's own matchless novel and its murderous debates about artistic style may seem to bear little relation to the questions raised by the *MLA Style Manual and Guide to Scholarly Publishing* in its third edition. Still, Pamuk's work dramatizes how significant professional, cultural, societal, and political issues are embedded in shifts in prescriptions for style, and this manual is no exception. To be sure, in the *MLA Style Manual* style does not include all aspects of creative production that concern the mode or form of expression; it does not even encompass rhetorical tropes, which treatises of proper style once contained. This manual focuses on disciplinary norms in the presentation of scholarship for publication, including conventions in spelling, punctuation, italics, capitalization, quotations, and most especially documentation and source reference, in the bibliography, text, and notes. The volume is indeed a manual or guide containing, as *Webster's* indicates, "in concise form the principles, rules, and directions needed for the mastery of an art, science, or skill" ("Manual").[2]

That presentational conventions embody rules of apprenticeship for attaining mastery is as true in scholarship today as it was in early modern Ottoman manuscript illustration. In every academic or artistic community or discipline, novices must master rules and conventions to gain essential skills and to establish and maintain membership in the order. We scholars may not view ourselves as "miraculously inspired, eagle-eyed, iron-willed, elegant-wristed, sensitive-spirited . . . calligraphers" and would certainly deny being masters living "half-saintly, half-senile lives" (Pamuk 60, 64–65), who succumb to blindness after staring at an illustration for weeks on end, eventually mingling their souls with the eternity of a picture (411). But, in a less exalted vein, a scholarly life in the academy is a calling, and its masters remain apprentices for life.

The title of the *MLA Style Manual* suggests that the conventions to be mastered are permanent. In fact, however, and despite their apparent fixity at any point of time, these protocols are historical, cultural, and contingent phenomena and thus provisional and subject to change. The note—footnote or endnote—emblematically reveals this intrinsic contingency. Historians of the footnote, such as Anthony Grafton and Chuck Zerby,[3] have documented that its earliest use coincided with the advent of the printed book (Zerby 18), in marginal glosses and annotations of the Bible and of esteemed secular works, such as the *Aeneid* (Grafton 27). Over time, variations in the forms and uses of the note became pronounced in humanistic fields. Thus, the grammarian's gloss differed from the marginal note in ecclesiastical history, just as footnotes that early modern playwrights (such as Ben Jonson) or novelists (such as Mme de Villedieu) used to assert their historical authority or to prove that their fictions were true differed from footnotes subversively deployed during the Enlightenment (in the *Encyclopédie*, for example) to articulate what the articles themselves could not state for fear of censure. The modern scholarly footnote was established in nineteenth-century Germany in the field of history, according to Grafton, only to be systematically assaulted and ridiculed, in Zerby's view, since the dawn of the twentieth century (113). In a gentle, ironic critique of the sometimes annoying, distracting, or interruptive effect of the note—which this foreword may well embody—Noël Coward observed that reading footnotes resembled having to go downstairs to answer the door while making love.[4]

Whether or not Zerby is right in asserting the existence of a conspiracy to eliminate footnotes and thus the need for an international commission to preserve them (4, 150), market forces in the economies of academic publishing are pressuring scholars to reduce their number and heft. This trend is bound to have a nefarious effect on scholarship. For notes essentially make critical exchange possible. They show how a scholar enters into ongoing intellectual conversations (Grafton 234), how a scholar engages with the primary issues and problems under debate in the past or the present, and in this way they help sustain and renew a community of discourse. Footnoting—or "endnoting"—also reveals how a scholar interacts with specific authorities in the field(s) that the work engages. By that token, noting is also a way for young scholars to gain credibility and to achieve authority in their own right. As Grafton suggests, footnoting is "bound up, in modern life, with the ideology and the technical practices of a profession. . . . Learning to make footnotes forms part of this modern version of apprenticeship" (4); it gives legitimacy to a scholar, much like membership in a guild of old. The failure to master this techne and the consequent judgment that one is not a good enough practitioner can result, in extreme cases, in condemnation by one's peers—and by authorities—for plagiarism and in symbolic or real expulsion from the profession. Notes can thus have career-threatening, if not murderous, consequences. In this light, noting is at once a protective, an authoritarian, and a companionate techne, both a freeing and a constraining cultural and historical practice.

The note is only one of the many signs that scholars emit as members of a particular reading and writing community.[5] It has been as subject to change as other conventions and key concepts, including scholarship and publication, notions that dominate the title of the *MLA Style Manual and Guide to Scholarly Publishing*. The 2006 report of the MLA Task Force on Evaluating Scholarship for Tenure and Promotion, for instance, advocates a more capacious conception of scholarship than was accepted in the past, one that does not merely embrace aspects of teaching and of service—thereby integrating the triad of scholarship, teaching, and service traditionally viewed as consisting of clearly demarcated parts—but that also transcends the reduction of scholarship to research and publication. Following the work of John Guillory, a task force member, this report defines research as only one component of humanistic scholarship, which can include archival, artifactual, and textual objects that involve human matters. In this acceptation, scholarship also requires reinterpretation (analysis or critique that revises or reconfigures what was previously thought), as well as a moment of reflection or theorization—an examination of concepts and arguments as they arise from and are altered by the practices of interpretation and research (Guillory 30). Moreover, in the task force's understanding, scholarship should not be equated with publication, which is basically a means of making scholarship public and should not be the raison d'être of scholarship.

In promoting an expansive redefinition of scholarship, the task force report emphasizes the need to rethink the dominance of the scholarly monograph. In an ever-growing number of institutional types, as the report's survey of 1,340 colleges and universities confirmed, the monograph is upheld as the only form of scholarship and publication acceptable for demonstrating mastery in one's chosen field and thus for achieving tenure. We tend to forget in this, as in other forms of scholarship, that a norm is a historical phenomenon subject to change: the monograph, for example, has emerged as the chief requisite for scholarly legitimation in the profession only since the 1970s. However, the monograph is clearly not the sole—or necessarily the best—form of scholarly communication; there can be equal value in a book of linked essays as well as in a stand-alone article. Edited collections of articles, critical editions, annotated translations of important primary texts, reviews and review essays, articles written for a general audience, trade books, textbooks, and pedagogically useful monographs can meet the highest standards of scholarship.

This is equally true of publications and other professional work in electronic form. Digital scholarship is becoming pervasive in the humanities, as the increased emphasis on electronic publications in this volume, when compared with the second edition of the *MLA Style Manual*, clearly shows. It is generating new forms of publication and dissemination—ranging from Web sites and e-journals to print-on-demand books—as well as significant new modes of scholarship, including digital archives and humanities databases. New media make new forms of scholarship possible, and scholarly quality can be assessed in those forms as rigorously as it is in print media. As new sources and instruments for knowing develop, the meaning of scholarship must expand to remain relevant to changing times.

Aside from changes in the definition of publication that have devolved from digital technology, there has been a notable shift in the border between what is and what is not a valid—or authoritative—scholarly style, which includes linguistic, rhetorical, structural, and evidentiary protocols of scholarship.[6] The 1970s, under the influence of structuralism and, more broadly, (social) science conventions, saw a mathematization of scholarly discourse in the humanities, but today the numbers, figures, formulas, and graphs characteristic of that decade have all but disappeared from the texture of books and articles. A number of broad factors, encompassing, among others, the feminist demystification of the universal *we* and of the abstracted, impersonal, authoritative male voice ubiquitous in scholarship before the 1970s, as well as the poststructuralist recognition that all knowledge and speakers are situated, have converged to make personal criticism, for instance, a significant feature of writing in humanities scholarship today.

In an essay that brings into dialogue deconstruction and feminism, Paul de Man's "The Resistance to Theory" and Margo Culley and Catherine Portuges's *Gendered Subjects: The Dynamics of Feminist Teaching*, Barbara Johnson writes that feminist theory aims

> to reintroduce the personal, or at least the positional, as a way of disseminating authority and decomposing the false

universality of patriarchally institutionalized meanings. Not only has female personal experience tended to be excluded from the discourse of knowledge, but the realm of the personal itself has been coded as female and devalued for that reason. In opposition, therefore, many of the essays of the volume [*Gendered Subjects*] consciously assume a first-person autobiographical stance toward the question of pedagogical theory. (69)

This type of feminist criticism—in fact, all personal criticism—has been criticized as "moi-ism," to cite Nancy K. Miller's ironic term in *But Enough about Me: Why We Read Other People's Lives*, published in the Columbia University Press series Gender and Culture. But Miller argues that reading a memoir, the most popular form of personal criticism within and outside the academy today, is "an excellent antidote to narcissism and nostalgia," because it invites both identification and disidentification (2, 9). A combination of the scholarly and the personal, this mode of criticism is a hybrid genre: Miller's memoir interweaves feminist theory, a historical-cultural study of the period 1950–90, and an analysis of a particular type of discourse.

Hybrid texts that aim to go beyond the traditional topics and rhetoric of scholarship and to reach broader reading communities are often presented as writerly projects for breaking down the confines of academic discourse. Marianna Torgovnick advocates "experimental critical writing" because it let her "out of the protective cage of the style I had mastered—a style I now call the thus-and-therefore style" (9), that careful, judicious style we pass on to our graduate students when we train them "to stay within the boundaries, both stylistically and conceptually"(10). She promotes experimental critical writing for its capacity to reach a larger audience, to "go somewhere new," and to stimulate "the profession to grow and to change" (8, 10). In "Being the Subject and the Object: Reading African-American Women's Novels," an essay that points to a similar frustration with scholarly discourse, Barbara Christian famously asked, "How does one respond to a language that is tonality, dance to these voices without mutilating them and turning them into logical progressions, mere intellectual concepts? How does one shimmy back to forms that soar beyond philosophical discourse or jargon?" (200).

The critique of academic style from within the institution and the experimentation with hybrid modes have had a less constructive counterpart, primarily outside the academy, in condemnations of purportedly incomprehensible jargon in humanities scholarship, what the editors of *Philosophy and Literature* dubbed "bad writing" in the notorious award they conferred annually from 1995 to 1998. The ideal of clarity propounded in such censure is associated with familiar, accessible discourse that can communicate widely. However, this association does not recognize that scholarship in the humanities involves rigorous definition and argument that may not be accessible to a lay audience or to journalists (Warner 116). As Michael Warner points out, there are different kinds of clarity for different audiences at different historical moments, and each kind is predicated on shared conventions and common references (115); what is clear to one reading community may be unclear to another. Besides, some readers, notably scholars, may prefer nuance, subtlety, and complexity and embrace what William Butler Yeats called "the fascination of what's difficult."[7] For, as David Palumbo-Liu has argued, new scholarly concerns or problems may call for discursive strategies and forms of linguistic expression that do not uphold a clear and distinct Cartesian idiom (175); indeed, to challenge preexisting ways of thinking, writers may feel impelled to defamiliarize language or to create a linguistic frame of "unknowing," to use Judith Butler's term ("Values" 214). Because views about reality are sedimented in everyday parlance, because language bodies forth norms, writers who call the status quo into question, Butler emphasizes, may engage language in nonconventional ways (200–01). Linguistic difficulty may thus be necessary for doing the demanding work of critical thinking (209).

The existence of different types and styles of scholarly discourse is recognized in a nomenclature that includes *scholarship*, *research*, *criticism*, *theory*, and *action research* and the corresponding terms for their practitioners: *scholar, researcher, intellectual, public intellectual, critic*, and *essayist*. The difficulty of distinguishing clearly each of these activities and practitioners from the others—in fact, their overlapping or hybrid nature—finds a correlative in the growing porousness or fluidity of disciplines over the past thirty years and in the defining presence of interdisciplinarity on United States campuses and its institutionalization in a number of seminal programs: women's, African American, postcolonial, subaltern, and queer studies, for instance, as well as American, Atlantic, and many other area or regional studies. Scholars can vary from one discursive practice or style to another depending on their goals, their circumstances, and the disciplinary, interdisciplinary, or general audience for a particular piece of writing.

That accepted definitions of publication, scholarship, and scholarly writing have shifted over time also means that scholars can work collaboratively and proactively with others to change the contingent and provisional protocols of scholarly presentation that the *MLA Style Manual* lays out. To be sure, a disciplinary community, by its nature, has a conservative bent and a constitutive modus operandi that excludes some procedures and includes others. But it is also the case, as Butler has argued broadly, that academic norms—of which presentational protocols are an integral part—are always being assessed, revised, rearticulated, and remade under pressure or in response to intellectual challenges, and in that process they produce new knowledge. Dissent from existing academic protocols can thus inaugurate new disciplinary and cross-disciplinary paradigms, Butler continues, and is thus "essential to the dynamic and historical life of academic norms, constituting the basis of a reflexive and critical approach that disciplines must take toward their own methodologies and customary modes of inquiry if they are not to stagnate as dogma or become calcified as rote formulas" ("Academic Norms" 114). Typically, such norms are in tension with one another, and these conflicts often define the theme and subject of academic work. As a result, innovation in a field "depends in part on elaborating new norms over and against established fields of knowledge," Butler observes, just as "professional norms are . . . often questioned and redefined by the work itself" (115, 112). This view in no way denies the importance of various kinds and levels of norms—including protocols of presentation—in situating and evaluating a body of scholarly work (114, 120).[8] But it does encourage us to engage norms as an integral aspect of critical thinking, interpretation, and innovation in academic work. We can be—and should become—conscious actors in such vital historical practices rather than defer to authorities or fear change as an assault on the existing system, even on civilization, as all but one or two apprentices and masters do in Pamuk's *My Name*

Is Red.[9] The *MLA Style Manual and Guide to Scholarly Publishing* should be read in that spirit: an open book that we can rewrite in future editions, for future generations.

NOTES

1. Hypothetically, it might be possible for a work to be so fully aligned with a dominant aesthetic or technique and its style so utterly naturalized in the eyes of the beholders that the style seems invisible, but Pamuk's novel suggests otherwise.

2. As the full title confirms—*MLA Style Manual and Guide to Scholarly Publishing*—this manual is also a guide: "something (as a guidebook . . . or instruction manual) that provides a person with guiding information" ("Guide").

3. The aim Grafton articulates for his "necessarily speculative essay" is "to find out when, where, and why historians adopted their distinctively modern form of narrative architecture," which he describes as "a curious arcade with its ornate *piano mobile* and its open bottom floor that offers glimpses of so many alluring wares" (33). As I go on to show, Zerby advocates saving the footnote from extinction at this moment of writing history.

4. Cited in Grafton 69–70. It could be argued that the historic shift from footnotes to endnotes in MLA style, as well as the adoption of parenthetical documentation in the text and a separate works-cited list, helps relieve the problem that Coward derides: those who want to read without interruption can do so, later looking up citational details and checking the endnotes for substantive elements of scholarship that suggest other avenues of research or tangential implications of the main argument. This "front door" and "back door" distinction allows scholars to address different reading demands. Of course, the conversation in the endnote should not wander off the topic or, worse, overwhelm and repulse the reader with excessive information, exhibiting what William Germano would call "footnote madness" (106–10)—hence the *MLA Style Manual*'s recommendation to avoid "lengthy discussions that divert the reader's attention from the primary text" (7.5.1).

5. Another such techne is bibliography, a historical and contingent practice subject to differences (as a comparison of the styles recommended in this manual and in *The Chicago Manual of Style* shows) and to change (as evolving norms for referencing texts online suggest).

6. The *MLA Style Manual* recognizes that "[t]he publication of scholarship takes many forms, depending on field, objective, medium, and audience" (1.1).

7. It is fair to say that there are no comparable expectations of accessibility for the sciences. The idea of a scholarly humanities discipline that departs from traditional, gentle(manly) humanistic writing is offensive to some journalists and pundits, who are the most vocal critics of scholarly difficulty, cast as incomprehensibility.

8. As Butler goes on to argue, the "very changeability and internal dissension [among standards and norms] implies that . . . we constantly have

to give reasons for invoking and commending the version of academic norms that we choose" (120).

9. In 1996 the American Association of University Professors changed the language of its statement on academic freedom to protect those who are skeptical about the foundations of their disciplines. See Scott 176.

WORKS CITED

Butler, Judith. "Academic Norms, Contemporary Challenges: A Reply to Robert Post on Academic Freedom." *Academic Freedom after September 11.* Ed. Beshara Doumani. New York: Zone, 2006. 107–42. Print.

———. "Values of Difficulty." Culler and Lamb 199–215.

Christian, Barbara. "Being the Subject and the Object: Reading African-American Women's Novels." *Changing the Subject: The Making of Feminist Literary Criticism.* Ed. Gayle Greene and Coppélia Kahn. London: Routledge, 1993. 195–200. Print.

Culler, Jonathan, and Kevin Lamb, eds. *Just Being Difficult? Academic Writing in the Public Arena.* Stanford: Stanford UP, 2003. Print.

Germano, William. *From Dissertation to Book.* Chicago: U of Chicago P, 2005. Print.

Grafton, Anthony. *The Footnote: A Curious History.* Cambridge: Harvard UP, 1997. Print.

"Guide." Entry 1. *Webster's Third New International Dictionary.* 1981. Print.

Guillory, John. "Evaluating Scholarship in the Humanities: Principles and Procedures." *ADE Bulletin* 137 (2005): 18–35. Print.

Johnson, Barbara. "Deconstruction, Feminism, and Pedagogy." *Teaching Literature: What Is Needed Now.* Cambridge: Harvard UP, 1988. 67–72. Print.

"Manual." Entry 2. *Webster's Third New International Dictionary.* 1981. Print.

Miller, Nancy K. *But Enough about Me: Why We Read Other People's Lives.* New York: Columbia UP, 2002. Print. Gender and Culture Ser.

MLA Task Force on Evaluating Scholarship for Tenure and Promotion. *Report of the MLA Task Force on Evaluating Scholarship for Tenure and Promotion. Modern Language Association.* MLA, Dec. 2006. Web. 1 Nov. 2007.

Palumbo-Liu, David. "The Morality of Form; or, What's 'Bad' about 'Bad' Writing?" Culler and Lamb 171–80.

Pamuk, Orhan. *My Name Is Red.* Trans. Erdağ M. Göknar. London: Faber, 2001. Print.

Scott, Joan W. "Academic Freedom as an Ethical Practice." *The Future of Academic Freedom.* Ed. Louis Menand. Chicago: U of Chicago P, 1996. 163–80. Print.

Torgovnick, Marianna. "Experimental Critical Writing." *ADE Bulletin* 96 (1990): 8–10. Print.

Warner, Michael. "Styles of Intellectual Publics." Culler and Lamb 106–25.

Yeats, William Butler. "The Fascination of What's Difficult." *The Collected Poems of W. B. Yeats.* New York: Macmillan, 1959. 91–92. Print.

Zerby, Chuck. *The Devil's Details: A History of Footnotes.* Montpelier: Invisible Cities, 2002. Print.

PREFACE

David G. Nicholls

For nearly twenty-five years, the *MLA Style Manual and Guide to Scholarly Publishing* has been the key guide for scholars in the humanities. In contrast to the *MLA Handbook for Writers of Research Papers*, which provides guidance for students in secondary school and college, the *MLA Style Manual* addresses graduate students and scholarly authors. The volume details the conventions of scholarly writing, describes the most common format for the preparation of manuscripts, and explains the MLA's recommendations on the documentation of sources. Users will find a full description of the protocols for submitting manuscripts to publishers for review and publication. Other resources include an extensive discussion of legal issues in scholarly publishing and an overview of the special requirements for formatting theses and dissertations. This edition builds on material in the first two editions, yet it is also fully updated and presents significant revisions—especially to MLA documentation style.

MLA style was first codified in 1951, when William Riley Parker, the association's executive director, compiled "The MLA Style Sheet" for publication in *PMLA*. The initial guidelines gained wide acceptance because they established the consensus practice among scholarly authors and publishers in the humanities. Over the years, MLA style has been revised and refined in response to trends in publishing and research practices. Advisory committees composed of MLA members regularly review the documentation style and propose changes, which are implemented in new editions of the *MLA Style Manual* and the *MLA Handbook* by publishing professionals on the MLA staff. Most recently, the Executive Council appointed the Ad Hoc

Committee on MLA Style (comprising David Bartholomae, chair; Donald Paul Haase; Eric S. Rabkin; David S. Shields; and Helene C. Williams) to study the format for documenting electronic publications. The committee concluded that MLA style placed a heavy burden on authors who cite electronic sources, requiring them to provide information in excess of that needed to find the sources, such as multiple dates (e.g., of print publication, of online posting, and of access), as well as information of dubious usefulness (e.g., URLs). In its report to the Executive Council, submitted in 2005, the committee defined a basic principle of citation: a citation should accurately identify the source consulted by the author. Accurate identification includes establishing the source's authority and accessibility and the context in which the author consulted it (e.g., on the Web). In addition, the committee called for a principle of sufficiency to be incorporated into MLA style: an entry in the list of works cited should present just enough information to identify the source accurately.

When MLA style was first developed, nearly every source of scholarship was a printed document. As electronic sources came into use, MLA style presented additional guidelines for recording features of them. Print continued to be considered the default medium of publication, and information for works in other media (e.g., publications on CD-ROM, articles in online databases) was added to the elements normally recorded for print sources. Given the ubiquity of electronic sources in contemporary research, it is now clear that we can no longer assume a common, default medium for the sources of scholarship. This revision of MLA style adds the medium of publication as an element of every entry in the list of works cited. While this new requirement will expand entries for print publications, it allows the recording of somewhat less information about publications on the Web. For reasons outlined in 6.7, the *MLA Style Manual* no longer recommends the inclusion of URLs in the works-cited-list entries for Web publications. There are additional refinements throughout chapter 6, mostly aimed at simplifying and standardizing the recommendations. Because issue as well as volume numbers are useful for finding articles in electronic databases, the manual now calls for inclusion of both for every journal article in the list of works cited. With the new attention to the medium of publication came adjustments to a number of subsections in

6.8, "Citing Additional Common Sources," addressing music, the visual arts, and other forms and media.

Though documentation style received a great deal of attention in this revision, other sections of the MLA Style Manual are significantly revised and updated here. The first chapter, on scholarly publishing, responds to the call from the MLA Task Force on Evaluating Scholarship for Tenure and Promotion to extend the definition of scholarship to encompass more forms than the monograph and the scholarly article: it gives expanded attention to reviews, review essays, and scholarly editions, among others. The chapter on legal issues in scholarly publishing is thoroughly updated. Several new guidelines in other chapters concern the preparation of manuscripts. For example, the manual now assumes the use of italics, rather than underlining, for text meant to be italicized in publication and provides new instructions on the preparation of figures, tables, and captions. Chapter 5 discusses considerations for students publishing their theses and dissertations electronically.

Each edition of the MLA Style Manual is created through the collaboration of many persons, as previous lists of acknowledgments make clear. The first edition was written by Walter S. Achtert and Joseph Gibaldi, and the second was prepared by Gibaldi. When I took on the task of writing the third edition, I knew that I would be carrying over much material from the previous one while introducing new material as well. I decided that the new edition should be considered a product of corporate authorship. Although I was responsible for revising or writing the entire volume, I had a great deal of assistance with my work. The chapter on legal issues received the most outside support. Arthur F. Abelman, an attorney, contributed the original chapter on this topic, for the second edition. In planning this edition, I commissioned a reading of Abelman's chapter from Daphne Ireland, director of intellectual property and documentary publishing at Princeton University Press and chair of the copyright committee of the American Association of University Presses. I then turned to Gloria C. Phares, a partner at Patterson Belknap Webb and Tyler LLP, who updated and revised the entire chapter and contributed new passages in several areas. For the preparation of other chapters, members of the MLA's book-publications department, which I direct, provided research assistance: Joshua Shanholtzer helped with chapter 4, Sonia Kane with chapter 5,

James C. Hatch with chapters 6 and 7, and Lucy Anderson with the index. Marcia Henry answered questions about permissions, and Joseph Gibaldi explained procedures used in the development of the previous editions. In the MLA's editorial department, headed by Judy Goulding, staff members played important roles in developing and producing the volume. Eric Wirth served as principal copyeditor, although his role was greater: I consulted him throughout the writing and revision of the manuscript. Laurie Russell assisted in preparing the index. Others in the department who provided advice and support include Judith Altreuter, Angela Gibson, David Hodges, Elizabeth Holland, Michael Kandel, Margit Longbrake, and Sara Pastel. Barbara Chen, director of bibliographic information services and editor of the *MLA International Bibliography*, reviewed sections on electronic databases and helped identify new sources of examples. Rosemary G. Feal, the MLA executive director, reviewed the entire manuscript and made comments and suggestions. MLA members make important contributions to all association publications, and this one is no exception. In addition to the assistance of the Ad Hoc Committee on MLA Style, noted above, I benefited from the counsel of the Committee on Scholarly Editions (on the description of kinds of editions) and the Committee on the Status of Graduate Students in the Profession (on the submission of electronic theses and dissertations). Officers of the Council of Editors of Learned Journals, an allied organization of the MLA, assisted in describing their mediation service. Heidi Byrnes provided advice on German spelling. Stephen E. Tabachnick advised me on documenting graphic narratives. The staff hears regularly from users of MLA style, and the following correspondents submitted suggestions or queries that are addressed in this edition of the *MLA Style Manual*: Damon Abilock, Grace Boyce, Laura Hammons, James L. Harner, Caroline E. Jones, Jan Phillips, Thomas G. Rice, Howard A. Rodman, and Mark Ziomeck. Last but certainly not least, this volume benefited from the leadership of Domna C. Stanton, MLA president in 2005. The work of the Task Force on Evaluating Scholarship for Tenure and Promotion, which she chaired, inspired many of the revisions here. She also graciously provided the foreword for this volume. I thank everyone who supported me in the creation of this new edition.

1

SCHOLARLY PUBLISHING

—————————————— 1.1 ——————————————
SCHOLARS AND SCHOLARLY PUBLISHING

To publish is to make public. When scholars make their work public, they educate, enlighten, stimulate learning, and further intellectual pursuit, serving the academic community and society at large. Scholarly publication is also often used within the academy as a measure when professional advancement is decided.

The publication of scholarship takes many forms, depending on field, objective, medium, and audience. Teaching is probably the most common way of making scholarship public. Other ways are contributing to an electronic discussion group and offering a presentation at a local, regional, national, or international meeting. This book primarily concerns itself with the more formal modes of academic publishing in the field of language and literature, especially journal articles and books. It also discusses such forms as reviews, review essays, translations, scholarly editions, anthologies, reference works, theses, dissertations, and pedagogical materials. This chapter provides guidance for authors on the protocols for working with the two major outlets for scholarly communication, journals and presses.

Scholarly publication is a collaborative enterprise that comprises diverse and complex relations among numerous persons besides you, as the author, and your reader. Academic authors normally submit their work to editors, who in turn customarily seek the advice and judgment of other scholars—for example, consultant readers (specialists in the field addressed by the author) and members of editorial boards. Various other persons, though perhaps less visible to the author, also play vital roles in making scholarship public; these include publishing professionals in areas like copyediting, design, typesetting, printing, electronic production, and marketing. Such intermediary figures add value to the author's work by enhancing its intellectual quality and communicative presentation and by helping to bring it to the attention of its potential audience.

Publishers are as intrinsic to the scholarly community as academic institutions and professional organizations are. While institutions provide a forum for teaching and organizations plan meetings that primarily promote the oral exchange of ideas and information among attendees, publishers make possible the dissemination of scholarship in finished forms to varied and broadly dispersed audiences. Book and journal publication, then, exists on a continuum with teaching and convention presentations. Scholars turn to a publisher when they believe they can make a contribution to scholarship that warrants wider circulation than the classroom and the conference hall permit. And libraries, by acquiring scholarly publications, preserve the record of scholarship and make it accessible to present and future readers.

1.2
REFEREED AND NONREFEREED PUBLICATIONS

Academic journals and presses can be divided into two broad categories: those that seek and rely on the advice of referees or consultant readers and those that do not. The editor of a refereed journal asks specialist readers to review a manuscript before it is accepted or rejected. Each consultant reads the work and sends the editor a report evaluating the manuscript and, in most instances, either recommending or not recommending it for publication. The editor, editorial staff, or editorial board—whichever is appropriate to the journal—refers to the consultants' evaluations and recommendations when deciding whether to publish the article. Most academic presses follow like procedures, soliciting reviews by experts before deciding on publication of a book manuscript or other scholarly work. (For more on the refereeing of articles and books, see 1.4.5 and 1.5.6, respectively.)

A nonrefereed journal, by contrast, generally publishes a manuscript without specialist review, as do some presses. The use of referees normally adds several months to the time between completion of the manuscript and its publication. Although it is desirable to get your work published as soon as possible, there are many advantages to seeking a publisher committed to a policy of refereeing.

Specialist readings constitute professional service to authors. As experts in the work's general subject, reviewers can identify scholarly errors and omissions and thus save the author the embarrassment of having a flawed manuscript reach publication. In addition, consultants often offer suggestions for revision that improve manuscripts or help make them publishable.

Academic institutions, moreover, invariably attach greater prestige to works that underwent formal review than to those that did not. Hiring, promotion, and tenure committees, whose members are frequently not specialists in the candidate's field, almost always assign a refereed publication significantly more professional standing and scholarly authority than they do a nonrefereed publication. Most scholars believe that the assistance derived from referees' reports and the value and prestige conferred on a published work that successfully passes through rigorous critical examination more than compensate for the publication delay that consultant evaluation necessitates.

1.3
DECIDING TO SUBMIT A MANUSCRIPT

Professional circumstances tend to press scholars to publish early and abundantly. Before you consider submitting a manuscript for publication, however, no matter the stage of your career, you will do well to ask a number of colleagues, especially other experts in your field, to read and assess your work, including revised versions of it; to advise you on whether the manuscript is appropriate and ready for publication; and to recommend possible publishers. These readers are likely to provide useful comments on intellectual and scholarly issues and on such matters as the organization and development of ideas, the coherence of the discussion, the cogency of the argument, and the clarity of expression. Many scholars share their work at conferences, workshops, and reading groups before seeking publication. Some scholars also place drafts—clearly labeled as works in progress—on the Internet and invite comments from interested readers.

You should not consider a work ready for submission to a publisher, moreover, until you have given it a final editorial review that includes, among other things, confirming the accuracy of all paraphrases, quotations, bibliographic references, and textual citations. Your manuscript should also follow the technical specifications discussed in chapter 4 of this manual.

You should be aware that most publishers adhere to a house editorial style, which dictates such features of scholarly presentation as the documentation system and mechanics of writing. Chapters 6 and 7 offer an authoritative and comprehensive explanation of the style followed by the Modern Language Association of America.

The submitted manuscript should also contain clear copies of illustrations you want to publish with the work. It is useful to consider at an early stage whether you will need permission to reproduce any quotations, photographs, charts, or other material that you take from others (see 2.2.13–14) and whether such permission will be easily obtained.

The author's concerns before submitting a manuscript, then, are many and wide-ranging: they include not only intellectual and scholarly but also stylistic and technical questions. Attention to this full range of authorial considerations before submission will facilitate the passage of a manuscript through the publishing process.

The next two sections discuss the typical procedures for placing a scholarly manuscript with a journal (1.4) and with an academic press (1.5). Because the two paths are not completely dissimilar, there is some inevitable repetition in the two sections that will permit you to consult these sections independently from each other. Particular attention is paid to the two most prevalent forms of scholarly publication, articles and books.

1.4
PLACING A MANUSCRIPT WITH A JOURNAL

1.4.1   SCHOLARLY JOURNALS

The scope of scholarly journals ranges from the broadly focused to the more specific. At one end of the spectrum, for example, is a journal like *PMLA*, which, according to its current statement of editorial policy, publishes "essays of interest to those concerned with the study of language and literature" and is "receptive to a variety of topics, whether general or specific, and to all scholarly methods and theoretical perspectives." Most journals, however, are more specialized, focusing on a specific literature, language, culture, period, genre, ethnicity, theory, methodology, theme, author, and so forth.

The editorial staff of a scholarly journal is usually identified on the copyright page, in the opening pages of each printed issue, in the opening section of an electronic journal, or as part of the journal's home page on the Internet. The roster typically designates at least one editor of the journal, and other persons may be listed as, for example, associate editor, book review editor, managing editor, manuscript editor, production editor, and editorial assistant.

The page also likely names the members of the journal's editorial board, sometimes given a title such as "advisory board" or "board of editorial consultants." This group of scholars, which may range in number from a half dozen to several dozen, assists the editorial staff in setting the direction of the journal as well as in evaluating submissions. Depending on the journal, publication decisions are made by the editor or editors or by the editorial board, sometimes in conjunction with the staff.

Most scholarly journals are associated with a sponsoring organization—a college, university, learned society, library, museum, foundation, research institute, or government agency. In addition, some journals have business affiliations with academic presses: the journal staff supplies the copy for each issue, and the press produces and distributes the publication.

TYPES OF SCHOLARLY ARTICLES

The typical issue of a scholarly journal in language and literature is devoted primarily to articles containing new research and original interpretations of texts and data. Some journals also publish book reviews, review essays, reviews of research, and translations. Other contributions include letters to the editor commenting on articles previously published in the journal or on general matters, interviews, notes, conference proceedings, and bibliographies. Most published articles are unsolicited, although some articles and even whole issues may be commissioned by the journal. Book reviews, review essays, reviews of research, and translations are almost always assigned.

Book Reviews. When commissioning book reviews, journal editors normally set the format, length, and coverage. A book review tends to be devoted to a single work, which is documented at the beginning (or sometimes at the end) of the review, usually with more information than a reference in a works-cited list gives. Besides the name of the author, title, city of publication, publisher, and date of publication, the reviewer often records the number of pages, price, and, if the book is not published by a major press, ordering information. If you would like to review books for a journal, you should write to the editor or the book review editor, if there is one, indicating your interest, your field of expertise, and your qualifications.

Review Essays and Reviews of Research. Review essays are extended book reviews, usually covering more than one recent book and giving full publication information for each work discussed. Review essays normally allow the writer greater compass to describe and compare the works under consideration and to place them in perspective. Reviews of research are extended review essays that describe, evaluate, and indicate the importance of significant works in a specific field or on a specific issue published over a broader period of time, often helping to set the terms of discussion for future work in the field. Normally longer than a book review and a review essay, the review of research generally provides only essential bibliographic information for sources (e.g., author, title, city of publication, publisher, and date of publication but not number of pages, price, and so forth). If you wish to contribute a review essay or a review of research, you should write to an appropriate journal to inquire if there is interest in such a contribution before you embark on it.

Other Features. Many journals also present bibliographies, exhibition reviews, interviews, little-known primary sources, performance reviews, and translations of articles and creative works originally published in other languages. If you are interested in submitting such a work to a journal that does not provide guidelines on doing so, you should write to the editor to see if the journal is willing to consider it.

1.4.3   SELECTING A JOURNAL

One of the keys to successful scholarly publishing is locating the right publishers. Your research will doubtless bring you in contact with numerous journals in your field. Colleagues might direct you to additional suitable journals. To learn of others, consult bibliographies and similar reference works in the discipline, library catalogs, and directories of periodicals.

The *MLA Directory of Periodicals*, a companion to the electronic *MLA International Bibliography*, is a guide to thousands of journals and book series that address the scholarship on and teaching of language, literature, film, and folklore. Each entry in this online directory provides contact information, a description of editorial aims, submission requirements, and information on subscriptions and advertisements. The entry includes the mailing address, e-mail address, telephone and fax numbers, and date of first publication, among other general information. The data on subscriptions include frequency of publication, circulation, and availability in electronic media (URLs and full-text providers may be noted). The entry describes the editorial scope of the periodical and gives such information as whether it reviews books, what languages submissions may be written in, and what its policy on author anonymity is (see 1.4.4). The entry gives specifications concerning submission, under categories like the following ones: restrictions on contributors, desired length of articles, editorial style followed, number of manuscript copies required, time between submission and publication decision, time between acceptance and publication, number of reviewers used, number of articles submitted to the periodical in a year, and number of articles published in a year. The *Directory* allows you to search all its entries by such topics as subject scope, sponsoring organizations, editorial personnel, and languages published. *Ulrich's International Periodicals Directory* is another useful source.

Once you have identified potential journals, you should consult recent issues of each to determine its nature and quality and to learn about any recent changes in editorial policy, about the editors' special interests, and about details of submission procedures. You might also consult with colleagues whose work has appeared in any of the journals to find out whether their experience was professionally satisfactory.

Journals frequently devote entire issues to specific topics. Editors planning special issues may seek submissions by announcing the topics in advance. (Editors' calls for papers can be found, for example, on the MLA Web site and in relevant electronic discussion groups and information lists.)

1.4.4   SUBMITTING A MANUSCRIPT TO A JOURNAL

In submitting a manuscript, follow the instructions in the journal concerning such matters as the number of copies required, submission fees (uncommon in the humanities), and any information you are expected to provide along with the manuscript. Be sure that your manuscript falls within the range of lengths requested and follows the appropriate editorial style. For journals published by professional organizations, check that you have the requisite membership status. If the journal has an anonymous-submission policy, your name should appear only on a separate or a duplicate title page (see 4.2.4), and the manuscript should not identify you in any other way; for example, cite yourself in the third person instead of using a self-identifying reference such as "See my article. . . ."

Unless the journal specifies otherwise, submit one printout of the manuscript prepared according to the guidelines in chapter 4. Some journals accept submissions by e-mail, disk, or an online interface, and most will request a copy of your electronic file if the manuscript is accepted for publication. Always keep a paper version of the manuscript, as well as electronic copies in at least two places.

Address the submission to the journal's editor. Include a brief cover letter that states the full title of the article, identifies you and any other author of the work, calls attention to special features (e.g., illustrations, tables), describes permissions that might be required and tells whether they have been or can easily be obtained, and supplies addresses for future correspondence. Send a printed manuscript by first-class mail, indicating in your cover letter if the manuscript is available in electronic format and enclosing a self-addressed mailer and unattached return postage if you wish the manuscript returned in case it is not accepted.

Journal editors do not have a common policy concerning the submission of manuscripts to more than one periodical at a time. Publications that have each manuscript evaluated by specialist readers often will not consider a submission that is under review elsewhere. If you decide to submit a manuscript to more than one journal simultaneously, you must inform each editor involved.

After submitting the manuscript, you should expect to receive a written acknowledgment of the journal's receipt of it within about two weeks. If there is no response within a month, you should inquire to see whether the manuscript was received.

1.4.5   EVALUATION OF A MANUSCRIPT

The editor of a refereed periodical generally reviews a manuscript soon after submission to verify that it is suitable for the journal. If it is not, the editor rejects the manuscript without further review. If it is suitable, the editor sends the manuscript for evaluation to consultant readers (usually two), sometimes simultaneously and sometimes consecutively. Although the questions asked of readers vary from journal to journal, most editors request comments on the importance of the subject, the originality and soundness of the argument, the accuracy of the facts, the clarity and readability of the style, and the validity of the documentation.

In addition, editors usually ask for a recommendation regarding publication — for example, one of the following choices: recommended without reservations or with only minor changes, not recommended without substantial revision, or not recommended. Consultants are typically encouraged to give specific reasons for their recommendations, to describe reservations in as much detail as possible, and to suggest ways to improve the manuscript.

With guidance from the readers' reports, the editor, editorial staff, or editorial board may accept the manuscript for publication, reject it, ask the author to revise and resubmit it, or accept it pending revision. The last two options have the potential for misunderstandings between editors and authors. If the editor asks for revisions, the requested changes and the conditions determining publication should be fully and clearly detailed in writing: you should understand whether the revisions are optional or required, whether there is a deadline for submitting a revised manuscript, whether revision will ensure acceptance or lead to another round of consultant review and publication decision, and, if there is to be a new evaluation, whether the same or different referees will be used. If you are unsure about any of these matters, do not hesitate to ask the editor for clarification.

Consider requests for revision carefully and deliberately. If you choose to undertake the revisions, inform the editor of your intent and give an expected date of resubmission or confirm that you will meet the deadline. When returning the revised manuscript, include in your cover letter a summary of the changes made.

If you do not agree with all the revisions requested, tell the editor in writing which changes you are willing to make and which you are not, giving explicit reasons for your decision, before reworking the article. If the editor does not concur with your plan of revision, you should withdraw the manuscript and submit it elsewhere.

Copies of the consultant readers' reports usually accompany requests for revision. Some journals remove the reviewer's name from each report whether it is favorable or not; others give consultants the option of anonymity. If the journal follows an anonymous review process, the editor is responsible for deleting references in the report (including metadata in electronic files) that may identify the reviewer. Many journal editors send the author copies of the reports—or excerpts from or summaries of them—regardless of the publication decision. Thus, even if the manuscript is rejected, the author might be able to use the reviews to improve it and make it publishable elsewhere.

The editor's acknowledgment letter at the start of the process may tell you approximately how long it will take before a decision is made. Many journals complete review of an article in about two or three months, although referees' schedules and the time of the academic year could delay the decision. If you do not hear again from the journal within four months after the initial acknowledgment, feel free to inquire about the status of the manuscript. When an editorial board, rather than an editor or editorial staff, decides on publication, the process can take longer because the board may meet only two or three times a year. If the journal is unable to make a decision after four to six months, depending on the type of journal, and the editor and you cannot agree on a timetable, you may send the manuscript to another journal after notifying the editor of your decision.

1.4.6   ACCEPTANCE OF A MANUSCRIPT

A journal generally accepts an article for publication either as is or subject to revisions that only the editor needs to review. Sometimes editors prescribe changes; sometimes they merely suggest them and allow the author to decide which to perform. Even if your article is accepted without the need for revision, you may receive an opportunity to update the manuscript or make final improvements before copyediting and production begin. Whatever the circumstances, make revisions as expeditiously as possible, carefully observing any deadline the editor sets. Submit the final version of the article in the form or forms required by the journal (e.g., printout and electronic file). When the journal receives the final version, the editor should be able to notify you of the projected date of publication. After accepting a manuscript, the journal usually offers the author a contract, or memorandum of agreement, for publication of the work (see 2.3.2).

Occasionally, communication between an author and a journal editor breaks down. The Council of Editors of Learned Journals mediates disputes between authors and the staffs of member journals. To request mediation, write the president at the address on the council's Web site.

On the production and publication of journal articles, see 1.6.

─────────────────── **1.5** ───────────────────

PLACING A MANUSCRIPT WITH A PRESS

1.5.1   SCHOLARLY PRESSES

Most scholarly books are published by university presses, professional organizations, commercial academic presses, and trade publishers. University presses and publication programs within professional organizations are usually headed by a director and include staff members in such areas as acquisitions, copyediting, design, production, marketing, sales, and business (e.g., contracts, royalties, rights, permissions). At both types of publishers, editorial boards composed of faculty members or association members normally make final decisions on publication (see 1.5.6, on evaluation).

By contrast, at commercial academic presses and trade publishers, which are rarely affiliated with an educational or a professional institution, decisions are usually made by staff editors rather than academic committees. Both types of publishers are set up to make a profit, but commercial academic presses, such as Blackwell Publishing or Greenwood Press, tend to issue the same kinds of works as university presses and professional organizations, whereas trade publishers, like Harper-Collins and Random House, generally seek out works that appeal to a wide general audience. Although commercial publishers are usually headed by presidents and vice presidents rather than directors, their staffs fulfill the same general functions (e.g., editorial, production, business) as those of nonprofit publishers.

1.5.2   TYPES OF SCHOLARLY BOOKS

Most scholarly books in the field of language and literature fall into one of the following categories: scholarly studies, collections of essays, translations, scholarly editions, reference works, and textbooks. Although presses have traditionally distributed these works in print form, scholarly books are increasingly being disseminated through electronic media.

Scholarly Studies. The most common form is the scholarly study, usually by a single author but occasionally by coauthors. A scholarly study typically begins with a clear statement of an original thesis and then explores that thesis by presenting and analyzing a significant body of evidence. In many humanities fields, such books are the primary means of advancing scholarly knowledge. A number of publishers maintain book series, often under series editors or editorial boards, that group studies according to subject.

Scholarly studies range from the monograph—an extended discussion of a narrowly focused topic (e.g., a single author or single text), aimed at a limited audience—to the nonfiction trade book, which reaches general readers as well as scholars. Nearly all presses tend to favor works that have wider scholarly audiences. A book with a small potential readership is more difficult to place than a book that promises to draw readers with different interests from various fields and disciplines. In general, moreover, most publishers will not consider unrevised dissertations, which are unlike books in nature, purpose, objectives, and intended audience, and, with few exceptions, publishers will review a revised dissertation only if it has been reconceived and rewritten to address the interests of a broad range of scholars (see William Germano, *From Dissertation to Book* [Chicago: U of Chicago P, 2005; print]; Eleanor Harman, Ian Montagnes, Siobhan McMenemy, and Chris Bucci, eds., *The Thesis and the Book: A Guide for First-Time Academic Authors* [2nd ed.; Toronto: U of Toronto P, 2003; print]; and Beth

Luey, ed., *Revising Your Dissertation: Advice from Leading Editors* [Berkeley: U of California P, 2004; print]).

Collections of Essays. A collection of original essays by different authors offers at its best a breadth of knowledge and diversity of perspectives and methodologies that no book by a single author can. To avoid problems of incoherence, unevenness, or confusion of purpose, the editor of a collection typically strives to identify a useful and important subject for the book, establish clear and attainable objectives, define the intended audience, divide the book's subject into specific topics, select appropriate contributors for these topics, establish unambiguous guidelines for writing the essays, maintain high scholarly and editorial standards, and communicate these goals and expectations to the contributors. If you are interested in editing such a collection, you might approach possible authors for tentative commitments at an early stage but should not formally invite anyone to contribute until a publisher expresses serious interest in the projected book and requests a manuscript.

Collections of previously published essays bring together studies from diverse sources, often giving wider circulation to important essays published in journals. Many such collections usefully and conveniently present major scholarly trends in an established field over a specific period, draw attention and help give definition and shape to an emergent field, or provide key essays on a certain topic for classroom use. Since identifying the most appropriate works for republication is essential to the success of the collection, its editor needs to consult widely with other scholars before selecting essays. Another consideration for the editor is to obtain permission from—and possibly pay requisite fees to—the holder of the copyright in each essay. If you plan to prepare such a book, you might make preliminary inquiries about permissions before approaching a potential publisher but should pay no fees until publication is certain. In any event, copyright holders usually do not grant permission or set fees until after they receive details of publication, such as the price of the book and the number of copies to be printed (see 2.2.14).

Translations. Translations of scholarly or creative works similarly expand readership. Like those who edit collections of previously published essays, the translator of a work under copyright or the translator's publisher needs to obtain rights from the copyright holder, normally the original publisher or the author, who will likely require a fee (see

2.2.14). Translations of works in the public domain—no longer protected by copyright law (see 2.2.7)—do not have this problem, but if the work has already been translated, the new translator has the challenge of making a convincing argument that the proposed rendition is necessary. Translators commonly prepare a sample translation to send to potential publishers, sometimes inquiring of the original-language publisher at the same time about the availability of translation rights, but do not translate the entire work or pay fees without a commitment to publish.

Scholarly Editions. A scholarly edition presents a version of a work based on explicit editorial principles. There are several kinds of scholarly editions. The editor of a single-text diplomatic edition reproduces a text (e.g., a manuscript) or version of a text (e.g., an important printed edition of the text) unemended—that is, as a historical document. The editor of an eclectic critical edition produces an original version of a text by combining the "best readings" drawn from several other versions (e.g., editions, manuscripts). The editors of variorum, genetic, and fluid-text editions use various means to track the sequence of revisions made to a work in manuscript, print editions, or both. Scholarly editions present textual variants and arguments for the editorial decisions in a textual apparatus. Like translators, scholarly editors usually seek a publication commitment before beginning a project, supplying a sample of the edition, along with a statement of editorial principles, to possible publishers. The MLA's Committee on Scholarly Editions establishes guidelines for best practices in scholarly editing. The committee's "Guidelines for Editors of Scholarly Editions," available at the MLA's Web site, is recognized by many editors, publishers, and funding agencies. The guidelines cover editorial practices for print and electronic editions. (For further information, see Lou Burnard, Katherine O'Brien O'Keeffe, and John Unsworth, eds., *Electronic Textual Editing* [New York: MLA, 2006; CD-ROM, print]; D. C. Greetham, ed., *Scholarly Editing: A Guide to Research* [New York: MLA, 1995; print]; and William Proctor Williams and Craig S. Abbott, *An Introduction to Bibliographical and Textual Studies* [3rd ed.; New York: MLA, 1999; print].)

Reference Works. Authoritative annotated bibliographies and other reference works (e.g., dictionaries, encyclopedias, handbooks) are useful, time-saving research tools for scholars and students. Such works are normally prepared only under contract to a publisher, since they usually involve a considerable investment of time and require close cooperation between author and publisher. Unlike most other scholarly books, reference works adhere to relatively strict editorial policies and follow numerous conventions intended to make them readily accessible to their users. Many multivolume reference works are created by teams of scholars working collaboratively over many years. (For further information on annotated bibliographies, see James L. Harner, *On Compiling an Annotated Bibliography* [2nd ed.; New York: MLA, 2000; print].)

Textbooks. Publishing textbooks allows scholars the opportunity to have their personally developed, perhaps theoretically based teaching approaches adopted by instructors for use in courses in other educational institutions. Textbooks can also be lucrative enterprises for authors as well as publishers. Because of the potential profits involved, commercial textbook publishing is a highly competitive area. To be successful, a textbook has to appeal not only to instructors, who must decide to adopt the book for their classes, often selecting it as a replacement for a previously used text, but also to students, whose experience with the book must be positive if it is to be reordered. Textbook publishers — often the textbook divisions of trade publishers — require extensive reviews of a proposed book. Reviewers number not just the two or three common to other scholarly publications but perhaps dozens, since the review process for textbooks serves both evaluative and marketing functions. If a textbook is accepted, the publisher's staff is likely to work closely with the author in the development of the book.

1.5.3   SELECTING A PRESS

Like selecting the right journal for an article, identifying an appropriate publisher will facilitate placing a book manuscript successfully. Your scholarly research and conversations with colleagues will help you know which publishers are apt to be interested in your work. Book advertisements in journals, publishers' catalogs and brochures, and visits to presses' Internet sites and to their exhibition booths at scholarly conferences will provide additional information about publishers' interests. Be especially alert to book series into which your project might fit. Just as journals devote issues to specific topics, many book publishers have series that group books according to kind (e.g., bibliographies, translations) or subject.

A useful reference work for selecting a book publisher is the annual directory of the Association of American University Presses (AAUP), which lists the more than 120 publishers that belong to the association. Each entry in this directory contains general information about the press; a comprehensive listing of staff members by department (e.g., administrative, acquisitions, manuscript editorial, marketing, design and production, business); facts on history and activity (e.g., year established, title output in the previous year, titles in print); and a description of the editorial program, including disciplines covered and book series and journals published. The AAUP directory also includes a subject-area grid that conveniently shows the interests of individual presses.

Other relevant, though less focused, directories are *Literary Market Place (LMP)*, *International Literary Market Place (ILMP)*, and *Books in Print (BiP)*. *LMP* is a directory of the book publishing industry in the United States and Canada. It lists virtually all publishers in the United States, offering primarily business-oriented information on each. This listing is indexed by geographic location, type of publication, and subject. The work also has a separate section on Canadian book publishers. *ILMP* is a companion to *LMP*, with similar data on book publishers in over 180 countries outside the United States and Canada. *BiP* lists all books currently published or distributed in the United States and includes general facts on publishers of listed books.

After you have identified potential publishers for your manuscript, you might look at some of their recent books to see the quality of work each produces. You might also learn how efficiently and professionally a press functions by asking colleagues whose work it has published.

1.5.4   SUBMITTING A PROSPECTUS FOR A BOOK

Every scholarly publisher includes among its staff an editor or a number of editors responsible for acquiring the manuscripts that the press publishes. Often such editors possess advanced degrees and a good sense of the scholarship in at least one field of learning. The acquisitions editor normally is the author's principal contact with the press; thus, it is essential that the two share a productive working relationship. Acquisitions editors at many presses solicit manuscripts, especially from well-known scholars who have written influential books and articles. Acquisitions editors also commonly attend professional meetings and make campus trips to seek manuscripts. Most authors who wish to publish scholarly books take the initiative by approaching editors at conventions, meeting with visiting editors on campus, or writing to presses.

When offering a book manuscript to publishers, submit a brief cover letter and a prospectus for the manuscript to the appropriate acquisitions editors. Since few publishers have the staff to read unsolicited manuscripts, do not send the complete manuscript unless invited to do so. Authors usually send the prospectus to the editor by first-class mail. Many editors now accept prospectuses by e-mail (with attached files). Presses prefer not to receive a prospectus by fax or on disk only. To find editors' names, consult the directories cited in section 1.5.3 or inquire directly of the presses; many presses keep contact information and submission guidelines up-to-date on their Web sites. If you cannot discover which editor to approach, write to the director or the editor in chief of the press, who will be able to route the prospectus to the right person. Alternatively, a colleague familiar with the press may be willing to introduce you to the editor who acquires books in your field.

Your prospectus should clearly and concisely describe the manuscript and provide a rationale for its publication. Usually no longer than ten double-spaced pages, the prospectus addresses such questions as the need for the book, its goals and purposes, its scholarly and professional significance, the qualities that distinguish it from other publications on the subject, and its intended audience. The prospectus also incorporates a summary of the book and provides biographical data indicating the author's credentials for the project, including previous publications, as well as information on the status of the manuscript and on relevant physical characteristics — scheduled completion date, expected length, word-processing software used, special features (e.g., illustrations, tables), and so forth. Typically accompanying the prospectus are selected materials from the manuscript, such as the table of contents, the introduction or preface, and a sample chapter. To facilitate future correspondence with the publisher, authors may include a self-addressed, stamped envelope for the acquisitions editor to use in acknowledging receipt of the prospectus and a self-addressed mailer with unattached postage if they wish the submitted materials returned.

After submitting the prospectus, you will likely receive a written acknowledgment of the press's receipt of it within about two weeks. If there is no response within a month, you should inquire whether the prospectus was received.

The acquisitions editor usually reads the prospectus first quickly to ascertain whether the proposed book is appropriate for the press. If it is not or if the prospectus seems ill-conceived, the editor normally rejects the prospectus immediately with a brief note stating that it does not meet the publisher's needs or requirements. Otherwise, the editor reads the prospectus again more carefully, perhaps circulating it to consultant readers for opinion and advice. After the evaluation, the editor responds to the author either to report that the press is not interested in the proposed book or to invite submission of the manuscript for full review. The consideration of a prospectus usually takes from one to three months. If you do not receive a decision or otherwise hear from the editor about the evaluation after three months, you should feel free to inquire about the status of the prospectus.

Experienced authors usually have a somewhat easier course in placing a book manuscript with a publisher. For one thing, they are more knowledgeable about which presses are apt to be interested in their work and may even have professional relationships with some acquisitions editors. If the scholar's previously published work was successfully received, editors from different presses may pursue and compete for the author's current manuscript. Such authors are likely to be offered advance contracts before submission of the manuscript (see 2.3.1) and to have a voice in such matters as how the work is published (e.g., in cloth, paper, or electronic versions) and marketed.

Academic authors, even experienced ones, seldom use literary agents to place their manuscripts. Since scholarly books rarely sell in large numbers and since agents receive a percentage of royalties as their fee, authors are reluctant to share their modest royalties with agents, and agents are reluctant to invest the time and effort required to place a manuscript for the small fee it will produce. The scholars who tend to use agents are those who write trade books — works that reach a wide general audience. If you wish to find an agent, seek the advice of colleagues who have used agents or consult the most recent editions of such reference works as *Literary Market Place (LMP)* and *International Literary Market Place (ILMP)*. *LMP* lists agents in the United States and Canada; *ILMP*, agents in other countries. Listings in *LMP* indicate whether the agent belongs to the Association of Authors' Representatives, a professional organization that sets ethical standards for its members.

1.5.5   SUBMITTING A MANUSCRIPT TO A PRESS

If a publisher invites you to submit a manuscript for consideration, follow the press's instructions, if any, on the method of submission and the number of copies to send. Unless the publisher specifies otherwise, submit one printout of the manuscript prepared according to the specifications in chapter 4. Always keep a paper version of the manuscript, as well as electronic copies in at least two places.

Send a manuscript by first-class mail, addressed to the editor who invited it. Include a brief cover letter that states the full title of the book, identifies you and any other author of the work, calls attention to any aspect of the manuscript that significantly differs from what was laid out in the prospectus, and supplies addresses for future correspondence. You should also enclose a self-addressed mailer and unattached return postage if you wish the manuscript returned in case it is not accepted.

Although it is common to send a prospectus simultaneously to more than one press, many publishers will not review a manuscript under consideration elsewhere, because of the time and expense the evaluation exacts. If two or more editors invite you to submit a manuscript and you decide to send it to more than one of them, you must inform each press involved.

After submitting the manuscript, you should expect to receive a written acknowledgment of the press's receipt of it within about two weeks. If there is no acknowledgment within a month, you should inquire to see whether the manuscript was received.

1.5.6   EVALUATION OF A MANUSCRIPT

The acquiring editor generally reviews a manuscript soon after submission to confirm that it fulfills the promise of the prospectus. If it does, the editor sends the manuscript for evaluation to consultant readers (usually two), sometimes simultaneously and sometimes consecutively. Some publishers ask authors for advice and suggestions concerning reviewers. Although the questions asked of readers vary from press to press, most editors seek comments on the importance of the subject, the originality and soundness of the argument, the accuracy of the facts, the logic and effectiveness of the organization, the clarity and readability of the style, and the validity of the documentation. The editor often also asks the readers to compare the work with other books on the subject and to comment on the potential audience for the manuscript.

In addition, editors usually ask for a recommendation regarding publication—for example, one of the following choices: recommended without reservations or with only minor changes, not recommended without substantial revision, or not recommended. Consultants are typically encouraged to give specific reasons for their recommendations, to describe reservations in as much detail as possible, and to offer suggestions on ways to improve the manuscript. Publishers usually pay readers an honorarium or offer them free books for preparing a report on a book-length manuscript.

If the press receives conflicting reports from two consultant readers, it may seek one additional evaluation or more. With guidance from the readers' reports, the press may accept the manuscript for publication, reject it, ask the author to revise and resubmit it, or accept it pending revision. The last two options sometimes result in misunderstandings between publishers and authors. If the press asks for revisions, the requested changes and the conditions determining publication should be fully and clearly detailed in writing: you should understand whether the revisions are optional or required, whether there is a deadline for submitting a revised manuscript, whether revision will ensure acceptance or lead to another round of consultant review and publication decision, and, if there is to be a new evaluation, whether the same or different referees will be used. If you are unsure about any of these matters, do not hesitate to communicate with your editor for clarification.

Consider requests for revision deliberately. If you choose to undertake the revisions, inform the editor of your intent and give an expected date of resubmission or confirm that you will meet the deadline. Notify the press of any subsequent delay, reporting on your progress and giving a new projected submission date. When returning the revised manuscript, include in your cover letter a summary of the changes made.

If you do not agree with all the revisions requested, tell the editor in writing which changes you are willing to make and which you are not, giving explicit reasons for your decision, before reworking the manuscript. If the press does not concur with your plan of revision, you should withdraw the manuscript and submit it elsewhere.

Copies of the consultant readers' reports usually accompany requests for revision. Some publishers remove the reviewer's name from each report whether it is favorable or not; others give consultants the option of anonymity. If the press follows an anonymous review process, the acquisitions editor is responsible for deleting references in the report (including metadata in electronic files) that may identify the reviewer. Many presses send the author copies of the reports—or excerpts from or summaries of them—regardless of the publication decision. Thus, even if the manuscript is rejected, the author might be able to use the reviews to improve it and make it publishable elsewhere.

When the readers' reports are favorable, the press usually considers whether to publish the manuscript. At most academic presses, the acquiring editor presents the manuscript for a publication decision to the editorial committee, normally a board of scholars who are not employed by the press. Faculty members constitute the committee at university presses; professional organizations with book publishing programs appoint association members to the board. The acquisitions editor shares with the committee representative excerpts from the manuscript (or sometimes the entire text), the readers' reports, the author's response to the reports (if deemed necessary), and any other material of importance to the decision. A covering document by the editor usually introduces the manuscript, supplying background information. At commercial academic presses and trade publishing houses, by contrast, staff editors usually make publication decisions.

The editor's acknowledgment letter at the start of the process may tell you approximately how long it will take before a decision is made. The typical waiting period is about two or three months, although referees' schedules and the time of the academic year could delay the decision. When an editorial board meets infrequently, the process can take longer. If you do not hear from the publisher within three months, feel free to inquire about the status of the manuscript. If the publisher is unable to make a decision after four to six months, depending on the type of press, and the editor and you cannot agree on a timetable, you may send the manuscript to another publisher after notifying the editor of your decision.

1.5.7   ACCEPTANCE OF A MANUSCRIPT

A press generally accepts a book manuscript for publication either as is or subject to revisions that only an editor needs to review. Sometimes publishers prescribe changes; sometimes they merely suggest them and allow the author to decide which to perform. Even if your book is accepted without the need for revision, you should expect to receive an opportunity to update the manuscript or make final improvements before copyediting and production begin. Whatever the circumstances, make revisions as expeditiously as possible, carefully observing any deadline the editor sets. If the publisher furnishes a set of editorial guidelines or a handbook for authors, prepare and submit the manuscript as requested. When the press receives the final version of the manuscript, your editor should be able to notify you of the projected date of publication, usually about a year from receipt of the final manuscript, depending on the length and complexity of the work, the time of the year, and the press's publication schedule.

The publisher usually offers the author a contract following acceptance of the book manuscript. Some scholarly book publishers, like most trade book publishers, offer contracts on approving a prospectus and inviting the manuscript for evaluation, but such advance contracts do not guarantee publication, since they normally stipulate that the manuscript must first satisfactorily pass through the evaluation process, including consultant review and approval by the editorial board. Sometimes the publisher offers the author a monetary advance against royalties, along with the contract (see 2.3.1). The press generally expects the author to secure before copyediting any permissions necessary for reproduction of illustrative matter and previously published text (see 2.2.13–14), typically asking the author to return a copy of the signed contract with the permission statements attached.

1.6
PRODUCTION AND PUBLICATION

Authors commonly submit the final version of their manuscript, as both a printout and an electronic file, to the journal editor or the book acquisitions editor, who reviews the manuscript and transmits it to editorial staff members for copyediting, design, and production. Book publishers normally ask authors to review both a copyedited and a typeset version of the manuscript and to supply an index for the book; journals usually require authors to review the article in at least one of the versions produced before publication.

1.6.1   COPYEDITING

Copyediting is an important intermediary stage between acceptance and publication, serving both the publisher and the author. The copyeditor's responsibilities embrace style and mechanics in addition to other aspects of the manuscript.

As Claire Kehrwald Cook notes in her book *Line by Line: How to Edit Your Own Writing* (Boston: Houghton, 1985; print), a principal task of copyediting is to eliminate "the stylistic faults" that "impede reading and obscure meaning" (viii). Copyeditors concern themselves with questions of grammar, usage, and punctuation as well as with the correctness and consistency of other mechanical matters, such as spelling, capitalization, the treatment of numbers and names, and the documentation of scholarship. This aspect of copyediting frequently centers on making the manuscript conform to the house style the journal or press follows. The copyeditor enables the publisher to ensure consistency in spelling, capitalization, italicization, and the like within a work and from one work to another. The copyeditor also marks up the manuscript for typesetting, specifying such design features as title, subheadings, set-down quotations, notes, and list of works cited.

Besides stylistic and mechanical questions, the copyeditor may call attention to more substantive matters that may not have been detected by the consultant readers and the acquisitions editor, such as errors of fact or logic, possibly unjustified generalizations, or even potential legal problems in the manuscript. The successful copyeditor, therefore, routinely renders a manuscript more cogent and accessible to its readers and sometimes saves the author and the publisher from various kinds of professional discomfiture.

Copyediting may be done on the paper or the electronic version of the manuscript. When working on a printout, editors use a set of symbols to indicate changes—deletions, insertions, transpositions, and so forth—in the manuscript. Frequently, the symbols are supplemented by explanations or clarifications in the margins or on slips attached to the page. Copyeditors also commonly use margins or slips to address queries to the author, requesting information or explication, for example, or suggesting alternative choices of wording. (See fig. 1.) A copyeditor who works on a computer usually produces at the end a new printout incorporating the editorial changes, which are often highlighted to allow the author to compare the original and copyedited versions easily. Normally, the publisher provides a key to understanding the highlighted editorial changes. Queries to the author may appear in the margins or elsewhere (e.g., in a list keyed to numbers embedded in the text). (See fig. 2.)

In returning the copyedited manuscript to the author for review, the editor usually sends a cover letter that, among other things, may call attention to special problems or give instructions about responding to changes and queries. The letter also normally specifies a deadline for the return of the manuscript. If you cannot meet the deadline, notify the editor immediately. Otherwise, the publisher will expect to receive the reviewed manuscript within the time requested, so that production can proceed on schedule. If no schedule is set, return the manuscript as quickly as possible.

When you receive a copyedited manuscript from your publisher, read the cover letter first, especially noting the deadline for return. Evaluate each suggested change and either accept the change or explain what is

A page reference is similarly unnecessary if ~~for example~~ you use

a passage from a one-page work. Of course, sources such as films,

television broadcasts, ~~and~~ performances and electronic sources

or other type of reference markers

with no pagination cannot be cited by ~~page~~ number. Such works

are usually cited in their entirety (see 7.4.1) and often by title

(see 7.4.4). Electronic publications *sometimes* ~~often~~ include paragraph   *OK? To avoid repet.*

numbers or other kinds of reference numbers (see 7.4.2).

Fig. 1. A sample of the copyedited manuscript
of this manual, which was copyedited on paper.

A page reference is similarly unnecessary if,
you use a passage from a one-page work.
Electronic publications sometimes include
paragraph numbers or other kinds of
reference numbers (see 7.4.2). Of course,
sources such as films, television broadcasts,
performances, and electronic sources with
no pagination or other type of reference
markers cannot be cited by number. Such
works are usually cited in their entirety (see
7.4.1) and often by title (see 7.4.4).

Deleted: , for example,

Comment: OK? To avoid repetition of "often."

Comment: Previous sentence moved from end of par.

Deleted: and

Deleted: page

Deleted: Electronic publications often include paragraph numbers or other kinds of reference numbers (see 7.4.2).

Fig. 2. A sample of the manuscript of this manual
copyedited electronically. Underlined passages are insertions.

wrong with it and, if the copyeditor has identified a problem, substitute a different revision. If you do not understand a change, ask for clarification. If the copyediting was done on paper, do not erase or otherwise obliterate any change or query. Try to respond unambiguously and as near as possible on the page to the query; if space is insufficient, place replies on a separate sheet, making evident the pages and lines involved.

The review of the copyedited manuscript is normally the author's last chance to make revisions, such as correcting or updating references, for from this time forward changes become costly (and are often charged to the author or not even made). If your revisions are brief, insert them within the manuscript; when lengthy or likely to lead to confusion if placed directly on the manuscript, revisions should be written on separate pages with clear indications of where they belong in the text.

Before returning the copyedited manuscript to the publisher, make sure you have answered all questions, supplied all requested information, and made all needed changes. Besides meeting the deadline, follow any special instructions the publisher gives for the return of the manuscript. Include a cover letter identifying any problems of which the copyeditor should be aware.

If problems remain unresolved, the copyeditor may return to you with further queries. The publisher normally transfers all changes to the electronic files containing the work. (Less frequently, some publishers ask authors to make the changes and to submit the final version electronically for composition.)

<table>
<tr><td>**1.6.2**</td><td>PROOFREADING</td></tr>
</table>

After your article or book is typeset, the publisher will send you for correction a set of proofs (your text converted into columns of type that will eventually constitute the actual publication), usually along with the final version of the manuscript.

Read proofs carefully, word for word against the manuscript. Do not assume that the manuscript was translated into type without omissions or other errors. If you are not an experienced proofreader, it may help to ask someone to read the manuscript aloud while you follow on the proofs. Make corrections on the proofs, using proofreading symbols (see 8.8), and respond to any queries from the editor or typesetter. To reduce production costs, many presses assign authors primary responsibility for proofreading and sometimes suggest they seek the services of a professional proofreader.

Because changes at this stage can prove costly (usually to the author if they are not corrections of the typesetter's errors) and also seriously delay the publication schedule, publishers will usually make changes only to remove factual errors and will not permit stylistic refinements. If you want to make alterations, explain their rationale and relative importance in a cover letter when returning the proofs, so that the publisher can make informed decisions about allowing the changes. Be sure to return the corrected proofs within the time agreed on or as quickly as possible if no schedule was set. Often the book publisher sends two sets of page proofs: one to correct and return, the other for preparing an index.

1.6.3   PREPARING AN INDEX

Creating the index for a scholarly book is usually the responsibility of the author, the person most familiar with the contents and intentions of the book; similarly, the editor of a collection of essays is responsible for preparing its index. In negotiating the contract, the author and publisher determine the type of index or indexes required: a name index, a subject index, a combined index of names and subjects, or another kind of index—a scholarly study of poetry, for example, might include an index of titles or an index of first lines. Another consideration is the mode of indexing. Whereas most books are indexed by page number, some works are more useful if indexed another way, such as by section number. This section explains how to prepare an index by page number.

Some authors hire a professional indexer rather than prepare the index themselves. The publisher can probably recommend an indexer if you are unsure about whom to hire. If you intend to have your press help you obtain the services of a freelance indexer, let the publisher know well in advance, so that the indexer's schedule can be coordinated with the publication schedule for the book. Since such an indexer is unlikely to be a specialist in your field, the press will ask you to review the index, deleting or adding entries as needed or making other refinements.

Ordinarily, the following parts of the book are indexed: the introduction, text, content notes, and appendixes. The following parts are usually not indexed: the preface and other front matter (e.g., title page, copyright page, dedication, table of contents, acknowledgments) and the list of works cited.

Although you cannot complete the index until page proofs are available, you can begin working on it at any time after acceptance. Before receiving proofs, for example, you can identify the terms for your index and arrange them in alphabetical order. For a subject index, you can select in advance what words and phrases you will use as headings and subheadings. Headings are key terms that guide readers to important ideas and issues discussed in the book; headings are normally divided into subheadings if the headings would otherwise be followed by long strings of undifferentiated page numbers. For a name index, you can extract all personal names from the manuscript and alphabetize them in advance. Once the index has been thus set up, all you then need do is add page numbers when you receive the proofs. Before beginning any such work, be sure to inquire about and follow any instructions the publisher provides for preparing the index.

Special indexing software or the indexing feature of your word-processing program can help produce the index, but you need to use such programs with care. Whereas software performs many valuable functions — for instance, it can automatically index terms the user marks; record headings, subheadings, and page numbers; and alphabetize entries — the indexer nonetheless must perform the most essential tasks: creating the list of terms to be marked, checking and modifying terms as indexing proceeds, editing entries, adding cross-references, and so forth.

Print out the final index copy double-spaced and in one column. Begin each entry flush with the left margin; indent the second and subsequent lines of the entry one-half inch from the margin (by setting a hanging indention of one-half inch in your word processor's ruler bar or paragraph formatting). Use commas to indicate inversions ("artists, reference works on") and qualifying phrases ("authors, as indexers" and "authors, and publishers"). Place a comma after the entry, type a space, and give the page number or numbers. Separate numbers with a comma and a space ("pragmatism, in editing, 489, 519, 536"). Use inclusive numbers if the subject continues for more than one page ("10–11, 110–11"; see 3.10.6, on inclusive numbers). If the page number refers to a note, add the lowercase letter *n* ("286n"). If the page contains more than one note, add the note number or numbers, preceded by the abbreviation *n* or *nn* ("286n3" or "286nn4–5"). Identify cross-references with *See* and *See also*, italicized ("acronyms *See* abbreviations" and "theater *See also* plays").

Although most indexes are printed in run-in style, prepare the copy in indented style (in which each subheading appears on a separate line indented under the major heading):

writing

    guides to, 38-40

    style manuals for, 260-61

Number every page of the index in the upper right-hand corner and otherwise follow the recommendations for manuscript preparation in chapter 4.

Indexes generally follow one of two systems of alphabetizing: letter by letter and word by word. The letter-by-letter system ignores spaces between words and alphabetizes by all letters up to the first comma indicating an inversion or a qualifier. The word-by-word system, in contrast, alphabetizes up to the first space and uses the letters that follow only when two entries begin with identical words.

LETTER BY LETTER	WORD BY WORD
Day, Dorothy	Day, Dorothy
daybooks	*Day of the Locust, The* (West)
Day of the Locust, The (West)	daybooks

The letter-by-letter system is more commonly used. In alphabetizing, disregard accents, hyphens, apostrophes, and commas indicating series, and follow the rules for names given in 3.6.

Check your manuscript of the index carefully, for at many presses the author has complete responsibility for the accuracy and correctness of the index. Unless otherwise instructed, submit the manuscript in both print and electronic form to the publisher. The manuscript of the index, like that of the rest of the book, will be copyedited and converted into proofs. Presses usually ask authors to review the copyedited manuscript or the proofs of the index.

There are many strategies and resources for creating indexes. *The Chicago Manual of Style* (15th ed.; Chicago: U of Chicago P, 2003; print, Web) briefly defines various kinds of indexes and gives considerable information about the mechanics of preparing an index (ch. 18). For a more extensive treatment of the topic, see Nancy C. Mulvany, *Indexing Books* (2nd ed.; Chicago: U of Chicago P, 2005; print).

1.6.4   DESIGN

Although publishers, not authors, are responsible for the design, production, and marketing of books and journals, it is useful for scholars to have some notion of what happens to their manuscripts apart from editing.

All scholarly publications have designs. A designer writes specifications that cover every aspect of the typography of the publication. For print publications, the designer's concerns include

- the trim size (the dimensions of a page of the publication)
- the margins (the space at the top, bottom, and sides of the page)
- the type page (the area of the page in which type appears, including any footnotes, running heads or running footers, and page numbers)
- the text page (the area of the page in which the text appears)
- the typeface and the type size for not only the text but also the running heads, chapter numbers, chapter titles, headings within the text, extracts, notes, list of works cited, and so forth
- the spacing between letters, words, and lines
- the indention of paragraph beginnings, extracts, notes, the list of works cited, and so forth

Designers of electronic publications make similar calculations about the rendering of the text on a computer screen.

The design of a book also includes such features as its cover and jacket (if there is one), the paper on which it is to be printed, the cloth or paper with which it will be bound, and the method of binding (e.g., case binding, adhesive binding). Publishers sometimes ask authors for design suggestions (e.g., a work of visual art to serve as an illustration for the cover or jacket of the book), but the press has the final say on all aspects of design.

1.6.5   COMPOSITION, PRINTING, BINDING,
ELECTRONIC PRODUCTION

The term *composition* covers a wide range of typesetting processes, old and new. Originally, typesetting involved selecting preformed metal characters from a case, arranging them into lines on a composing stick, and then, after the lines were laid out in galleys and a proof impression taken, locking them into rectangular chases, or frames. Then inking the type and pressing it against paper yielded first galley or page proofs and eventually the final printed product. The terminology of publishing still reflects these procedures, which held sway for four centuries. Typesetting was mechanized in the late nineteenth century, with the invention of the Linotype and the Monotype, which automated the selection of the metal characters.

Recent decades have seen rapid changes in composition methods. Today electronic text files—usually originating with the author but sometimes created when the typesetter keyboards a paper manuscript or scans it with an optical character reader—are imported into a pagination or page-layout program, where the text can be corrected and formatted and pages generated. Pagination programs vary in their ability to lay out a document. Some are virtually automatic, programmed with rules to create an aesthetically pleasing page. Most programs, however, work through a combination of automation and manual intervention (in page-spread alignment, page breaks, hyphenation, line justification, etc.). A heavily illustrated book, for example, requires more manual work than a book with text only.

Working with a typesetter, the publisher prepares proofs for review, usually by copyeditors and the author. The typesetter makes corrections after each stage of review and generates new pages. This cycle repeats until there are no further corrections and the pages are deemed ready for printing. This version is then sent as electronic files to the printer for reproduction.

The text pages for a clothbound book are sewn or glued together to form a book block, and the endpapers are pasted to both the book block and covered boards. Text and sometimes designs are stamped or printed on the covering material before it is glued to the boards. The book may then be wrapped in a printed jacket. The collated pages of a paperbound publication are glued to a printed paper cover.

The final typesetting files can be converted and used for online publication. In some cases, you may be asked to review electronic proofs in a staging area before your work is posted for public viewing. If your publisher intends to prepare electronic files for readers with print disabilities, you may be asked to provide additional information (e.g., a detailed description of an illustration).

1.6.6   MARKETING

Publishers use marketing to try to bring their publications to the fullest potential audiences. Scholarly publications are usually marketed through promotional mailings to individuals and libraries, advertisements, displays at professional conferences, listings on the press's Web site, and efforts to have the works reviewed.

The marketing plan for a publication depends on the nature of the work and on its intended audience. For example, for a trade book aimed at a general audience, a press might place an advertisement in the *New York Review of Books* or arrange author interviews and book signings, but for a more specialized book it might rely on direct mailings and reviews in scholarly journals and in periodicals consulted by academic librarians, such as *Choice*.

A book publisher is likely to ask you to play an active advisory role in the marketing of your book. The press will customarily send you a questionnaire or similar form requesting information that will assist the marketing staff. You might be asked, for instance, to supply a brief description of the book and biographical data to be used in the copy for the jacket or cover and for direct-mail materials (flyers, brochures, catalogs).

In addition, you will probably be asked to provide a list of journals whose reviews are respected (and whose advertisements are read) by scholars in your field. Although publishers rely on their own lists of customers as well as lists rented from professional and scholarly associations and from list services, you can assist in direct-mail advertising by telling the press of any organizations and groups whose members might be particularly interested in the book; some groups will allow the publisher to post notices in their newsletters or electronic mailing lists. Similarly, many publishers exhibit their books at meetings of major scholarly associations, but you can help direct the press to specialized meetings that have exhibit opportunities. In addition, you might mention any awards and prizes for which the book is eligible.

It might not be possible for your publisher to pursue every suggestion you offer. Keep in mind that the marketing staff needs to promote many new and backlist titles at the same time, that the costs of advertising are high, and that the plan for each title is limited by a budget and largely shaped by the projected income from the book. Nevertheless, you should expect your press to do its best to inform potential readers of the existence and importance of your book.

1.7

CONCLUSION

Scholarly publication ideally constitutes a collaboration between author and publisher, characterized by complementary and mutually supportive and sustaining interests and goals. Authors wish to gain publication of manuscripts that have usually taken them years to conceptualize, research, and write. Publishers wish to disseminate new and important ideas and scholarship and must invest considerable time and money in reviewing, editing, designing, composing, publishing, and marketing each work. Authors and publishers alike seek to have the publications they produce reach as wide a readership as possible.

Scholarly publishing typically relies on evaluations and advice from consultant readers or referees. Such specialist readings help the publisher verify the soundness and quality of the submitted work's thought, scholarship, and writing and help the author discover ways in which the manuscript might be improved.

Cooperation between the two parties enhances the efficacy and the efficiency of the publishing process. Toward this end, an author prepares and submits a manuscript for an article or a prospectus for a book in a commonly accepted form or as prescribed by the journal or press; tells the publisher if the work, or any part of it, is being considered elsewhere; agrees to make necessary revisions; reviews the copyedited manuscript and corrects proof; supplies an index, if required; provides advice on design and information for marketing, as requested; and, most important, meets the publisher's deadlines.

For its part, the publisher in this ideal relationship promptly notifies the author of every significant development (and of any delay) during the review stage, from the receipt to the approval of the manuscript; clearly indicates what revisions it wants the author to make and whether the revisions are optional or required; keeps the author informed of the publication schedule; and establishes reasonable deadlines for making revisions, reviewing the copyedited manuscript, correcting proof, and preparing an index.

The author and the publisher enter into a contract for the publication of the manuscript. In book publishing, they commonly share any income derived from the work. And finally, by making important scholarship public in conveniently accessible form, both parties also share in the other rewards — intellectual, professional, and personal — that successful scholarly publication renders.

2

LEGAL ISSUES IN SCHOLARLY PUBLISHING

2.1
INTRODUCTION

Scholars who publish their works inevitably become involved in a network of legal issues, including copyright, contracts, libel, and the right of privacy. These issues have been shaped by a complex history of laws, court decisions, and international agreements that may be unfamiliar and are often confusing. Since common sense is not always a reliable guide to proper legal conduct in publishing, it is important for potential authors to protect themselves by an acquaintance with the fundamentals of legal issues in scholarly publishing.

In our information-based society and economy, intellectual property has drawn increasing attention. New conditions of publication rendered possible by the electronic exchange of texts are making it necessary to reconsider and redefine long-standing copyright law in the United States and abroad. In addition, the globalization of regional economies is creating pressure for the standardization of intellectual-property laws across national borders. Such developments in copyright law affect scholars both as creators who want to protect their writings from unauthorized uses and changes and as researchers who want to use and build on the writings of others. Although scholars as researchers often encounter obstacles when trying to gain access to and use texts, they manage copyright in their own works with relative ease. This is particularly so since, despite the efforts of some scholars and librarians to liberalize the use of intellectual property, changes in the law have for the most part increased protection, lengthened copyright duration, and decreased the risk that material could fall into the public domain.

2.2

COPYRIGHT

2.2.1

DEVELOPMENT OF COPYRIGHT LAW
IN THE UNITED STATES

The principal method of protecting the rights of authors and other creators of original material fixed in a tangible medium of expression is copyright. There has been statutory copyright protection since 1710, when the English parliament enacted the Statute of Anne, the first copyright act. After the American Revolution, most of the former colonies enacted copyright statutes, many influenced by the Statute of Anne. When the nation's founders met in Philadelphia to draft the Constitution, a copyright clause was inserted without opposition or even significant discussion. However, the copyright clause of the Constitution, instead of directly protecting authors' and other creators' interests, gave Congress "power . . . to promote the progress of science and useful arts, by securing for limited times to authors and inventors the exclusive right to their respective writings and discoveries . . ." (art. 1, sec. 8). By reason of this language in the Constitution, copyright in the United States has developed as a limited monopoly, a group of exclusive rights granted to authors with exceptions or limits for the benefit of the public.

Congress proceeded to enact a series of copyright statutes, the first of which, enacted in 1790, protected maps, charts, and books. By far the most important statute today is the 1976 Copyright Act (Pub. L. 94-553, 90 Stat. 2541–602, 19 Oct. 1976, codified at 17 USC), the first major revision of copyright law in three-quarters of a century, because it took account of new and emerging technology and because it laid the groundwork for the United States to afford greater protection of authors' rights through international treaties. Also still relevant is the Copyright Act of 1909, which governs the ownership of copyrights in works published before 1 January 1978, the effective date of the 1976 Copyright Act. The Sound Recording Amendment Act of 1971 extended federal protection to sound recordings and was incorporated into the 1976 Copyright Act.

Much more than prior copyright acts, the 1976 Copyright Act tries to codify copyright law instead of relying on case law to develop a general statutory framework. In part because of this greater reliance on statutory guidance, there have been several amendments of the statute, including the Computer Software Copyright Act of 1980, extending federal protection to computer programs; the Berne Convention Implementation Act of 1988, which amended copyright law so that it met the basic standards necessary for the United States to join the Berne Convention (the major international copyright treaty), whose members protect the existing copyrights of other member countries; the 1990 Visual Artists Rights Act (codified at 17 USC, sec. 106A), which grants rights of attribution and integrity ("moral rights") to certain works of the visual arts; the Copyright Amendments Act of 1992, which clarifies congressional intent about the fair use of unpublished works; the Copyright Renewal Act of 1992, which provides for the automatic renewal of copyright in works copyrighted from 1 January 1964 through 31 December 1977; the 1994 Uruguay Round Agreements Act, which, among other things, restored to United States copyright foreign works that were still in copyright in their country of origin but had fallen into the public domain in the United States for failing to comply with United States copyright formalities; the Digital Millennium Copyright Act, which encompasses several other acts, the most pertinent of which are the WIPO Copyright and Performances and Phonograms Treaties Implementation Act of 1998 (which prohibits circumvention of copyright-protection systems and provides protection for copyright-management information) and the Online Copyright Infringement Liability Limitation Act (which limits the liability of Internet service providers for specified conduct so long as they comply with the statute's requirements); the 1998 Sonny Bono Copyright Term Extension Act, which extended the terms of copyright by twenty years; and the Technology, Education, and Copyright Harmonization (TEACH) Act of 2002, which permits the performance and display of specified copyrighted materials by government bodies and accredited nonprofit educational institutions as part of distance-learning class sessions, so long as the use complies with certain restrictions and affirmative statutory duties.

2.2.2   SUBJECT MATTER OF COPYRIGHT

Copyright is based on *authorship* of *original* works that are fixed in any *tangible medium* now known or later developed. The Supreme Court has defined an author as a person "to whom anything owes its origin; originator; maker" (*Burrow-Giles Lithographic Co. v. Sarony*; 111 US 53–61; 1884; print; 58). (For the authorship of works made for hire, see 2.2.5.) Originality means that the author's work is the product of the author's own creation and judgment, even if the original elements are only modestly creative, and is not copied from other work. To be fixed in a tangible medium, a work must be able to be perceived, reproduced, or otherwise communicated either directly or with the aid of a machine or other device. The Copyright Act lists the following examples of works of authorship (sec. 102):

- Literary works, which include literary criticism, scholarly writing, and computer programs
- Musical works, including accompanying words
- Dramatic works, including accompanying music
- Pantomimes and choreographic works
- Pictorial, graphic, and sculptural works
- Motion pictures and other audiovisual works
- Sound recordings
- Architectural works

The subject matter of copyright also includes compilations, such as collective works. A *compilation* is defined by the Copyright Act as a work formed by the collection and assembling of preexisting materials, which may or may not be protected by copyright, in such a way that the result constitutes an original work of authorship. Compilations include *collective works*, defined as journal or other periodical issues, anthologies, or encyclopedias, in which separate and independent contributions, each separately copyrightable, are assembled into a whole. Copyright in a compilation itself, as distinct from copyright (if any) in the materials included in the compilation, arises from originality either in the selection of the included materials or in the arrangement of them. A 1991 Supreme Court decision (*Feist Publications, Inc. v. Rural Telephone Service Co., Inc.*) made clear that an alphabetical listing of the names and addresses of all people with a telephone number in a town does not qualify as an original work because inclusion of all the service subscribers reflects no original selection and alphabetical order reflects no original arrangement. The Court rejected the idea that considerable effort ("sweat of the brow") expended in the compilation of a work could qualify the work for copyright protection.

Also protected by copyright are *derivative works*, which consist of editorial revisions, annotations, elaborations, and other modifications of one or more preexisting works. A derivative work may be a translation, a musical arrangement, a dramatization, a fictionalization, a motion picture version, a sound recording, an art reproduction, an abridgment, a condensation, or any other recasting, transformation, or adaptation of an underlying work. The right to make a derivative work is controlled by the author of the original work. Authors of derivative works own the material they contributed to create the derivative works.

Copyright protects only the author's expression and does not extend to facts, ideas, procedures, and methods of operation regardless of the form in which they are embodied or illustrated. For example, theories about history, such as a theory about the destruction of the dirigible *Hindenburg*, or scientific discoveries are unprotectable, but the words by which an author expresses ideas, theories, or discoveries are protected.

Questions about whether a particular work is protected by copyright, in whole or in part, can be complex. Authors who plan to use another's work but doubt whether they have the right to do so should refer the question to copyright counsel. In the absence of an opinion from counsel, it is prudent to assume that there is copyright protection. (On the fair use of copyrighted works, see 2.2.13.)

2.2.3   OWNERSHIP OF COPYRIGHT

Except for a work made for hire (see 2.2.5), the author of a work owns the copyright in it from the moment the work is first fixed in a tangible medium of expression (e.g., paper, film, hard drive, DVD, CD). An author is not required to comply with any formalities, such as publication with a copyright notice or registration, to obtain copyright protection. The copyright owner can alter ownership by assigning the copyright or licensing (see 2.2.12) any of the copyright rights encompassed in it (see 2.2.11).

The copyrights in the contributions to collective works remain with the authors unless the copyrights are expressly transferred in writing. The compiler of a collective work owns the copyright in the collective work—that is, the rights to the original selection or arrangement of the collected materials (or to both). Unless the contributing copyright owners granted greater use by contract, ownership of the copyright in the collective work conveys only the privilege of reproducing the contributions together in that collection, in a revision of that collection, or in a later collective work in the same series (17 USC, sec. 201(c)). The Supreme Court confirmed this point in *New York Times Co. v. Tasini* (2001). When newspaper and magazine publishers licensed the contributions of freelancers to electronic-database publishers, the freelancers sued, arguing that the publishers were not authorized to do so. The publishers responded that their use fell within section 201(c), so the issue before the Supreme Court was whether the electronic databases—*Lexis/Nexis* and the *New York Times Ondisc*, each of which contained text only, without the original formatting or accompanying images, and *General Periodicals Ondisc*, an image-based system that reproduced a contribution exactly as it appeared on the printed page but did not allow users to flip to another page—were revisions of the original collective work. The Court decided that they were not, because the databases permitted users to search for and produce each contribution by itself without reference to the other contributions with which it was originally published. In other words, a publisher intending to sublicense a collective work to an electronic publisher was not privileged to do so without first obtaining licenses from (and paying) contributors to the collective work who had retained the copyrights in their contributions. Many publishers responded to the decision by revising their agreements with contributors to collective works to include this sublicensing right.

2.2.4   CO-OWNERSHIP OF COPYRIGHT

Co-ownership of copyright results from two situations. The first is the creation of a *joint work*. The Copyright Act of 1976 and interpreting case law define a joint work as one prepared by two or more authors with the intention both that their separate copyrightable contributions be merged into inseparable or interdependent parts of a unitary whole and that the authors will own the copyright jointly. A common example of a joint work is a song with words and music by different parties who intend to produce an integrated work and own the copyright jointly. An interview can also be a joint work. Co-ownership of copyright can also occur when a person acquires ownership after the work's creation. For example, the owner of a copyright may transfer a portion of it to another—a business partner, a spouse, or a child—or the children of a deceased author may together inherit their parent's copyright under a will. Unless the co-owners specify differently in a written agreement, it is assumed that they own equal interests in the copyright.

Co-owners of a copyright may transfer their respective interests in it separately, without approval of the other owners, but all the co-owners must join in an assignment or exclusive license of the entire copyright.

In the United States, any co-owner of a copyright may license the entire copyright on a nonexclusive basis without the consent of the other co-owners, but one who does so is required to account for the proceeds to the other co-owners and pay them their just shares. As a practical matter, most users of copyrights willing to pay substantial sums for a license will require an exclusive license.

2.2.5   WORKS MADE FOR HIRE

The Copyright Act provides that the employer or other person for whom a *work made for hire* is commissioned is considered the author of that work. A work made for hire can be created in only two ways: either (1) the work is prepared by a regular employee within the scope of employment or (2) the work is commissioned from an independent contractor, the contractor and commissioning party agree in a written agreement, signed by both of them, that the work is made for hire, and the work is one of the following:

- A contribution to a collective work
- Part of a motion picture or other audiovisual work
- A translation
- A supplementary work (i.e., a work prepared for publication as a secondary adjunct to a work by another author for the purpose of introducing, concluding, illustrating, explaining, revising, commenting on, or assisting in the use of the other work, such as a foreword, an afterword, a pictorial illustration, a map, a chart, a table, editorial notes, a musical arrangement, answer material for tests, a bibliography, an appendix, or an index)
- A compilation
- An instructional text (i.e., a literary, pictorial, or graphic work prepared for publication and for use in systematic instructional activities)
- A test
- Answer material for a test
- An atlas

If the work is not described by one of these nine categories, it cannot be commissioned from an independent contractor as a work made for hire.

Under the first statutory definition of work made for hire (employees working within the scope of their employment), the work of faculty members at scholarly institutions could be considered work for hire.

This conclusion is not consistent with case interpretations of the 1909 Copyright Act, and there is considerable argument that the conclusion is not consistent with decades-old practice and would not be satisfactory as public policy. Case law is too scarce to offer reliable guidance. In response to the unsettled legal guidance, many institutions have addressed the problem by written contract or policies that state that faculty members will own the copyrights in their writings and courses except, perhaps, for works that the employer specifically requested, such as a curriculum intended for long-term use by the institution.

Some institutions try to carry out what is essentially an assignment of copyright by means of institutional policies, but because the Copyright Act requires an assignment of copyright to be in writing and signed by the assignor (see 2.2.12), there is a good argument for questioning whether an unsigned policy can legally accomplish that objective; at least one trial court has said that it cannot where there is no clarity about what copyright is being transferred and there is no signature. Scholars should consider this issue when discussing copyright ownership with their employers.

2.2.6   MATERIAL OBJECTS

Copyright law has long provided that the ownership of a copyright or of any right under a copyright, such as an exclusive license, is distinct from ownership of the material object embodying the copyrighted work. The sale or other transfer of the material object does not convey any rights in the copyright unless they are separately granted in writing. Conversely, ownership of a copyright or a right under a copyright does not convey any right in the material object embodying the copyrighted work.

Accordingly, owners of letters, manuscripts, and original works of art have no copyright rights in those works unless the copyright owner specifically conveys copyright rights in writing. The recipient of a letter, for example, owns the physical letter but may not exercise any copyright rights in it, including copying or distributing copies of it. Those rights belong to the author of the letter. Similarly, the owner of a work of art may not exercise any of the copyright rights in the work (including copying or authorizing copying of it) without having received the right to do so from the copyright owner. The Copyright Act makes one exception to this rule, granting the owner a license to display publicly a lawfully made copy of a work (including the original work), such as a book, work of art, letter, or manuscript. If the copyright in a unique work (such as a painting or sculpture) has expired, the owner of the material object may nevertheless be able to regulate copying of the work by controlling physical access to the object.

2.2.7   TERM OF COPYRIGHT

Under the Copyright Act of 1909, which applies to works published before 1 January 1978, a work that was published with a copyright notice (or an unpublished work registered with the Copyright Office) had a term of copyright of twenty-eight years, which could be extended for an additional twenty-eight years if the appropriate claimant filed a renewal application in the Copyright Office in the last year of the first term. Under the 1909 Copyright Act, the consequence of publishing a work without a copyright notice or failing to renew it in the last year of the first term was harsh: the work automatically went into the public domain. (See 2.2.9 on the use of copyright notices after 1 January 1978 and 2.2.10 on automatic renewal for works published in 1964 and after.) The same consequence befell a foreign work that did not comply with the copyright notice, registration, and renewal formalities applicable to the work in the United States. (See 2.2.16 on restoration of foreign copyrights.)

Under the 1976 Copyright Act, as amended, the term of copyright for works first published on or after 1 January 1978 and for works unpublished as of that date is the life of the author plus seventy years after the author's death. The term of copyright for a joint work is the life of the last surviving author plus seventy years. Works that are anonymous, pseudonymous, or made for hire (see 2.2.5) have a copyright term of ninety-five years after first publication or 120 years from creation, whichever expires first.

Works published under the Copyright Act of 1909 that were in their first term of copyright on 1 January 1978, the effective date of the Copyright Act of 1976, have a term of protection of twenty-eight years from the date copyright was secured and a renewal term of sixty-seven years (for a total of ninety-five years of copyright protection) if the renewal copyright was secured as provided in the Copyright Act. A different rule applies to a category of works that were nearing the end of their second, renewal terms when Congress began work on what became the Copyright Act of 1976. Believing that the revision would take a short time, Congress extended the renewal terms of copyrights that would have expired on 19 September 1962 and after so that they would have the benefit of the longer term. But it took Congress approximately fifteen years to revise and pass the 1976 Copyright Act. In the end, Congress passed nine acts that extended until 31 December 1976 terms that otherwise would have expired between 19 September 1962 and 31 December 1976. Then the 1976 Copyright Act provided that the terms of copyright of works that were in their renewal terms at any time between 31 December 1976 and 31 December 1977, inclusive, or were due to be renewed (and were renewed) during that period were extended to endure for seventy-five years from the date copyright was originally secured. Consequently, works published before 1923 are now in the public domain because their terms expired before the 1998 Sonny Bono Copyright Term Extension Act.

Calculating whether a work published before 1 January 1978 is still protected by copyright can be difficult, because learning whether a copyright owner complied with the many formalities requires searching the records of the Copyright Office. Although the Copyright Office plans to put all its records on its Web site, at present only documents filed or recorded on or after 1 January 1978 are available there. To determine whether a work published before 1 January 1978 is under copyright protection, you should check its renewal status. Renewal records for books are available in Stanford University's *Copyright Renewal Database*, an online searchable collection of renewals received by the Copyright Office from 1950 through 1992 for books published in the United States from 1923 through 1963.

In 1994 Congress amended the Copyright Act to implement the obligations of the United States to countries that are members of the Berne Convention and to strengthen protection abroad for United States works (see 2.2.16). The amendments automatically restored to copyright as of 1 January 1996 works that (1) were first published in a foreign country (but not published in the United States within thirty days of that publication) if the country was or would become a member of the Berne Convention or the World Trade Organization and (2) were still protected by copyright in their country of origin but had fallen into the public domain in the United States either because of their failure to comply with the formalities under the Copyright Act of 1909, such as publication with notice, renewal, or compliance with the manufacturing clause, or because the United States had no copyright relations with the country of origin. The legislation also restored to copyright pre-1972 foreign sound recordings, which are not protected by United States copyright law. (Sound recordings published in the United States before 1972 are still not protected by United States copyright.) When copyright was restored, these works were granted the remainder of the term of copyright that they would have had under United States law if the works had never entered the public domain in the United States (and if they had complied with all formalities, such as renewal).

A scholar should carefully investigate the facts before reaching a conclusion about the copyright status of a foreign work. The Copyright Office's Web site includes a list of works for which the copyright owners filed a notice of their intent to enforce their restored copyrights against so-called reliance parties, those who had exercised rights in the works in the period before restoration when they were in the public domain in the United States. The notice of intent to enforce filed with the Copyright Office is considered "constructive notice" (because available for consultation but not served directly on reliance parties) to all reliance parties that they must cease using the works or arrange a license to continue doing so. But that list is not the complete list of works whose copyright owners are enforcing these rights. In addition to the constructive notice provided to the Copyright Office, copyright owners have the option of serving actual notices of their intent to enforce restored copyrights directly on parties that exercised rights in the works before restoration.

Any work published before 1923 is in the public domain in the United States. But determining a work's term of protection in the United States does not determine whether the work is still protected by copyright in other countries of the world. The term of copyright in a particular country is determined by the law of that country. However, the many countries that are and have been members of the Berne Convention for many years measure the term of copyright by the Berne Convention's minimum term of life of the author plus fifty years. When the members of the European Union harmonized their terms of copyright, they extended the term to life of the author plus seventy years. In doing so, many of these countries also granted the longer term to works that had passed into the public domain under the old life-plus-fifty-years rule but that would have still been in copyright under the new life-plus-seventy-years rule. Scholars relying on the public domain status of a work in the United States should consider whether their publications also will be published in a country where the work is still protected by copyright.

2.2.8   REGISTRATION OF COPYRIGHT

Registration has not been required as a condition of copyright protection since 1 January 1978. But the Copyright Act offers advantages to owners who register their copyrights. First, a registration provides an evidentiary presumption in a lawsuit. If the Copyright Office verifies that the work meets the formal requirements of the Copyright Act, registers the claim, and issues a certificate of registration, then in a judicial proceeding this certificate, if issued before publication or within five years after, is prima facie evidence that the copyright and the facts stated in the certificate are valid.

Second, a registration enables an owner of copyright in a United States work to initiate an action for infringement; registration gives the court jurisdiction. The registration of a collective work in the name of the owner of the collective work will not serve as the required jurisdictional registration for an infringement action brought by an author of a contribution to the collective work if the author retained the copyright in the contribution. The author must obtain a separate registration in order to commence an infringement action. Owners of copyrights in foreign works protected under the Berne Convention are exempt from the requirement to register before initiating an action for infringement.

Third, in an action for infringement of an unpublished work, the plaintiff is not entitled to an award of statutory damages or attorney's fees if the infringement began before the effective date of registration. Similarly, a plaintiff is not entitled to statutory damages or attorney's fees for infringement of a published work if the infringement began after first publication and before the effective date of registration, unless registration was made within three months after first publication. But whenever the infringement and the registration occur, the owner of an infringed work is always entitled to actual damages, such as lost income, as well as the infringer's profits attributable to the infringement, so long as they are not considered in the computing of actual damages. (See 2.2.15 on actual damages.)

The owner of a copyright may register it by depositing with the Copyright Office an application form, the prescribed fee, and the number of copies of the work that the office specifies (usually one copy or two of the edition of the work that is first published in the United States). Often the author's publisher undertakes this process, and the author can provide in the publishing agreement for the publisher to register the copyright in the author's name (see 2.3). Forms for registration vary according to the class of work being registered, and all are available from the Copyright Office through its Web site. Instructions accompany each form, including the Copyright Office's address, the appropriate fee, and a description of the kind and number of deposit copies required. Even if copyright is not registered, however, deposit of the work is required by law within three months of publication. This deposit requirement is intended to build the collection of the Library of Congress, of which the Copyright Office is a division. The deposit for registration can satisfy both the deposit requirement and the registration procedure.

2.2.9   COPYRIGHT NOTICE

Even after the effective date of the 1976 Copyright Act (1 Jan. 1978), copyright notice was required on works published in the United States and elsewhere that claimed the protection of United States copyright law. But failure to include a copyright notice on first publication did not put a work in the public domain if the copyright owner followed statutory directions for remedying the omission. On the effective date of the Berne Convention Implementation Act of 1988—1 March 1989— notice was no longer required, because the Berne Convention stipulates that there be no conditions to obtaining copyright.

Nevertheless, it is advantageous for all works to bear a copyright notice. The notice should be visible either directly or with the aid of a device, such as a computer. The form of the notice consists of three elements (17 USC, sec. 401):

1. The word *Copyright*, the symbol ©, or the abbreviation *Copr.*
2. The year of first publication of the work
3. The name of the owner of the copyright in the work, an abbreviation by which the name can be recognized, or some other designation of the owner of the copyright

The phrase *All rights reserved* that appears after many copyright notices was required by the Pan American Conventions, to which the United States and many Latin American countries were parties. Now that all the signatories of those treaties are also signatories of Berne by virtue of their membership in the World Trade Organization, omission of that phrase does not result in the loss of copyright protection in those countries. Moreover, there is a good argument that requiring a notice that "rights are reserved" would be, like requiring a copyright notice, inconsistent with the Berne Convention's prohibition of such conditions.

If a notice following the requirements of the Copyright Act is placed in or on a work, then a court must give no weight to a defendant's defense that the infringement was innocent and that damages should be mitigated. Further, the use of the symbol ©, though not of the term *Copyright* or *Copr.* alone, in a notice gains rights for the copyright owner in countries that belong to the Universal Copyright Convention

(UCC) but not to the Berne Convention. (Not all members of the UCC are also members of the Berne Convention.)

It is possible for someone to print less than all the pages of a work published online, thus separating the portion read from the copyright notice that may appear in a preliminary part of the work. It may be advisable to ensure that a copyright notice appears on each page of a work in electronic form to alert readers that copyright should be respected.

A notice of copyright on a collective work in the name of the proprietor of the collection protects all the component parts, even if they are of different ownership and were originally published in various years. Separate notices of copyright for component parts may be properly used if the publisher is willing to print them. No notice of copyright renewal is required for works in which copyright was renewed. Under the Copyright Act, the year of first publication of the work is the proper year for the notice even in the renewal term and even when a work is republished long after the initial publication.

2.2.10   RENEWAL OF COPYRIGHT

Renewal of copyright applies only to works under the 1909 Copyright Act—that is, works published before 1 January 1978. But authors should be aware of the relevant law when trying to determine whether a work they wish to reproduce is in the public domain. Before 1992 copyright-renewal applications had to be filed in the twenty-eighth year of the copyright for all works published before 1 January 1978. If a copyright was not renewed, the work fell into the public domain. After a 1992 amendment to the Copyright Act, copyrights secured in 1964 and later renew automatically even if no application is filed. In the case of works that are owned by a proprietor other than by assignment from an author, a post-1963 copyright renews automatically in the name of the proprietor if no application is filed. These works can include posthumous works, periodicals, encyclopedic and composite works owned by the proprietor or its predecessor in interest in the original term, and works created for hire (see 2.2.5).

When copyright in a work is owned by an author, the Copyright Act gives the renewal term to the author, if living; to the widow, widower, or children as a class if the author is not living; to the author's executor if the author and author's spouse and children are not living; or to the author's next of kin if the author left no will. The renewal follows the order specified in the statute and does not follow state inheritance law or the author's will. Furthermore, an author's grant of the renewal term is not effective if the author does not live into the renewal term, which is why an author may not leave by will a renewal copyright that has not yet vested in the author. The reason for this restriction is that the author does not own the renewal term unless the author is alive when the renewal application is filed in the twenty-eighth year of the copyright or when the renewal term commences. As these arrangements make evident, copyright is not property in the ordinary sense. It is created by Congress, and the renewal term is also created by Congress, which decides who is entitled to the renewal term.

2.2.11   RIGHTS OF COPYRIGHT OWNERS

The proprietor of copyright in a work is given by statute the exclusive right to do or authorize others to do any of the following actions (17 USC, sec. 106):

- Reproduce the work
- Distribute copies of the work to the public by sale or other transfer of ownership or by rental, lease, or lending
- Prepare derivative works based on the work
- Perform the work publicly if it is a literary, musical, dramatic, or choreographic work; a pantomime; or a motion picture or another kind of audiovisual work
- Display the work publicly if it is a literary, musical, dramatic, or choreographic work; a pantomime; or a pictorial, graphic, or sculptural work, including the individual images of a motion picture or of another kind of audiovisual work
- Perform the work publicly by means of a digital audio transmission if it is a sound recording

The Copyright Act provides numerous specific exceptions to these exclusive rights and a general exception for fair use (see 2.2.13). For example, section 110(1) of the Copyright Act permits performance and display of an audiovisual work, such as a motion picture, in face-to-face teaching activities of a nonprofit educational institution. In 2002, in response to new technology, Congress passed the TEACH Act, codified in section 110(2) and in a section of definitions following 110(10), which permits additional exceptions for distance education when conducted in accordance with several requirements. Section 105 states that a work created by a federal (but not a state) government officer or employee as part of that person's official duties is in the public domain. This includes judicial decisions, legislative reports, works of federal agencies, and presidential speeches. Section 108 provides exceptions to the copyright owner's exclusive rights for libraries and archives. As of this writing, the Copyright Office is conducting studies intended to lead to revisions that recognize digital technology. In 1996 Congress added section 121 of the Copyright Act, which provides that it is not an infringement for certain nonprofit organizations and government agencies to reproduce or distribute copies of a nondramatic literary work made for the blind or other persons with disabilities.

2.2.12   TRANSFERS AND TERMINATIONS

Copyright ownership resides with the author unless the author transfers it to another party. The term *transfer of copyright ownership* is defined to include an assignment, an exclusive license, and any other conveyance of any of the exclusive rights comprised in a copyright, but it does not include a nonexclusive license. Ownership of a copyright may also be bequeathed. A transfer of copyright ownership is not valid unless it is in writing and signed by the author or the author's authorized agent. (See 2.2.5 on the writing requirement for the creation of a work for hire.)

The 1976 Copyright Act contains a provision (sec. 203) that permits termination of an assignment of copyright or an exclusive or nonexclusive license of any right under a copyright in a work, other than a work made for hire, executed by the author on or after 1 January 1978. Congress's purpose in creating this termination provision was to protect authors against unremunerative transfers by giving them an opportunity to recapture the rights and transfer them anew. Termination may be effected during a period of five years after the expiration of thirty-five years from the date of the grant, but if the grant covers the right to publish the work, the five-year period begins thirty-five years after publication of the work or forty years after the date of the grant, whichever is earlier.

The 1976 Copyright Act also contains an analogous provision (sec. 304(c)) permitting termination of an assignment of copyright or an exclusive or nonexclusive license of any right under a copyright in a work, other than a work made for hire, executed before 1 January 1978 by the author, the author's spouse or children, the author's executors, or the author's next of kin. But this termination right is not effective during the same periods as the one under section 203. The objective of the termination right under section 304(c) is to permit the copyright owners to terminate and renegotiate rights at the beginning of the extended renewal term granted by the 1976 Copyright Act (i.e., at the end of fifty-six years from first publication) or, if the termination right is not exercised then, at the beginning of the further extended term granted in 1998 by the Sonny Bono Copyright Term Extension Act (i.e., at the end of seventy-five years from first publication).

The Copyright Act (under secs. 203 and 304(c)) specifies who may terminate a grant, the type of notice of termination required, and when the notice must be given. Whenever an assignment is terminated, all copyright rights that were covered by it revert to the author or other parties owning termination rights. Failure to give proper and timely notice and to file it in the Copyright Office, in Washington, DC, results in an irrevocable lapse of the termination right, and the grant continues for the balance of the copyright term for works subject to section 203 termination or until the second termination period for works subject to section 304(c) termination.

The Copyright Act of 1976 makes clear that an author may terminate an assignment or license of copyright rights even if the eligible terminating party agreed not to do so. Congress added this provision to ensure that authors (or their heirs) would not be forced by weak bargaining postures to give up the termination right as had happened with the renewal copyright under the 1909 Copyright Act.

2.2.13   FAIR USE OF COPYRIGHTED WORKS

The rights of copyright owners are not absolute. The Copyright Act provides many limitations on these rights (see 2.2.11); the most important limitation is known as *fair use*. The purpose of fair use is to advance creativity and public knowledge. Under this doctrine, someone who does not own the copyright in a work may be entitled to make limited use of the work without permission of the owner for purposes "such as criticism, comment, news reporting, teaching . . . , scholarship, or research." The Copyright Act of 1976 for the first time set forth criteria for fair use, which previously had been enunciated and interpreted through judicial decisions. The law now provides that the fair use of a copyrighted work is not an infringement of copyright. The statute lists four nonexclusive factors to be considered in determining whether a use of a copyrighted work is fair (17 USC, sec. 107):

1. The purpose and character of the use, including whether it is of a commercial nature or for nonprofit educational purposes

2. The nature of the copyrighted work
3. The amount and substantiality of the portion used in relation to the copyrighted work as a whole
4. The effect of the use on the potential market for or value of the copyrighted work

Congress intended the statutory provisions above to restate the fair use doctrine that existed before passage of the act, not to change, narrow, or enlarge it in any way, as the reports of the House and Senate committees make clear. Accordingly, all decisions of the courts before and after the enactment of the 1976 Copyright Act are relevant to determining the application of fair use to any question of copyright law. This means that factors other than those listed in the statute may be considered if they are relevant to the particular case. A factor not listed in the statute that courts often consider is the good faith of the party using the material. Furthermore, the Copyright Act makes no statement about the relative importance of the factors, and the Supreme Court clarified in *Campbell v. Acuff-Rose Music, Inc.* (1994) that no one factor is more important than the others, nor must the use be supported by all four factors to be fair. In a determination of fair use, each fact involved must be considered and weighed against the others. Because the analysis depends so much on the facts of the particular use, this weighing of the four factors has been referred to as the most difficult issue in copyright.

In discussing the first factor, the purpose and character of the use, the courts give greater latitude to uses "such as criticism, comment, news reporting, teaching . . . , scholarship, or research" and to uses that are for nonprofit educational rather than commercial purposes. The courts consider whether the use is "transformative." In the first years following the Supreme Court's *Campbell v. Acuff-Rose* decision, which enunciated this transformative requirement, courts interpreted it to mean that the use adds to the original work something new and possibly different in form, as a parody does.

More recently, courts have also shown a willingness to consider whether the context of the use of the work or the way the work is used is transformative. For example, an appellate court, recognizing the robust indexing capability of the Internet, held in *Kelly v. Arriba Soft Corp.* (2002) that reproduction on a Web site of small, low-resolution thumbnails of images for the purpose of showing what pictures were available on the Internet was a fair use. In another appellate case, *Bill Graham Archives v. Dorling Kindersley Limited* (2006), the court held that the use of reduced images of seven of the famous posters that advertised the rock concerts of the Grateful Dead in a biography of the group was a transformative use because they, along with other visual materials and text, served to create the historical context of the group. But reproduction that essentially substitutes for the original work is more likely to be considered an infringement.

The second fair use factor, the nature of the copyrighted work, looks at whether the original work is fictional or nonfictional. Factual works tend to be accorded less protection because, unlike a work of fiction, they are not wholly creative and contain unprotected material, including facts, theories, and ideas (see 2.2.2). In addition, their expression is less likely to be creative because it is dictated by the factual nature of the subject matter.

The third fair use factor considers the amount of the underlying work used, both quantitatively and qualitatively. In general, this factor cautions against use of more than is necessary, but use of even a small part of the original work may weigh against the user if the part is critical. For example, in *Harper and Row Publishers v. The Nation Enterprises* (1985), the Supreme Court concluded that the use of only 350 words from President Gerald Ford's entire memoir was not a fair use because the passage, which recounted Ford's pardon of President Richard Nixon, was the portion of the memoir most interesting to readers and so was qualitatively too significant. This does not mean that use of an extensive part, even the entire work, is impossible, but the second author must be able to justify it. Although one occasionally hears that it is acceptable to use some percentage of a work or some specified number of words, neither the statute nor any regulation nor case law sanctions such guidelines on the quantity of material protected by copyright that may be taken without permission, and authors should not rely on them.

The last fair use factor considers the effect of the use on the potential market for or value of the original work. This consideration does not mean that the owner of the copyright in the original work can preempt all subsequent uses by licensing the work. A court could still find that the use did not substantially diminish the copyright owner's market or that the other factors outweighed this one.

Fair use of unpublished works is more restricted than that of published works. In 1992 Congress added the following sentence to section 107 of the Copyright Act: "The fact that a work is unpublished shall not itself bar a finding of fair use if such finding is made upon consideration of all the above factors." This amendment responded to a series of cases in which the United States Court of Appeals for the Second Circuit denied fair use to users of unpublished letters by J. D. Salinger and L. Ron Hubbard. Letters, manuscripts, and other archival materials are examples of works that may be unpublished.

Authors evaluating whether their use is fair, just like a court considering a claim of fair use, must weigh all the factors in the light of the ultimate purpose of the fair use doctrine. In evaluating a use, authors should begin by thinking about why they need to use the copyrighted work. Why is it essential to the work being created? The more the use is necessary to commentary, critique, or the expression of scholarly opinion, the more likely the use will be viewed as transformative. Authors should guard against using a copyrighted work because it would make their own work more amusing or entertaining. That objective is not among the ones the statute says are permissible, "such as criticism, comment, news reporting, teaching . . . , scholarship, or research."

If a creative work—which is usually accorded more protection than a nonfiction work involving unprotectable facts—is being used, the author should consider whether the other fair use factors justify proceeding without permission. The author should also consider whether more of the copyrighted work is being used than is necessary to the author's goal. Is the other work unpublished, and is the author depriving the original author of the right to publish it? If so, that should be a factor in not using the work or not using much of it, and if the author cannot avoid publishing a large amount of an unpublished work, that alone, depending on the nature of the work, may decide the question against the use. Finally, the author should candidly consider whether the use is likely to affect a meaningful market for the copyright owner's work. Even if it does, the other factors may outweigh this consideration in the context of the particular use, but the possible harm to the first author should not be ignored.

The same kind of analysis applies to visual material, but here the need to use all the work should figure more strongly in the author's analysis. Is the use of all of an image justified by being transformative, and what is the nature of the image that is being reproduced? This issue frequently arises for books involving art. Although a public domain work may be reproduced, many authors are hesitant to do so in the belief that a photograph of a public domain work is itself the subject of copyright. No appeals court has addressed this question, but a well-reasoned decision from a federal trial court in New York, *Bridgeman Art Library, Ltd. v. Corel Corp.* (1999), concluded that, as a matter of public policy, a photograph faithfully reproducing a two-dimensional public domain work should not be accorded copyright protection, because doing so would have the effect of potentially keeping the work in copyright forever. The court did not extend its analysis to photographs of three-dimensional works, recognizing that the choice of how to photograph such objects entails greater originality. But because this case has limited application, authors should be careful about relying on it without first consulting with their editors.

The fair use analysis is different for an image on the cover of a book. The cover of a work is seen as serving an advertising and promotional purpose that weighs against fair use because of its commercial objectives.

2.2.14   REQUESTING PERMISSION

The Supreme Court has said that requesting permission to use a copyrighted work should not be interpreted to mean that the requester thinks that the use is not fair, recognizing that even where a use is believed fair, it may still be prudent to ask for permission. Written permission to reproduce copyrighted materials should be obtained if there is a substantial question whether the use is fair or if there is no other specific statutory exception allowing the use. Part of the reason for caution is that authors usually warrant to a publisher that they have all the rights necessary to publish and that doing so will not infringe another copyright, and they promise to indemnify the publisher if the warranty is breached. Litigating a fair use question can be enormously expensive because the courts have to examine in detail each of the four factors described in 2.2.13. A defendant found to have infringed a copyright may be liable for damages (see 2.2.15).

An author should allow a substantial amount of time for obtaining permission. It is not a defense against a copyright-infringement claim that there was insufficient time to obtain permission or that a rights holder failed to respond to an inquiry about permission. A request for permission should specify the full extent of the material intended to be used as well as particulars of the use, including the type of publication in which the material would appear and the geographic distribution of the publication. The name of the publisher, the date of publication, and the price of the projected work are helpful in a permission request if they are known. Most presses provide written guidelines on how to obtain permissions, and some provide forms or sample letters to help authors accomplish this task. In addition, rights holders' Web sites often contain instructions and forms for authors who apply for permission.

DAMAGES FOR COPYRIGHT INFRINGEMENT
                    AND ATTORNEY'S FEES

While infringement litigation is pending, a court may issue a preliminary injunction if the court is persuaded that the plaintiff is likely to prevail at trial. A variety of remedies are available to someone whose copyright has been infringed. The court may issue an injunction to prevent or restrain the infringement and may order the impounding of copies made in violation of the copyright owner's rights as well as all film, plates, digital files, and other production materials from which copies could be reproduced. In addition, an infringer is liable for the actual damages that the copyright owner suffered as a result of the infringement and for profits the infringer made from the infringement so long as they do not duplicate the copyright owner's actual damages. However, not all copyright owners whose rights have been infringed can prove that they suffered damages, and not all infringers make profits. The Copyright Act gives the copyright owner the right to elect statutory damages instead of actual damages and profits. For each work (not each infringement), statutory damages consist of not less than $750 or more than $30,000. When the court finds that the infringer was not aware and had no reason to believe that the acts committed were infringing, it may reduce the award to not less than $200; when the court finds that the infringement was willful, it may increase the award to $150,000. In a jury case, the jury determines the amount of the award.

In addition to damages, the court may at its discretion award the copyright owner reasonable attorney's fees and other costs of bringing the action. An unsuccessful plaintiff in an infringement action may have to pay the defendant's costs and attorney's fees if the court determines that the case was objectively unreasonable. No award of statutory damages or attorney's fees may be made for an infringement of an unpublished work that began before copyright registration or for an infringement of a published work that began before the effective date of registration unless registration was made within three months after first publication of the work. (On registration, see 2.2.8.) The award of attorney's fees may be less than the amount charged by the attorney, who is not bound by the award to reduce the fee.

The term *plagiarism* is not used in the Copyright Act. Plagiarism brings a moral stigma and penalties in institutions, but it is legally punishable only to the extent that it qualifies as copyright infringement. (On plagiarism, see 6.2.)

2.2.16   INTERNATIONAL COPYRIGHT

For the first one hundred years of American history, the United States was a copyright piracy center, extending no copyright protection to foreigners. Beginning in 1891, foreigners were permitted to obtain some copyright rights in the United States by complying with complicated formalities. The Berne Convention, which affords a high level of protection, was adopted by many countries of the world in 1886. Instead of joining Berne, the United States negotiated with individual countries to arrive at bilateral treaties affecting copyright. These treaties continued until 1955, when the United States joined a multinational copyright convention it had proposed, the Universal Copyright Convention, called the UCC. It is from this treaty that the copyright world outside the United States acquired the symbol © as a part of the notice claiming copyright.

In the meantime, however, United States publishers attempted to secure Berne Convention rights for their works by the so-called back door to Berne. The Berne Convention covers works first or simultaneously published in a Berne member country. As a result, some quintessentially American works were first published in England, including *Tom Sawyer*, *Huckleberry Finn*, and *Moby-Dick*. It later became common practice for United States publishers to publish their books simultaneously in the United States and Canada, a member of the Berne Convention.

The United States signed the Berne Convention in 1988 and the terms of the convention became effective on 1 March 1989. Because Berne standards do not allow a member country to require that copyright owners comply with formalities in order to secure copyright, Congress had to amend the Copyright Act to exempt Berne claimants from procedures such as notice, registration, and deposit as requirements for copyright. (These formalities became optional for United States copyright owners as well, although to encourage registration Congress made certain benefits—e.g., eligibility for statutory damages and attorney's fees—contingent on registration before infringement [see 2.2.15].) The accession of the United States to Berne afforded protection in the United States for works from member countries and protected works of United States origin in those countries, more numerous than the membership of the UCC, without resort to the problematic back door to Berne.

But the United States did not fully carry out its obligation to accord rights to works in Berne member countries until it signed the World Trade Organization Agreement in 1994. This treaty contained several subsidiary agreements, including the Agreement on Trade-Related Aspects of Intellectual Property Rights (TRIPs), which required the restoration to copyright of certain foreign works that were in the public domain in the United States but were protected in a country of origin belonging to Berne. This obligation was implemented by the enactment in 1994 of the Uruguay Round Agreements Act, which automatically restored to copyright, on 1 January 1996, foreign works that were in copyright in the country where they were created but that had fallen into the public domain in the United States for failing to comply with some formality of United States copyright law.

Berne sets out broad minimal guidelines, but each member country implements them in its own way. The rights accorded an author's work in a particular country depend on the law there. For example, the concept of fair use, a central aspect of United States copyright law, plays no part in the law of most countries. Not all countries recognize the concept of work made for hire. And while Berne prescribes a term of copyright of the life of the author plus fifty years, many countries have adopted life plus seventy years or longer.

The laws of many European countries, especially France, recognize a series of moral rights of authors, such as the right to claim authorship of one's work, the right to prevent others from using one's work or name in a manner that harms one's reputation as an author, and the right to prevent distortion of one's work. Moral rights reflect a tradition of copyright in which authors' writings are considered a part of their personalities. An author usually retains these moral rights even after transferring all economic rights in a copyright to another party. The Berne Convention expressly recognizes some moral rights—for example, the rights to claim authorship and to prevent distortion or other modification of the work. United States law extends Berne Convention moral rights to certain works of visual art, though not to works of other kinds. Still, for any work, claims of severe distortion may be actionable under state laws as defamation or on other grounds.

2.2.17   COPYRIGHT AND COMPUTER NETWORKS

With the advent and growth of computer networks, including the Web and online databases, came questions about using copyrighted materials in these new environments, about the liability of service providers that give access to the Internet, and about the liability of entities that provide software and hardware that can be used to infringe copyrights. Lawsuits led to efforts to achieve solutions on a global scale, such as ratification by the United States of two World Intellectual Property Organization (WIPO) treaties, and then in 1998 to passage of the Digital Millennium Copyright Act (DMCA), including the WIPO Copyright and Performances and Phonograms Treaties Implementation Act and the Online Copyright Infringement Liability Limitation Act. But because of the rapid changes in technology, there still are no definitive decisions on many applications of copyright in the digital environment. The courts are grappling with how law designed to deal with physical copies should be applied in the digital realm, where anyone can make and distribute an unlimited number of copies of a work with minimal effort and without giving up possession of the work.

Copyright principles, including fair use and other statutory exceptions, apply in electronic environments, such as the Internet and databases, although not always smoothly. While all the relevant issues are not settled, visitors to Web sites should assume, as they do when reading print material, that works that are subjects of copyright are protected by it unless the term of protection has expired and therefore are not available for copying without permission or a statutory exception. Although not required to do so, many Web sites state—usually on a page labeled "Legal Notices" or "Terms and Conditions" or "User Agreement"—whether users are permitted to download or print a copy of a copyrighted work and, if they are, for what purpose. If a site offers a mechanism for printing a work or e-mailing it to someone, the site owner implies a license to copy or distribute the work in that way. The owner probably is not authorizing users to download the work to a hard drive for later copying and distribution and almost certainly not for commercial exploitation.

Downloading and uploading (transferring works from and to network servers) are essentially copying. There is an argument that uploading a work for viewing by others is also an exercise of the public display right. Because of the way the Internet functions, arguments have arisen about when and how the display right is implicated. Sup-

pose that a search engine used for finding images on the Internet re-
trieves an image from the Web site that provides it and seamlessly
integrates the image into the search engine's results page so as to give
the user the impression that the image is reproduced there. Which entity is displaying the image—the site that provides it or the search engine that frames the image on its own page for viewing? One appellate
decision holds that it is the former, but it would be a mistake to think
that a decision from one court settles the issue.

Courts have also addressed fair use online and held that when a
search engine shows thumbnails of images (i.e., small, low-resolution
copies) for the purpose of indexing the images available on the Internet, the copying is a fair use. Analyzing and balancing the four fair
use factors, the courts have concluded that the function of indexing
and improving access to images on the Internet is transformative and
does not interfere with or substitute for the aesthetic experience of
viewing the original, full-size images; the photographs were already
published, so publication of the thumbnails does not deprive the pho-
tographer of the right of first publication; copying only a portion of
the images would not fulfill the transformative function; and the reso-
lution of the thumbnails is not high enough to deprive the photogra-
pher of the market for selling copies or licensing use of the original
works.

Before passage of the DMCA, several cases considered the question
whether the operator of a service that provided access to the Internet—an Internet service provider, or ISP—should be liable when one
of its subscribers transmitted infringing material through a Web site or
a bulletin board, even when the ISP was unaware of the transmission.
This problem was addressed by a part of the DMCA, the Online Copyright Infringement Liability Limitation Act (17 USC, sec. 512). For in-
fringements made possible by certain functions of an ISP—routing
or providing connections for material through a system or network
that the ISP owns or controls, caching material on a system or network that the ISP owns or controls, storing material placed by a third
party on a system or network that the ISP owns or controls, and link-
ing to an infringing site from a system or network that the ISP owns or
controls—the statute bars anyone from obtaining monetary damages
from the ISP and allows only narrow injunctions against it, so long as
the ISP complies with requirements that the statute specifies.

The initial major cases involving the Internet related not to direct copyright infringement but to the secondary (contributory and vicarious)

liability of providers that offered free, peer-to-peer software that facilitated the unauthorized sharing of copies of copyrighted sound recordings among users of the software. *A&M Records v. Napster, Inc.* (2001) and *In re Aimster Copyright Litigation* (2003) found that two such providers were vicariously or contributorily liable for direct infringement by the users of their software. The courts found liability because the providers in these cases controlled central indexes or servers. In response to these decisions, providers offered software that was decentralized. Movie studios and recording companies challenged this new software in a case, *Metro-Goldwyn-Mayer Studios, Inc. v. Grokster, Ltd.*, that made its way to the Supreme Court. In its decision, the Court announced a new theory of secondary liability, "inducement," explaining that if an entity "distributes a device with the object of promoting its use to infringe copyright, as shown by clear expression or other affirmative steps taken to foster infringement," that entity is "liable for the resulting acts of infringement by third parties" (545 US 913–66; 2005; print; 936–37).

The dazzling capabilities of the Internet, which include the easy copying and distribution that distress copyright owners, have for the first time made the general public intensely aware of (and often hostile to) copyright laws. The challenge for the future will be to accommodate the legitimate interests of copyright owners with this new technology in a way that does not stifle it or unduly frustrate the public.

2.3
PUBLISHING CONTRACTS

2.3.1   BOOKS

The most common form of license by which exclusive rights under a copyright are transferred is the contract between author and publisher for publication of a book. Authors of scholarly books and textbooks usually negotiate their own contracts with publishers, whereas authors of trade books are commonly represented by agents. The subjects that must be covered by a publication contract are the grant, the term, the compensation, subsidiary rights and payments for them, the acceptability of the manuscript, the correction of proofs, the copyright notice and credit, the index, permissions, warranties and indemnities, and the publisher's agreement to publish the work. Other subjects covered may be revisions and subsequent editions, competing publications, an option on the author's next work, the author's termination of the contract and recapture of rights, and the publisher's termination of the contract. A brief explanation of these subjects follows.

Grant. The contract for a scholarly book or textbook normally has the author transfer the copyright to the publisher, although there is no legal requirement that the author do so. Because publishers cannot accept competition on the same work, most contracts contain a grant of exclusive rights to publish the work in book form. The contract usually calls for the author to "grant and assign" to the publisher "any and all" rights associated with the work for "any and all" purposes in "any and all" languages, forms (e.g., clothbound, paperbound), and media (e.g., print, electronic), whether now known or later developed, throughout the world. If the author is granting exclusive rights and not assigning the copyright, the word *assign* should not be used in the granting language.

A publisher sometimes fashions the contract so that it commissions the work as a work made for hire. A consequence of this arrangement is that the publisher is considered the author for copyright purposes, although the publisher may be willing to give writer's credit to the original author. Under the Copyright Act, only nine categories of works can be commissioned as works for hire (see 2.2.5). No other kind of work can be commissioned as a work made for hire.

As copyright owner or exclusive licensee, the publisher takes on the responsibility of not only filing the proper forms with the Copyright Office and paying the appropriate fee but also guarding against unauthorized use of the work, negotiating subsidiary rights, and looking after administrative work related to licensing (e.g., receiving and responding to requests for permission, setting and collecting fees).

Term. The publisher customarily requests as a term the life of the copyright and any renewals or extensions of it, including extensions provided for by future legislation. The reference to "renewals" is now anachronistic because renewal rights arose only under the 1909 Copyright Act and do not apply to works published on or after 1 January 1978.

Compensation. Compensation to the author may take the form of royalties, based on a percentage of sales. Not all publishers offer royalties, and when they do, rates vary considerably. Customary rates range from five to fifteen percent. For scholarly books, the rate may be based on the publisher's net receipts from sales, while trade book royalties are based on the publisher's suggested retail price. The royalty offered on a clothbound edition of a book may be higher than that offered on a paperbound edition. In addition, while some publishers pay the same rate for all copies sold, others use a sliding scale, paying a higher royalty after a certain number of copies have been sold (e.g., eight percent on the first one thousand clothbound copies sold and ten percent thereafter). For a book with multiple authors, the publisher may divide the royalties among the authors or pay honoraria in lieu of royalties.

The author may receive an advance payment against future royalties earned, a fixed sum paid before the publication of the book. After gaining income from sales of the book, the publisher records the royalties due to the author. When the royalties due exceed the amount of the advance payment, the publisher makes additional payments on the schedule established in the contract. The author should ensure that an advance is nonreturnable so that if the book does not earn sufficient royalties to cover the advance, the author is not responsible for repaying the publisher. No royalty is typically paid for works made for hire, but a fixed fee may be paid. Publishers usually do not make royalties reports (or payments of royalties) more than once (for scholarly books) or twice (for trade books) a year. The statement, reporting the sales or revenues and computing the royalties for each period, precedes or accompanies the check from the publisher to the author. The contract may state that if the royalties for a period fall below a certain amount (e.g., fifty dollars), the publisher will hold the sum over until the royalty account reaches the minimum figure. Publishers also may claim the right to retain part (usually ten percent) of an author's royalties as a reserve against books that are sold but later returned. In general, such a reserve is unnecessary after three or four royalty periods. Authors are also commonly given a stated number of free copies of the book and the opportunity to purchase additional copies at a reduced price. None of these copies may be resold, and royalties are not paid on them.

Subsidiary Rights and Payments. The rights the publisher exercises through sublicenses to others are called subsidiary rights (or, colloquially, "subrights"). All the subsidiary rights in other publication forms and media granted by the author to the publisher should be stated in the contract, and the division of proceeds that result from such rights should be specified. Subsidiary rights usually include copublication by a foreign English-language publisher; translation; republication of parts of the work by other publishers in periodicals (first serial rights if before book publication and second serial rights if after book publication), anthologies, and electronic databases; and classroom photocopying of a portion of the work. Usually the publisher splits equally with the author the proceeds from licensing of subsidiary rights.

Acceptability of the Manuscript. The author normally agrees to deliver a manuscript of a specified length, often together with such supplements as "illustrations, maps, and charts" (typically qualified as "camera-ready" or "reproducible without redrawing"), in a specified form (e.g., on computer disks as well as printed) or a specified number of legible copies, on or before a certain date, "time being of the essence." (The latter phrase enables the publisher to cancel the contract and to retrieve any advance against royalties if the author does not deliver the manuscript by the date specified.) Publishers contract for an acceptable literary property, not labor and services. Hence, the contract also specifies that the work must be acceptable (or satisfactory) to the publisher, unless the work is already written before the signing of the contract (and even then the contract form may contain such a clause). Much litigation has arisen over the meaning of the term *acceptable (or satisfactory) to the publisher.* Although the term is usually interpreted to favor the publisher, courts in recent years have been less willing to uphold a publisher's rejection of a work based on its view that the work will not sell well when the view is formed after the contract is signed and the author has submitted an otherwise satisfactory manuscript.

Correction of Proofs. The author will be required to correct proofs within a reasonable time and to share the cost of large changes to the proofs other than corrections of printer's (typesetter's) errors. The author normally also agrees that the publisher may proceed to publish the manuscript if the author does not return the proofs at a specified time. The typical contract does not oblige the publisher to accept any of the author's changes in proof and provides that the publisher may charge the author for the cost of proofreading should the author fail to read and return proofs.

Copyright Notice and Credit. The publisher usually undertakes to register the copyright in accordance with United States copyright law. Since the law no longer requires copyright registration or notices, authors should be sure that the contract obligates the publisher to register the work with the Copyright Office (within three months of publication, which ensures damage benefits to the publisher and author if the work is ever infringed) and to include in each copy of the work a copyright notice in the author's name (unless the author has assigned the copyright or agreed to the commissioning of a work made for hire). Authorship is not usually the subject of a publishing contract, although it is customary for a publisher to credit the author. But without a contract provision requiring that the author be credited, failing to do so is not considered a breach of contract. After the 1993 Supreme Court decision in *Dastar Corp. v. Twentieth Century Fox Film Corp.*, it is recommended that an author ask for a provision ensuring that the author will be acknowledged on the work as the author.

Index. Authors are usually required to provide an index for the book, preparing it themselves (see 1.6.3) or having it prepared at their expense, within a stated number of days after receiving page proofs from the publisher. The contract normally provides that if the author fails to do so, the publisher will have an index prepared and charge the cost to the author's royalty account.

Permissions. The publisher expects the author to obtain written permission to use copyrighted material included in the book, usually requiring the author to furnish a copy of each permission to the publisher (see 1.3 and 2.2.14). Since copyrighted material may be subject to fair use and thus included without permission, the author should be knowledgeable about fair use (see 2.2.13) and should consult with the publisher if there is uncertainty about whether permission is required. While many scholarly publishers employ fair use boldly, some of them make determinations about the necessity of permission by considering their own interest; to avoid all risks of litigation, such publishers are less likely to rely on fair use, even if applicable.

Warranties and Indemnities. The author is typically asked to warrant that the work is original, that the author is the sole author (or has obtained permission for any copyrighted material included in the book) and has full power to make the agreement, that the work was not published previously, and that it is not the subject of any other publishing agreement. In addition, the author is asked to warrant that the work violates neither the law nor the rights of third parties with respect to copyright infringement, libel, and invasion of privacy and publicity rights. The author should be knowledgeable about fair use (see 2.2.13) and should secure permission for the inclusion of copyrighted material only when necessary. The contract may also include warranties that procedures or other matters that the author advises the reader to do or use are not injurious and that factual statements are supported by research. The contract requires the author to indemnify the publisher against loss from the author's breach (and usually also from claims of breach) of the warranties and to pay reasonable attorney's fees expended by the publisher in defense of the book.

Publisher's Agreement to Publish the Work. The publisher typically agrees to publish the manuscript in "such manner and style" as the publisher deems "best." The agreement to publish thus makes the publisher the final arbiter of the appropriate design and content of the book and normally gives the publisher the sole right to set the price of the work. Some publishers stipulate an outside date for publication, measured from the signing of the contract. Even if no outside date is set, the publisher legally cannot hold exclusive rights indefinitely without exercising them and paying the author.

Revisions and Subsequent Editions. A revision clause is important to a publisher for certain scholarly and trade books and for all textbooks. The contract may provide that the publisher, when planning, for example, a new edition of the work, may obtain revisions from a third-party expert if the author refuses to make them or disagrees about their necessity and that the cost will be deducted from the author's royalties. The contract should provide that the original author and the revising author be given separate credits.

Competing Publications. Many publishing contracts contain a provision prohibiting the author from writing, editing, or contributing to a competing publication. The problem with such a provision is that a precise definition of a competing publication is difficult to frame and an overbroad definition is unfair to the author. Factors that can be used to limit the scope of such a provision are the nature of the book (e.g., scholarly vs. coffee-table), the audience for the book (scholarly vs. popular), and price. When an author writes exclusively in a particular field of scholarship, such a clause can hamper all the author's future writing projects. Even in the absence of such a provision, the author makes an implied promise not to deprive the publisher of the benefits of the contract. Writing a second book that captured all or part of the publisher's market for the first book would breach this promise. At the same time, the nature of an author's field may necessitate that passages in subsequent works be "substantially similar," the test for copyright infringement, to passages in a prior published work. For example, an expert on art may have to describe the same painting in more than one work. Even if the descriptions are not identical, they might necessarily be substantially similar, because there are only so many ways a painting can be described. An author should consider requiring a contractual provision in which the publisher acknowledges the nature of the author's profession and agrees that the kind of substantial similarity just described will not amount to a breach of the author's agreement not to publish a competing work or of the warranty that the work is original.

Option. Contracts for many trade books and for some scholarly books contain a provision granting the publisher some form of option on the author's next work. An option that defines the author's compensation for the next book deprives the author of the opportunity of gaining a greater royalty if the current work is successful. If possible, therefore, authors should negotiate to delete terms specifying compensation for future work or to limit the option to a right of negotiation rather than to specific terms.

Author's Termination of the Contract and Recapture of Rights. There are two principal ways to terminate a contract—one is statutory and will not be mentioned in a publishing agreement; the other is contractual. Authors should understand these provisions and know when and how to use them.

The termination right provided for in the Copyright Act is described in 2.2.12, and it applies even if the contract says that it does not. (According to the statute, the termination right applies "notwithstanding any agreement to the contrary.") Under the statute, authors or certain of their family relations or legal representatives are entitled to terminate an assignment or license of rights, even when the original term is for the entire term of copyright. The statute specifies who may terminate, when termination may occur, and the procedures for doing so, which include a notice that must contain specified information.

If the author assigns the copyright to the publisher, as is common in scholarly publishing, then the publisher controls the rights for the term of copyright unless the statutory termination right is exercised by the author or by others specified in the statute. But if the author licenses the copyright rights in the work to the publisher for the term of copyright, as is common in trade publishing, the agreement likely includes a provision for the recapture of publishing rights from the publisher and specifies the protocol for termination. For example, an agreement may state that the publisher must release the rights if, following a written notice from the author and the elapse of a specified time (usually six to nine months), the publisher fails to make the book available for sale in print. Such a provision usually defines whether a book is out of print by referring to whether the work is in print in any edition.

The provision for termination and recapture of rights has been known as the "out-of-print clause." But with the development of technology that permits printing on demand, a work is arguably always in print. Recognizing that development, some authors have advocated basing the definition of whether a work is out of print on whether a specified number of copies of all editions or a specified edition were sold in a twelve-month period. In 2007 one major trade publisher, without consultation with authors or authors' representatives, deleted the out-of-print clause from its form trade publishing contract on the theory that its printing-on-demand technology made the provision obsolete. The publisher rescinded the change in response to contentions from authors and the Authors Guild that contracts should continue to provide for termination and recapture of rights. The publisher agreed to negotiate a "revenue-based threshold" to determine whether a book was in print, although, as the Authors Guild noted, that approach raises new issues, such as whether revenues should be measured by income to the publisher or the author, what level of revenues meets the threshold, and how authors without agents will fare under the policy. As publishing technologies and business practices evolve, authors should make sure that any provisions for termination and recapture of rights are up to date before signing a contract.

Once rights have reverted to the author, they may be licensed to another publisher. However, the first publisher's failure to discern a sufficient demand for the book to justify keeping it in print suggests that a second publishing license may be difficult to achieve, at least at that time. But if a publisher is not publishing a work, the author is advised to recapture the rights so that the author controls them if approached by another publisher in the future. Prompt recapture of rights may also ensure that the publisher does not republish the book when it is no longer current.

Publisher's Termination of the Contract. Many contracts give the publisher the right to terminate the contract after a stated number of years following publication of the work, often stipulating that the author then be allowed to purchase any remaining stock of the work. If the author declines to purchase it, the publisher is free to dispose of it at will.

Any negotiations over provisions of the contract usually take place before the publisher draws up a final contract. Authors whose books generate significant income and numerous requests for subsidiary rights frequently hire lawyers or agents to negotiate and review contracts.

2.3.2   JOURNAL ARTICLES AND CONTRIBUTIONS
                                TO EDITED WORKS

The agreement covering publication of a journal article or of a contribution to an edited work ("collective work") may be a formal contract or a letter of agreement. The publisher often requires an assignment of the copyright to itself. The transfer of copyright allows the publisher to publish and republish the work and to license other uses of it, such as classroom photocopying, translation, and republication in print or electronic forms by others. In return for transfer of copyright, the publisher may grant the author the right to republish the article in any work of which the author is the author or editor, as long as proper credit to the first publisher is given in the new publication. The publisher may also permit an author to upload a copy of the work to the intranet of the author's employer (e.g., a research or scholarly institution) but will usually not consent to placement on a public Web site since such publication could compete with its own sales or conflict with licensed republication in digital databases. In addition, the publisher may agree to share with the author any fees received from licenses for subsidiary rights. If there is no written transfer of copyright, the publisher acquires only the privileges of publishing the article nonexclusively in the collective work, any revision of that collective work, and any later collective work in the same series (see 2.2.3).

In the typical formal contract for publishing an article, the author warrants that the manuscript is new, original, and unpublished and that it does not violate the copyright or another right (e.g., through defamation or violation of privacy or publicity rights) of any person or entity. Commonly the publisher agrees to publish the work and to allow the author an opportunity to review the copyedited manuscript or to correct proofs (or both), and the author agrees to obtain any permissions needed for the reproduction of material from other sources, to pay fees related to those permissions, and to read and return the copyedited manuscript or proofs by a reasonable date set by the publisher. (On fair use and permissions, see 2.2.13–14.)

Authors rarely receive royalties or fees from the original publication of a journal article but may be given free offprints of the contribution, copies of the issue, or a year's subscription to the journal. For a contribution to a book, compensation may take the form of a single payment or free books.

2.4
DEFAMATION

LIBEL

The tort of defamation was recognized and remedied by English law for hundreds of years before the American Revolution. The concepts underlying the English common law of defamation were taken into American common law early in American history. With the exception of federal decisions in the second half of the twentieth century to protect the freedom of the press guaranteed by the First Amendment to the United States Constitution, there has been little change in the law of defamation since the eighteenth century.

In law defamation is a false statement of fact about a living person that is made to a third party (and is not privileged), exposing the person to public hatred, ridicule, contempt, or disgrace, inducing an evil opinion of the person in the minds of others, or depriving the person of friendly relations in society, so long as the one who made the statement acted at least negligently. Defamation has traditionally been divided into two branches—slander, or oral defamation, and libel, or written defamation. With the prominence of the broadcast media, the distinction between these two branches of defamation has become confused. Legal treatises have commented on the difficulty of distinguishing between slander and libel. In this chapter, libel (written defamation) is the focus of discussion. Not all false statements about a person are libelous. False statements that are merely annoying or unpleasant, even if the statements include words of abuse and epithets, or that subject someone only to jests that hurt feelings are not defamatory and therefore are not legally actionable.

In assessing whether a statement is defamatory, courts are guided by standards of construction. The words are read in the context of the communication taken as a whole, including all reasonable inferences. Language is given its plain, ordinary meanings, with a fair, not an extreme, interpretation. Most important is to consider the context in which the statement is made. A statement made on the playing field is likely not to be interpreted the same as one made at a shareholders' meeting. The same statement may be understood as joking or hyperbole if made in one place and as a claim of incompetence or criminality if made in another. To be defamatory, a statement must be so understood by those likely to receive it, not necessarily by any reasonable person. To focus only on the average, reasonable person would permit someone to libel another if the libel would be understood only by a minority of knowledgeable people.

But in an evaluation of whether a statement is libelous, context is only one factor that must be considered. Also relevant are changes in social standards and attitudes over time. For example, falsely asserting someone suffers from a "loathsome disease" is often cited as an example of a libel, although courts and commentators now question that conclusion or characterize it as historical. But in some contexts a false claim that someone suffers from a disease could still be libelous, especially where it might affect employment. As social standards and attitudes have changed, the same allegations that were once libelous per se primarily against women have in recent decisions been found to be libelous per se against men. Questions of sexual libel are still not treated identically for men and women, however. A false claim that someone is homosexual, once commonly perceived as a libel, in part because it implied violation of criminal laws, has now been held by many courts not to be libelous.

The terms *libel per se* and *libel per quod* refer to two kinds of defamatory statements. A *libel per se* is a false statement that is defamatory on its face. The false statement that a professor is a plagiarist, for example, is damaging in itself, because the personal and professional reputation of the professor is assumed to be harmed and the professor's employment jeopardized if the statement is believed true.

A *libel per quod* requires an additional allegation of facts and a proof of harm. For example, a business owner sued after a report understated his sales and the size of his staff. While the report's statement that the plaintiff had a staff of 10–15 employees was not in itself damaging, he argued that since he actually had 650 employees, readers of the report would conclude that his business had suffered a major retrenchment. Showing the difficulty of alleging *libel per quod*, the court observed that to prove the claim, the plaintiff would have to demonstrate that those who received the report already knew about his business's size and presence in the industry, that they were reasonably capable of interpreting the report in the light of those facts, and that they would have imputed a defamatory meaning to the statements. The plaintiff would also have to prove that his business was damaged by the false report.

2.4.2   OPINION

Statements of pure opinion are not actionable no matter how offensive they are. This follows from the definition of defamation as a false statement of fact. However, an opinion that would be libelous if asserted as fact and that is accompanied by an implication that it is based on undisclosed facts is actionable. Thus, when writing an unflattering opinion, an author should be careful to set forth the facts on which it is based. Rhetoric and hyperbole are closely related to pure opinion and, in the absence of other factors, are not actionable. It is therefore safer to express a harsh judgment or conclusion in the form of hyperbole than as an unsupported statement of fact.

The determination whether an offensive statement is opinion rather than an allegation of fact is a frequent subject of judicial opinions. The determination is based on what an average person reading the statement would understand it to mean. This judgment, difficult at best, is largely a question of the context in which the statement is made. The context in which offensive words appear can alter their status from opinion to fact. For example, words that might be regarded as opinion or rhetoric and not be actionable if uttered in the heat of a dispute could be found to be a statement of fact and therefore actionable if appearing in a book based on research. Verbal qualifications can shift a statement from fact to opinion. A writer without conclusive proof of an offensive statement should not hesitate to say that the statement is the writer's opinion or belief instead of propounding it as factual. Nonetheless, a court may not be bound by qualifying language in extreme cases, such as the accusation of a heinous crime. The type of writing may also make a difference. Offensive language appearing in reviews or humorous writing is likely to be found to be protected opinion. There would be no purpose to such writing if unfavorable comment could not be made. Indeed, one who appears in a public performance, writes a book, or opens a restaurant may even be deemed to have consented to a review, no matter how unfavorable. Not only is such work protected by the common law of most states, but some courts have found it to be constitutionally protected as well.

2.4.3   TRUTH AS DEFENSE

Truth is a complete defense in all actions for libel. However, belief in the truth of an offending statement is different from the ability to prove the truth of such a statement. Government records and believable witnesses with pertinent knowledge are the best proofs of truth. Many publishers are willing to accept a potentially offensive statement as true if it appeared in a publication with a large circulation and if no rebuttal is known to have been made. Nonetheless, such a precedent is not proof of truth; it would at most mitigate damages if an author who repeated the statement lost an action for libel. The judge or jury would have to consider whether it was the prior publication, as well as the author's repetition, that injured the plaintiff's reputation. Publishers may still be justified in refusing to publish such material, since damages are not always mitigated on these grounds and since a libel action carries expenses and risks besides damages, such as the costs of defense. The defense of truth is further complicated because although in some states a plaintiff may be required to prove that an offensive statement is false, in other states the statement may be presumed false without proof. In the latter case, the defendant has the burden of proving the truth of the potentially libelous statement.

2.4.4   ACTUAL MALICE

State libel law has not changed much in the last two hundred years. In 1964, however, the United States Supreme Court, deciding the case *New York Times Co. v. Sullivan*, drastically altered the law of libel about persons involved in public matters. The court was asked for the first time the extent to which the United States Constitution limits the power of the states to award libel damages to public officials. In this case, L. B. Sullivan, a public official in Montgomery, Alabama, brought a libel action against the *New York Times* for publication of a political advertisement in support of Martin Luther King, Jr., placed by a group advocating civil rights in the South. The advertisement, which did not mention Sullivan by name, charged that civil rights were being abridged in the South and specifically referred to actions of public officials in Montgomery. It contained some errors of fact. A jury awarded Sullivan $500,000, and the Alabama Supreme Court affirmed the award. The United States Supreme Court, on appeal, held unanimously that the First Amendment to the Constitution bars any award to a public official for defamatory statements unless the statements were made with what the court called "actual malice," defined by the court as knowledge that the published material was false or as reckless disregard of the truth. In a libel case, "actual malice" does not mean ill will or spite. As a result of the *Sullivan* case, a public official claiming to have been libeled by statements in a publication protected by the First Amendment has to prove both that the statements are false and that the defendant published them with actual malice.

In 1967 the Supreme Court decided two cases that expanded the protections of the *Sullivan* case to statements about public figures who were not officials. In *Curtis Publishing Co. v. Butts*, a nationally known football coach and athletic director charged the *Saturday Evening Post* with libeling him because it printed an article accusing him of fixing a football game. The Supreme Court again applied the protection of the First Amendment and the actual-malice standard. The court found the magazine's investigative practices so bad as to constitute actual malice and permitted recovery for libel, but it also clarified that the rule of the *Sullivan* case applied to public figures who were not public officials. In the second case, *Beckley Newspapers Corp. v. Hanks*, the Supreme Court made it clear that publication with a bad or corrupt motive or out of personal spite did not constitute actual malice under the standard of the *Sullivan* case. Rather, the publication had to have been made with knowledge that the material was false or with reckless disregard of the truth.

Despite the expansion of the actual-malice standard established in the *Sullivan* case, plaintiffs who are public figures have sometimes been able to prove actual malice and to recover damages for libel. Further, the Supreme Court has held that as long as states do not impose liability for defamation without fault, they may define appropriate standards for liability for publication of defamatory material about individuals who are not public figures. Consequently, great care in research and writing is still required. The key to liability for defamation of private individuals, which may vary from state to state, is usually neglect of the procedures of reporting that a prudent journalist or scholar would follow.

To be able to counter accusations of recklessness or negligence, a prudent author should keep careful notes, tapes of interviews, copies of documents in support of contentions made in writing, and copies of reports making the same charges that the author intends to make. Someone who suspects the possibility of defamation in an upcoming publication may ask to see an author's work before publication. The author should discuss such a request with the prospective publisher.

It is customary to refuse such a request unless the person making it will provide the author with important facts or material otherwise unavailable.

2.5

RIGHT OF PRIVACY

2.5.1   EMERGENCE OF PRIVACY LAW

Unlike copyright and defamation, the law of privacy is a development of the twentieth century. In 1890 Samuel D. Warren and Louis D. Brandeis, later a justice of the United States Supreme Court, wrote an article entitled "The Right to Privacy" (*Harvard Law Review* 4.5 [1890]: 193–220; print), which called for the law to recognize the right of anyone to be let alone. In an early privacy case (*Roberson v. Rochester Folding Box Co.*), involving the use of the plaintiff's likeness in an advertisement for a product, New York's highest court held in 1902 that the right of privacy did not exist in New York in common law or equity. In response to this decision, the New York legislature enacted in 1909 a limited statutory right of privacy that made it a misdemeanor to use without permission the name, portrait, or picture of any living person for advertising or purposes of trade. The New York legislature has resisted adding further provisions regarding the circumstances actionable as invasion of privacy. Most states proceeded to recognize by statute or case decision four kinds of violation of the right of privacy:

1. Unreasonable intrusion on the seclusion of others
2. Appropriation without permission of another's name or likeness for advertising or purposes of trade
3. Unreasonable publicity of another's private life
4. Publicity placing another in a false light

Not every state recognizes all four categories of invasion of privacy as legally actionable; New York, for example, recognizes only the second category. Other states have recognized all the types of invasion of privacy but by judicial decision rather than by statute.

2.5.2   UNREASONABLE PUBLICITY OF PRIVATE LIFE

In many states, publication of private facts about someone who is not of public concern is considered an invasion of privacy. Although existing cases in this area involve disclosure in the mass media, it is not impossible that publication before a limited audience, such as the readers of a scholarly book or journal, could be actionable. The facts disclosed must be private, however, to be the basis for an action. When they are in the public record, even if not widely known, there is no invasion of privacy. According to some commentators, the publicized facts must be very offensive to reasonable people. There has been little guidance from the United States Supreme Court concerning this type of invasion of privacy.

2.5.3   PUBLICITY PLACING ANOTHER IN A FALSE LIGHT

Publicity that places the person who is its subject in a false light is an actionable invasion of privacy. This tort seems to be nothing more than a variant form of defamation. To clarify the false-light tort, courts and commentators have added the requirements that the publicity be highly offensive and that the person creating it act in reckless disregard of the truth or with knowledge of the falsity of the publicity. When there is significant misrepresentation of fact or outright fictionalization, the publicity is clearly actionable. Omission of important facts can also contribute to a false-light claim. Not all states recognize false light as an actionable invasion of privacy, but this area of law is still developing. It is thus unwise to place someone in a false light. Another reason to avoid false-light characterizations is that it is difficult to determine which state law could apply, since a plaintiff may make a claim under the law of the state in which the plaintiff lives at the time of publication.

2.5.4   CONSENT AS DEFENSE

For a defendant in an action of invasion of privacy, proof that the plaintiff consented to the invasion is a complete defense. Some states require that the consent be in writing. Many users of material that may invade privacy, including publishers, require before publication written consent forms from those who are subjects of the material. State laws that recognize consent as a defense against an invasion-of-privacy claim may base this recognition on the existence of a contract. To be enforceable, however, such a contract requires a payment of money or of something else of value. A consent form given without consideration is revocable at will and could be revoked after substantial funds have been expended on the project. Therefore, publishers and other producers may require both a recitation of consideration in the consent form and a payment to the subject signing the consent.

2.6
FURTHER GUIDANCE

Publications of the Copyright Office

The following publications are available from the Copyright Office, Library of Congress, 101 Independence Ave., SE, Washington, DC 20559-6000. Most of them can be read on the Internet.

Copyright Basics. Circular 1.
Copyright Notice. Circular 3.
Renewal of Copyright. Circular 15.
Duration of Copyright: Provisions of the Law Dealing with the Length of Copyright Protection. Circular 15a.
Extension of Copyright Terms. Circular 15t.
Reproduction of Copyrighted Works by Educators and Librarians. Circular 21.
How to Investigate the Copyright Status of a Work. Circular 22.
International Copyright Relations of the United States. Circular 38a.
Highlights of Copyright Amendments Contained in the URAA (Uruguay Round Agreements Act). Circular 38b.
Copyright Registration of Books, Manuscripts, and Speeches. Fact sheet 109.

On Copyright and Publishing Agreements for Books

Abrams, Howard B. *The Law of Copyright*. 2 vols. Eagan: Thomson, 2006. Print.
Association of American Publishers. "Copyright." *The Association of American Publishers*. Assn. of Amer. Pubs., 2007. Web. 13 July 2007.
Association of American Publishers, Association of American University Presses, Copyright Clearance Center, National Association of College Stores, and Software and Information Industry Association. *Questions and Answers on Copyright for the Campus Community*. 7th ed. N.p.: Assn. of Amer. Pubs., AAUP, Copr. Clearance Center, Natl. Assn. of Coll. Stores, Software and Information Industry Assn., 2006. Print, Web. 16 July 2007.
Association of American Universities, Association of Research Libraries, Association of American University Presses, and Association of

American Publishers. *Campus Copyright Rights and Responsibilities: A Basic Guide to Policy Considerations. Association of American University Presses*. AAUP, Dec. 2005. Web. 13 July 2007.

Association of American University Presses. "Copyright and Permissions Resources." *Association of American University Presses*. AAUP, n.d. Web. 13 July 2007.

Authors Guild, Inc. *Authors Guild Model Trade Book Contract and Guide*. New York: Authors Guild, 2000. Print.

Balkin, Richard. *A Writer's Guide to Book Publishing*. 3rd ed. New York: Dutton, 1994. Print.

Bielstein, Susan M. *Permissions, a Survival Guide: Blunt Talk about Art as Intellectual Property*. Chicago: U of Chicago P, 2006. Print.

Crawford, Tad, and Kay Murray. *The Writer's Legal Guide: An Authors Guild Desk Reference*. 3rd ed. New York: Authors Guild; Allworth, 2002. Print.

Fischer, Mark A., E. Gabriel Perle, and John Taylor Williams. *Perle and Williams on Publishing Law*. 3rd ed. New York: Aspen, 2006. Print.

Fishman, Steven. *The Copyright Handbook: What Every Writer Needs to Know*. 9th ed. Berkeley: Nolo, 2006. CD-ROM, PDF file, print.

Geller, Paul Edward, gen. ed. *International Copyright Law and Practice*. New York: LexisNexis Matthew Bender, 2006. CD-ROM, print.

Goldstein, Paul. *Goldstein on Copyright*. 3rd ed. New York: Aspen, 2006. Print.

Kirsch, Jonathan. *Kirsch's Handbook of Publishing Law: For Authors, Publishers, Editors, and Agents*. 2nd ed. Venice: Acrobat, 1995. Print.

Lindsey, Marc. *Copyright Law on Campus*. Pullman: Washington State UP, 2003. Print.

Nimmer, Melville B., and David Nimmer. *Nimmer on Copyright*. 10 vols. New York: LexisNexis Matthew Bender, 2006. CD-ROM, print.

Patry, William F. *Patry on Copyright*. 7 vols. Eagan: West, 2007. Print.

Stanford University Libraries and Academic Information Resources. *Copyright Renewal Database. Stanford University*. Stanford U, 2006. Web. 13 July 2007.

United Nations Educational, Scientific, and Cultural Organization. *Copyright Laws and Treaties of the World*. Washington: Bureau of Natl. Affairs, 2000. Print.

On Defamation and Privacy

Forer, Lois G. *A Chilling Effect*. New York: Norton, 1989. Print.

McCarthy, J. Thomas. *The Rights of Publicity and Privacy*. 2nd ed. 2 vols. New York: Thomson, 2007. Print.

Media Law Resource Center. *MLRC Fifty-State Survey: Media Libel Law 2007–08*. New York: Media Law Resource Center, 2007. Print.

———. *MLRC Fifty-State Survey: Media Privacy and Related Law 2007–08*. New York: Media Law Resource Center, 2007. Print.

Sack, Robert D. *Sack on Defamation: Libel, Slander, and Related Problems*. 3rd ed. 2 vols. New York: Practising Law Inst., 2006. Print.

Sanford, Bruce W. *Libel and Privacy*. 2nd ed. Gaithersburg: Aspen, 2006. Print.

Smolla, Rodney A. *Law of Defamation*. 2nd ed. 2 vols. New York: Clark, 2006. Print.

3

BASICS OF SCHOLARLY WRITING

3.6 Names of Persons

3.7 Capitalization

3.8 Titles of Works in the Manuscript

3.9 Quotations

3.1

AUDIENCE, GENRE, AND THE CONVENTIONS OF SCHOLARSHIP

Scholarly writing takes various shapes and forms, depending on genre (e.g., research article, book review) and audience. An accurate assessment of your intended audience will help you answer many of the formal and stylistic questions that arise in preparing a manuscript. For a general audience, such as that for a book review in a newspaper, you would usually keep documentation to a minimum and give only in English translation any quotations from works originally written in other languages; for somewhat more knowledgeable readers, such as those for an article in a periodical like the *American Scholar*, you might mention sources, either in the text or in a bibliography, and offer occasional words and phrases in another language, along with English translations; but a scholarly audience expects full, precise documentation and quotations in the original language (and translations may be subordinated, if provided at all).

This book assumes a scholarly audience and presents recommended guidelines for scholarly publication. At times you may need or choose to consider variations of these guidelines, but since conventions by definition are general agreements about basic principles and since conventional practices are readily understood by others, most scholars do not depart from such guidelines without weighing advantages against disadvantages.

In some situations, departures from convention result in greater clarity or enable you to meet the needs of a particular audience. Normally, you should alter established practices only by expanding them—for instance, by giving publishers' names in full or by not using abbreviations. Where conventions do not exist or are not established, you should adopt clear, workable, and consistent procedures. In general, closely follow the conventions outlined in this manual when you write articles for periodicals (or essays for collections) addressed to other scholars. Publishers usually allow more latitude for books; some types of manuscripts, such as scholarly editions and reference works, often require special practices. Many publishers define editorial conventions, or a house style, for the works they publish; if you are preparing your work for a particular publisher, be certain to ask your editor for guidance on the house style.

3.2
LANGUAGE AND STYLE

Whereas conventions govern such matters as documentation and format of scholarly manuscripts, there are no special directives for scholarly prose style. Scholars usually aim for the qualities that distinguish all effective expository prose. (The works listed in 3.12 provide guidance.) Like most other authors of nonfiction prose, scholars generally work toward writing that is direct and clear, organized and coherent, lively and persuasive. In presenting arguments, they strive for fairness and balance while maintaining clarity and focus. In addition, the scholarly authors who have been most influential over a long period have usually conveyed their ideas without jargon, which presumes a specialized audience, seeking instead terminology comprehensible to a wide range of educated readers, no matter how complex the subject.

Careful writers do not use language that implies unsubstantiated or irrelevant generalizations about such personal qualities as age, birth or family status, disability, economic class, ethnicity, political or religious beliefs, race, sex, or sexual orientation. Many journals and book publishers have strong editorial policies concerning the avoidance of such language. Since 1981, for example, *PMLA*'s statement of editorial policy has urged "its contributors to be sensitive to the social implications of language and to seek wording free of discriminatory overtones."

Discussions and statements about nondiscriminatory language have generally focused on wording that could be labeled sexist. For example, many writers no longer use *he, him,* or *his* to express a meaning that includes women as well as men. The use of *she, her,* and *hers* to refer to a person of no particular sex can also be distracting and momentarily confusing. Both usages can often be avoided through a revision that recasts the sentence into the plural or that eliminates the pronoun altogether. Another technique is to make the discussion refer to a person who is identified, so that there is a reason to use a specific singular pronoun. *They, them, their,* and *theirs* cannot logically be applied to a single person, and *he or she, her or him,* and *her or his* are cumbersome alternatives to be used sparingly. Many authors now also avoid terms that unnecessarily integrate a person's sex with a job or role. For instance, *anchorman, policewoman, stewardess,* and *poetess* are commonly replaced with *anchor, police officer, flight attendant,* and *poet.* For advice on current practices, see the guides to nondiscriminatory language listed in 3.12.

Effective scholarly writing depends on clarity and readability as well as on content. The organization and development of ideas, coherence of presentation, and fitness of sentence structure, grammar, and diction are all essential considerations, as is the correctness of the mechanics of writing—capitalization, punctuation, spelling, and so on. Although the scope of this book precludes a detailed discussion of grammar, usage, and related aspects of writing, the sections that follow address mechanical questions scholarly authors encounter in their writing: spelling, punctuation, italics, names of persons, capitalization, titles of works, quotations, numbers, and romanization.

3.3
SPELLING

3.3.1   CONSISTENCY AND CHOICE OF SPELLING

Spelling, including hyphenation, should be consistent throughout the manuscript—except in quotations, which must retain the spelling of the original, whether correct or incorrect. To ensure accuracy and consistency, always use a single widely recognized authority for spelling, such as *Merriam-Webster's Collegiate Dictionary* or, if the word is not listed there, *Webster's Third New International Dictionary.* Other standard dictionaries are *The American Heritage Dictionary* and *The New Oxford American Dictionary.*

Where entries show variant spellings, use the form given first or, if the variants have separate listings, the form that appears with the full definition. Inform your editor, before copyediting begins, of any necessary deviations from this practice—for example, a variant commonly used in your discipline.

3.3.2   WORD DIVISION

Dividing words at the ends of lines makes the manuscript less readable and can cause typesetting errors. If a word will not fit on a line, leave the line short and begin the word on the next line. The "word-wrap" feature of word-processing programs performs this operation automatically, provided that any automatic-hyphenation option is turned off. If you choose to divide a word, consult your dictionary about where the break should occur.

3.3.3   PLURALS

The plurals of English words are generally formed by addition of the suffix -s or -es (*laws, taxes*), but there are exceptions (e.g., *children, halves, mice, sons-in-law, bison*). The tendency in American English is to form the plurals of words naturalized from other languages in the standard manner. The plurals *librettos* and *formulas* are therefore now more common in American English than *libretti* and *formulae*. But some adopted words, like *alumnus* and *phenomenon*, retain the original plurals (*alumni, phenomena*). Consult a dictionary for guidance. If the dictionary gives more than one plural form for a word (*appendixes, appendices; syllabi, syllabuses*), use the first listed. (See 3.4.7 for plurals of letters and for possessive forms of plurals.)

3.3.4   ACCENTS

In quoting, reproduce all accents and other diacritical marks exactly as they appear in the original. Handwrite marks that your word processor lacks. Accented letters do not always retain the accent mark when capitalized (the accent in the French word *école* may be omitted in *Ecole*, for example), but an accent is never unacceptable over a capital letter that would require one if it were lowercase (*École*). When transcribing words that appear in all capitals and changing them to lowercase (as in transcribing a title from a title page), insert the necessary accents.

3.3.5   UMLAUTS

In German words the umlaut should not be replaced with *e* (*ä, ö, ü* rather than *ae, oe, ue*), even for initial capitals (*Über*). But common usage must be observed for names: *Götz*, but *Goethe*. In alphabetizing such words, Germanists treat an umlauted vowel as if the letter were followed by an *e*; thus, *Götz* would be alphabetized as *Goetz* and would precede *Gott* in an alphabetical listing. Nonspecialists, however, and many libraries in English-speaking countries alphabetize such words without regard to the umlaut; for publications addressed primarily to speakers of English, this is the recommended practice. (For more on the arrangement of entries in the list of works cited, see 6.4.3.)

3.3.6   LIGATURES AND OTHER SPECIAL CHARACTERS

A ligature is a combination of letters that is united in print: *æ* and *Æ* in Danish, Norwegian, and Old English; *œ* and *Œ* in French; and *ß* in German. When addressing a specialist audience, you should reproduce these characters in your manuscript, through your word processor or by hand notation, if they appear in the source you are duplicating. When addressing a general readership, you may omit the connection between letters (*ae, Ae, oe, Oe, ss*). For words adopted into English from other languages, omit the connection between letters (*aesthetic, oeuvre, schuss*). Other special characters—for example, Old English and Middle English letters that are not used in modern English, quotation marks following alternative typographic conventions outside English—should be reproduced from the source regardless of your audience.

─────────── **3.4** ───────────
PUNCTUATION

3.4.1   PURPOSE OF PUNCTUATION

The primary purpose of punctuation is to ensure the clarity and readability of writing. Punctuation clarifies sentence structure, separating some words and grouping others. It adds meaning to written words and guides the understanding of readers as they move through sentences. The rules set forth here cover many of the situations common

---

Many of the usage examples in 3.4–5 are quotations or adaptations of quotations. The sources are listed on pages 305–08.

in scholarly writing. For the punctuation of quotations in the text, see 3.9.7. For the punctuation of parenthetical references and bibliographies, see chapters 6 and 7. See also the individual listings in the index for specific punctuation marks.

3.4.2   COMMAS

a. Use a comma before a coordinating conjunction (*and, but, for, nor, or, so,* or *yet*) joining independent clauses in a sentence.

> Synonyms have a basic similarity of meaning, but at the margins they can differ greatly.

> Inexpensive examples of literary annuals still turn up in secondhand stores, for the craze leaped the Atlantic, and the books became as popular in the United States as in England.

But the comma may be omitted when the sentence is short and the connection between the clauses is not open to misreading if unpunctuated.

> Wallace sings and Armstrong plays cornet.

b. Use commas to separate words, phrases, and clauses in a series.

Words

> Priests, conjurers, magicians, and shamans have long known the importance of using words correctly in prayers, petitions, hexes, and incantations.

Phrases

> To some writers the computer is a subtle saboteur, subverting their intentions, reconstituting their words, and redirecting their attention to the layout of the page.

Clauses

> Originally the plantations were rather small, there were fewer slaves than colonists, and social discrimination was less harsh than in the eighteenth century.

But use semicolons when items in a series have internal commas.

Perhaps the most ambitious English-language poem of the decolonized Third World, Walcott's *Omeros* fills hundreds of pages with rolling hexameters in terza rima; alludes abundantly to Homer, James Joyce, and Aimé Césaire; and ranges historically from precolonial Africa to contemporary Ireland and Saint Lucia.

c. Use a comma between coordinate adjectives—that is, adjectives that separately modify the same noun.

> For men, heroism was usually described as bravery and the active, successful overcoming of adversity.
>
> (The adjectives *active* and *successful* each modify *overcoming*.)

but

> The dialogue soon reveals the reason for her mysterious daily sojourns there.
>
> (The adjective *mysterious* modifies *daily sojourns*.)

d. Use commas to set off a parenthetical comment, or an aside, if it is brief and closely related to the rest of the sentence. (For punctuation of longer, more intrusive, or more complex parenthetical elements, see 3.4.5.)

> A title or a headline, for instance, functions as a signal and determines our approach to the ensuing text.
>
> It is not, I submit, about the body at all.

e. Use commas to set off a nonrestrictive modifier—that is, a modifier that is not essential to the meaning of the sentence. A nonrestrictive modifier, unlike a restrictive one, could be dropped without changing the main sense of the sentence. Modifiers in the following three categories are either nonrestrictive or restrictive. (For the use of parentheses and dashes around complex nonrestrictive modifiers, see 3.4.5b.)

Words in Apposition

NONRESTRICTIVE

> Baron François-Pascal-Simon Gérard, court painter to Louis XVIII, made Duras's heroine the subject of a painting.

RESTRICTIVE

The painter Baron François-Pascal-Simon Gérard made Duras's heroine the subject of a painting.

Clauses That Begin with *Who, Whom, Whose, Which,* and *That*

NONRESTRICTIVE

All these subjects seemed irrelevant to Seneca, who thought that the only valid use of literature was as a model for conduct.

A brief comparison with the most famous chivalric drama, which was written fifteen years earlier, clarifies the uniqueness of Thon's play.

RESTRICTIVE

All these subjects seemed irrelevant to philosophers who thought that the only valid use of literature was as a model for conduct.

A brief comparison with a chivalric drama that was written fifteen years earlier clarifies the uniqueness of Thon's play.

Many writers prefer to use *which* to introduce nonrestrictive clauses and *that* to introduce restrictive clauses.

Adverbial Phrases and Clauses

NONRESTRICTIVE

After the separation, she moved to Lunéville, where she was under the protection of the ducal court.

RESTRICTIVE

After the separation, she moved to a town where she was under the protection of the ducal court.

f. Use a comma after a long introductory phrase or clause.

PHRASE

In this charged atmosphere of cultural victory and cultural defeat, Americanists undertook the search for a central myth of America.

CLAUSE

When Zilia begins learning how to write French, she is writing to Aza.

g. Use commas to set off alternative or contrasting phrases.

Fin de siècle Spain was simply not receptive to feminism, especially not to the fundamental feminism that formed the basis of Pardo Bazán's thought on sex roles.

Sometimes this is where the deeper motives for the work are most clearly, if inadvertently, revealed.

but

Alexander Pope uses classical myths and allusions for incidental yet incisive contributions to his overarching satiric design.
(The conjunction *yet* links *incidental* and *incisive*, making commas unnecessary.)

h. Do not use a comma between subject and verb.

What makes Sartre's theory of commitment relevant to our discussion [no comma] is its insistence that choice in today's world can be only political.

i. Do not use a comma between verb and object.

In 1947 Allen Walker Read devoted to dialect geography [no comma] only the fifth day of his twenty-eight-day course.

j. Do not use a comma between the parts of a compound subject, compound object, or compound verb.

COMPOUND SUBJECT

Bakhtin's notion of novelistic languages as "ideologically saturated" [no comma] and his conception of them as "rejoinders" in a dialogue with the extraliterary (271, 274) are heuristic tools that can be applied not only to the analysis of prose fiction but also to the interpretation of poetic texts.

COMPOUND OBJECT

Miller has taken pride in citing the civic function of the theater [no comma] and the way in which the spectacle influences the private tensions of the individual.

COMPOUND VERB

In the afterlife, the poem suggests, African artists such as Wheatley will have "gem-blaz'd" crowns of their own [no comma] and will take their rightful places in "the heav'nly choirs."

k. Do not use a comma between two parallel subordinate elements.

From his darkness, Lear has gained insight into himself as fallible man and negligent king [no comma] and into the evil of Goneril and Regan.

The current political and cultural climate has given rise to a public that demands training in basic literacy [no comma] but that is unwilling to pay for it.

l. Use a comma in a date whose order is month, day, and year. If such a date comes in the middle of a sentence, include a comma after the year.

Martin Luther King, Jr., was born on January 15, 1929, and died on April 4, 1968.

But commas are not used with dates whose order is day, month, and year.

Martin Luther King, Jr., was born on 15 January 1929 and died on 4 April 1968.

m. Do not use a comma between a month and a year or between a season and a year.

The events of July 1789 are as familiar to the French as those of July 1776 are to Americans.

The prime minister announced his resignation in spring 2007.

See 3.9.7 for commas with quotations.

3.4.3   SEMICOLONS

a. Use a semicolon between independent clauses not linked by a conjunction.

> Shelley remarks that "the blank incapability of invention . . . is the greatest misery of authorship" (x); that misery overcome, she is pleased to write the "Author's Introduction" to a tale in which authorship proves a misery to her protagonist.

b. Use semicolons between items in a series when the items contain commas.

> Thérèse, the washerwoman; Sethe, the cook; Eva, the shelter giver and caretaker; and Baby Suggs, the churchless preacher, negotiate this paradox successfully within the narrative context.

3.4.4   COLONS

The colon is used between two parts of a sentence when the first part creates a sense of anticipation about what follows in the second. Leave only one space after a colon, not two.

a. Use a colon to introduce a list, an elaboration of what was just said, or the formal expression of a rule or principle.

LIST

All five of the relatively distinct types of early Japanese religious belief and practice are present in the book: Shinto, Buddhism, Taoism, Confucianism, and folk religion.

ELABORATION

As Emerson's friend at Walden Pond suggested, it takes two to speak the truth: one to speak and another to hear.

RULE OR PRINCIPLE

Most such standards no doubt point to the *delectare* and *prodesse* of Horace's advice to the poet: Delight and benefit your reader!
(A rule or principle after a colon should begin with a capital letter.)

But do not use a colon before a list if the list is grammatically essential to the introductory wording.

> Atwood's other visual art includes a drawing for the cover of *Good Bones*, collages in *The Journals of Susanna Moodie*, and comic strips. (The list is the object of the verb *includes*.)

> Atwood has produced other visual art, such as a drawing for the cover of *Good Bones*, collages in *The Journals of Susanna Moodie*, and comic strips.
> (The list continues the expression *such as*.)

b. Use a colon to introduce a quotation that is independent from the structure of the main sentence.

> The new art relation of modernism is a concept that was most memorably given expression by Walter Pater: "All art constantly aspires towards the condition of music" (140).

A quotation that is integral to the sentence structure is generally preceded by no punctuation or, if a verb of saying (*says, exclaims, notes, writes*) introduces the quotation, by a comma. A colon is used after a verb of saying, however, if the verb introduces certain kinds of formal literary quotations, such as long quotations set off from the main text (see 3.9.2–4, 3.9.7–8). On colons separating titles and subtitles, see 3.8.1.

3.4.5   DASHES AND PARENTHESES

Dashes make a sharper break in the continuity of the sentence than commas do, and parentheses make a still sharper one. To indicate a dash, type two hyphens, with no space before, between, or after. (Your word processor may convert the two hyphens into a dash, as seen in the examples below.) Your writing will be smoother and more readable if you use dashes and parentheses sparingly. Limit the number of dashes in a sentence to two paired dashes or one unpaired dash.

a. Use dashes or parentheses to enclose a sentence element that interrupts the train of thought.

> The human race has survived, and the planet seems to have replenished itself—there are fish, oceans, forests—but what kind of society exists in 2195?

b. Use dashes or parentheses to set off a parenthetical element that contains a comma and that might be misread if set off with commas.

> Most newcomers to both states soon accommodate to the "correct" pronunciation—that is, to the pronunciation used by most westerners.

> The Italian sonnet (which is exemplified in Petrarch's *Canzoniere*, along with other kinds of poems) developed into the English sonnet.

c. Use a dash to introduce words that summarize a preceding series.

> Whether we locate meaning in the text, in the act of reading, or in some collaboration between reader and text—whatever our predilection, let us not generate from it a straitjacket.

A dash may also be used instead of a colon to introduce a list or an elaboration of what was just said (see 3.4.4a).

3.4.6   HYPHENS

Compound words of all types—nouns, verbs, adjectives, and so on—are written as separate words (*hard drive, hard labor*), with hyphens (*hard-and-fast, hard-boiled*), and as single words (*hardcover, hardheaded*). The dictionary shows how to write many compounds. A compound not in the dictionary should usually be written as separate words unless a hyphen is needed to prevent readers from misunderstanding the relation between the words. Following are some rules to help you decide whether you need a hyphen in compounds and other terms that may not appear in the dictionary.

a. Use a hyphen in a compound adjective beginning with an adverb such as *better, best, ill, lower, little,* or *well* when the adjective precedes a noun.

> better-prepared ambassador
> best-known work
> ill-informed reporter
> lower-priced tickets
> well-dressed announcer

But do not use a hyphen when the compound adjective comes after the noun it modifies.

> The ambassador was better prepared than the other delegates.

b. Do not use a hyphen in a compound adjective beginning with an adverb ending in *-ly* or with *too, very,* or *much.*

> thoughtfully presented thesis
>
> very contrived plot
>
> too hasty judgment
>
> much maligned performer

c. Use a hyphen in a compound adjective ending with the present participle (e.g., *loving*) or the past participle (e.g., *inspired*) of a verb when the adjective precedes a noun.

> hate-filled speech
>
> sports-loving throng
>
> fear-inspired loyalty

d. Use a hyphen in a compound adjective formed by a number and a noun when the adjective precedes a noun.

> twelfth-floor apartment
>
> second-semester courses
>
> early-thirteenth-century architecture

e. Use hyphens in other compound adjectives before nouns to prevent misreading.

> children's-book library
>
> (The hyphen indicates that the term refers to a library for children's books and not to a library belonging to children.)
>
> Portuguese-language student
>
> (The hyphen makes it clear that the term refers to a student who is studying Portuguese and not to a language student who is Portuguese.)

f. Do not use hyphens in familiar unhyphenated compound terms, such as *social security, high school,* and *liberal arts,* when they appear before nouns as modifiers.

> social security tax
>
> high school reunion
>
> liberal arts curriculum

g. Use hyphens to join coequal nouns.

> writer-critic
>
> scholar-athlete
>
> author-chef

But do not use a hyphen in a pair of nouns in which the first noun modifies the second.

> father figure
>
> opera lover

h. In general, do not use hyphens after prefixes (e.g., *anti-, co-, multi-, non-, over-, post-, pre-, re-, semi-, sub-, un-, under-*).

antiwar	overpay	semiretired
coworker	postwar	subsatellite
multinational	prescheduled	unambiguous
nonjudgmental	reinvigorate	underrepresented

But sometimes a hyphen is called for after a prefix.

> post-Victorian
> (Use a hyphen before a capital letter.)
>
> re-cover
> (The hyphen distinguishes this verb, meaning "cover again," from *recover*, meaning "get back.")
>
> anti-icing
> (Without the hyphen, the doubled vowel would make the term hard to recognize.)

APOSTROPHES

A principal function of apostrophes is to indicate possession. They are also used in contractions (*can't, wouldn't*), which are rarely acceptable in scholarly writing, and the plurals of the letters of the alphabet (*p's and q's, three A's*).

a. To form the possessive of a singular noun, add an apostrophe and an *s*.

> a poem's meter

b. To form the possessive of a plural noun ending in *s*, add only an apostrophe.

> photographers' exhibit

c. To form the possessive of an irregular plural noun not ending in *s*, add an apostrophe and an *s*.

> women's studies

d. To form the possessive of nouns in a series, add a single apostrophe and an *s* if the ownership is shared.

> Palmer and Colton's book on European history

But if the ownership is separate, place an apostrophe and an *s* after each noun.

> Palmer's and Colton's books on European history

e. To form the possessive of any singular proper noun, add an apostrophe and an *s*.

> Dickens's reputation
>
> Descartes's philosophy
>
> Marx's precepts
>
> Venus's beauty

f. To form the possessive of a plural proper noun, add only an apostrophe.

> the Dickenses' economic woes
>
> the Vanderbilts' estate

g. Do not use an apostrophe to form the plural of an abbreviation or a number.

> MAs   fours
>
> PhDs   GRE score in the 1400s
>
> 1990s

On using apostrophes to abbreviate dates, see 3.10.5.

QUOTATION MARKS

a. Place quotation marks around a word or phrase given in someone else's sense or in a special sense or purposefully misused.

> Teachers often make use of visual "texts" from current exhibits at the college's art gallery.

> Baillie relies on metaphors that contrast "bad" ancien régime-style formal gardens to "good" British natural landscapes.

> One commentator would go so far as to say that nothing is less traditional than "primitive" societies.

If introduced unnecessarily, this device can make writing heavy-handed. Quotation marks are redundant after *so-called*.

> One commentator would go so far as to say that nothing is less traditional than so-called primitive societies.

b. Use quotation marks for a translation of a foreign word or phrase.

> From its inception in the *tragosodos*, the "goat songs" whose dithyrambic intensity galvanized early Greek audiences of tragedy, the tragic has served this self-reflexive purpose.

> During the Meiji period, the emperor was recuperated as a divine monarch embodying the national polity (*kokutai*, literally "national body").

You may use single quotation marks for a translation that follows the original directly, without intervening words or punctuation.

> In a 1917 letter to the publisher Kurt Wolff, for example, Kafka refers to "[der] tief in mir sitzende Beamte" 'the deep-seated bureaucrat inside me' (*Briefe, 1902-1924* 158; *Letters* 134).

On quotation marks with titles, see 3.8.3–4. On quotation marks with quotations and with translations of quotations, see 3.9.7 and 3.9.8, respectively.

3.4.9   SQUARE BRACKETS

Use square brackets around a parenthesis within a parenthesis, so that the levels of subordination can be easily distinguished.

> The editor decided to use the Leningrad Codex (preserved in the Saltykov-Shchedrin State Public Library in Leningrad [now Saint Petersburg]).

For square brackets around an ellipsis or an interpolation in a quotation, see 3.9.5 and 3.9.6, respectively. For square brackets around missing, unverified, or interpolated data in documentation, see 6.6.2, 6.6.22, and 6.6.24.

3.4.10   SLASHES

The slash, or diagonal, is rarely necessary in formal prose. Other than in quotations of poetry (see 3.9.3), the slash has a place mainly between two terms paired as opposites or alternatives and used together as a noun.

> The essay traces a number of crossings over hypothetical borders or divisions: East/West, female/male, homosexual/heterosexual, colonized/colonizer, among others.

> The class studies Meyer Schapiro's discussion of such pictorial properties of painting as right/left or frame/center.

But use a hyphen when such a compound precedes and modifies a noun.

> nature-nurture conflict
>
> either-or situation
>
> East-West relations

3.4.11   PERIODS, QUESTION MARKS, AND EXCLAMATION POINTS

A sentence can end with a period, a question mark, or an exclamation point. Periods end declarative sentences. (For the use of periods with ellipsis points, see 3.9.5.) Question marks follow interrogative sentences. Except in direct quotation, avoid exclamation points in scholarly writing.

Place a question mark inside a closing quotation mark if a question mark occurs there in the quoted passage. But if the quotation ends a sentence that is a question, place a question mark outside the quotation. If a question mark occurs where a comma or period would normally be required, omit the comma or period. Note the use of the question mark and other punctuation marks in the following sentences:

> Whitman asks, "Have you felt so proud to get at the meaning of poems?"

> Where does Whitman speak of "the meaning of poems"?

> "Have you felt so proud to get at the meaning of poems?" Whitman asks.

3.4.12   SPACING AFTER CONCLUDING PUNCTUATION MARKS

In an earlier era, writers using a typewriter commonly left two spaces after a period, a question mark, or an exclamation point. Publications in the United States today usually have the same spacing after concluding punctuation marks as between words on the same line. Since word processors make available the same fonts used by typesetters for printed works, many writers, influenced by the look of typeset publications, now leave only one space after a concluding punctuation mark. In addition, some publishers' guidelines for preparing a manuscript's electronic files ask professional authors to type only the spaces that are to appear in print. Because it is increasingly common for manuscripts to be prepared with a single space after all concluding punctuation marks, this spacing is recommended and shown in the examples in this manual.

3.5
ITALICS

In preparing manuscripts, authors commonly italicize text meant to be italicized in the final publication. This practice is assumed in the discussion and examples in this manual. In manuscripts that will be submitted for production by editors, typesetters, and the like, the clarity of every detail of the text is important. Choose a type font in which the italic style contrasts clearly with the regular style.

The rest of this section discusses using italics for words and letters referred to as words and letters, foreign words in an English text, and emphasis. (See 3.8.2 for the italicizing of titles.)

3.5.1   WORDS AND LETTERS REFERRED TO AS WORDS AND LETTERS

Italicize words and letters that are referred to as words and letters.

> The exercise is designed to help students understand critical terms like *irony, symbol,* and *metaphor.*

> Shaw spelled *Shakespeare* without the final *e.*

3.5.2   FOREIGN WORDS IN AN ENGLISH TEXT

In general, italicize foreign words used in an English text.

> The Renaissance courtier was expected to display *sprezzatura,* or nonchalance, in the face of adversity.

The numerous exceptions to this rule include quotations entirely in another language ("Julius Caesar said, 'Veni, vidi, vici'"); non-English titles of works published within larger works (poems, stories, essays, articles), which are placed in quotation marks and not italicized ("El sueño," the title of a poem by Quevedo); proper nouns (the Entente Cordiale), except when italicized through another convention (SS *Normandie* [see 3.8.2]); and foreign words anglicized through frequent use. Since American English rapidly naturalizes foreign words, use a dictionary to decide whether a foreign expression requires italics. Following are some adopted foreign words, abbreviations, and phrases commonly not italicized:

ad hoc	et al.	lieder
cliché	etc.	raison d'être
concerto	genre	sic
e.g.	hubris	versus

3.5.3   EMPHASIS

Italics for emphasis is a device that rapidly becomes ineffective. It is rarely appropriate in scholarly writing.

3.6

NAMES OF PERSONS

3.6.1   FIRST AND SUBSEQUENT USES OF NAMES

In general, the first time you use a person's name in the text of your manuscript, state it fully and accurately, exactly as it appears in your source.

> Arthur George Rust, Jr.
>
> Victoria M. Sackville-West

Do not change Arthur George Rust, Jr., to Arthur George Rust, for example, or drop the hyphen in Victoria M. Sackville-West. In subsequent references to the person, you may give the last name only (Rust, Sackville-West)—unless, of course, you refer to two or more persons with the same last name—or you may give the most common form of the name (e.g., Garcilaso for Garcilaso de la Vega). In casual references to the very famous—say, Mozart, Shakespeare, or Michelangelo—it is not necessary to give the full name initially. In some languages (e.g., Chinese, Hungarian, Japanese, Korean, and Vietnamese), surnames precede given names (see 3.6.7 and 3.6.12).

3.6.2   TITLES OF PERSONS

In general, do not use formal titles (Mr., Mrs., Miss, Ms., Dr., Professor, Reverend) in first or subsequent references to men or women, living or dead (Churchill, not Mr. Churchill; Mead, not Professor Mead; Hess, not Dame Myra; Montagu, not Lady Montagu). A few women in history are traditionally known by their titles as married women (e.g., Mrs. Humphry Ward, Mme de Staël), although the tendency is to omit such titles (Lafayette, not Mme de Lafayette). Treat other women's names the same as men's.

The appropriate way to refer to persons with titles of nobility can vary. For example, the full name and title of Henry Howard, earl of Surrey, should be given at first mention, and thereafter Surrey alone may be used. In contrast, for Benjamin Disraeli, first earl of Beaconsfield, it is sufficient to give Benjamin Disraeli initially and Disraeli subsequently. Follow the example of your sources in citing titles of nobility.

3.6.3   NAMES OF AUTHORS AND FICTIONAL CHARACTERS

It is common and acceptable to use simplified names of famous authors (Vergil for Publius Vergilius Maro, Dante for Dante Alighieri). Also acceptable are pseudonyms of authors.

> Molière (Jean-Baptiste Poquelin)
>
> Voltaire (François-Marie Arouet)
>
> George Sand (Amandine-Aurore-Lucie Dupin)
>
> George Eliot (Mary Ann Evans)
>
> Mark Twain (Samuel Clemens)
>
> Stendhal (Marie-Henri Beyle)
>
> Novalis (Friedrich von Hardenberg)

Refer to fictional characters in the same way that the work of fiction does. You need not always use their full names, and you may retain titles (Dr. Jekyll, Mme Defarge).

3.6.4   DUTCH AND GERMAN NAMES

With some exceptions, especially in English-language contexts, Dutch *van*, *van der*, and *van den* and German *von* are generally not used with the last name alone.

> Beethoven (Ludwig van Beethoven)
>
> Droste-Hülshoff (Annette von Droste-Hülshoff)
>
> Kleist (Heinrich von Kleist)
>
> Vondel (Joost van den Vondel)

but

> Van Dyck (Anthony Van Dyck)
>
> Von Braun (Wernher Von Braun)

See 3.3.5 for German names with an umlaut.

3.6.5   FRENCH NAMES

With some exceptions, especially in English-language contexts, French *de* following a first name or a title such as *Mme* or *duc* is not used with the last name alone.

    La Boétie (Étienne de La Boétie)

    La Bruyère (Jean de La Bruyère)

    Maupassant (Guy de Maupassant)

    Nemours (Louis-Charles d'Orléans, duc de Nemours)

    Ronsard (Pierre de Ronsard)

    Scudéry (Madeleine de Scudéry)

but

    De Quincey (Thomas De Quincey)

When the last name has only one syllable, however, *de* is usually retained.

    de Gaulle (Charles de Gaulle)

    de Man (Paul de Man)

The preposition also remains, in the form *d'*, when it elides with a last name beginning with a vowel.

    d'Arcy (Pierre d'Arcy)

    d'Arsonval (Arsène d'Arsonval)

The forms *du* and *des* — combinations of *de* with *le* and *les* — are always used with last names and are capitalized.

    Des Périers (Bonaventure Des Périers)

    Du Bos (Charles Du Bos)

A hyphen is frequently used between French given names, as well as between their initials (Marie-Joseph Chénier, M.-J. Chénier). Note that *M.* and *P.* before names may be abbreviations for the titles *Monsieur* and *Père* (M. René Char, P. J. Reynard).

3.6.6   GREEK NAMES

In Greek books, the author's name appears on the title page in the genitive case ("Hypo ["by"] Perikleous Alexandrou Argyropoulou"). The first name and usually the surname of a man are nominative (some surnames, however, are always genitive). The second, or patronymic, remains genitive because it means "son of" (Periklés Alexandrou Argyropoulos, Konstantinos Petrou Kavafis). The first name of a woman is nominative, the patronymic and surname both genitive (Roxanes Demetriou Argyropoulu). On romanization, see 3.11.

3.6.7   HUNGARIAN NAMES

In Hungarian, the surname precedes the given name.

> Bartók Béla
>
> Bessenyei György
>
> Illyés Gyula
>
> Molnár Ferenc
>
> Nagy László
>
> Szabó Magda

In English texts, Hungarian names usually appear with given name first and the surname last.

> Béla Bartók
>
> György Bessenyei
>
> Gyula Illyés
>
> Ferenc Molnár
>
> László Nagy
>
> Magda Szabó

3.6.8   ITALIAN NAMES

The names of many Italians who lived before or during the Renaissance are alphabetized by first name.

> Bonvesin da la Riva
>
> Cino da Pistoia
>
> Dante Alighieri
>
> Iacopone da Todi
>
> Michelangelo Buonarroti

But other names of the period follow the standard practice.

> Boccaccio, Giovanni
>
> Cellini, Benvenuto
>
> Stampa, Gaspara

The names of members of historic families are also usually alphabetized by last name.

> Este, Beatrice d'
>
> Medici, Lorenzo de'

In modern times, Italian *da*, *de*, *del*, *della*, *di*, and *d'* are usually capitalized and used with the last name alone.

> Da Ponte (Lorenzo Da Ponte)
>
> D'Azeglio (Massimo D'Azeglio)
>
> Del Buono (Oreste Del Buono)
>
> Della Casa (Giovanni Della Casa)
>
> De Sica (Vittorio De Sica)
>
> Di Costanzo (Angelo Di Costanzo)

3.6.9   RUSSIAN NAMES

See J. Thomas Shaw's *The Transliteration of Modern Russian for English-
Language Publications* (1967; New York: MLA, 1979; print) for a more extended discussion of which system of romanization to use for Russian
names in various circumstances and when to use common Western
forms of names. The following is adopted from Shaw.

Russian names have three parts: prename, patronymic, and surname (Anton Pavlovich Chekhov). Prenames of Russians should be
romanized according to the appropriate system rather than given in
their English equivalents (Ivan, not John). The only exception is the
prename of a Russian ruler used alone (without the patronymic); in this
case, use the English equivalent (Michael I, but Mikhail Pavlovich).

The form of patronymics in Russian varies by sex, as the form
of surnames often does. For example, Aleksandr Sergeevich Pushkin
was the husband of Natalia Nikolaevna Pushkina. The treatment of
such names in an English text depends on the audience, on the pre-
dominance of masculine or feminine names in the text, and particularly on whether the text uses names without prenames. In general,
the feminine forms should be used for the feminine names and the
masculine forms for the masculine names. On occasion, however, especially in a casual reference to Russians in a work not on Russian
studies, some modifications may be acceptable. Scholars not familiar
with Russian names must exercise care in balancing accuracy with
clarity.

3.6.10 SPANISH NAMES

Spanish *de* is not used before the last name alone.

>   Las Casas (Bartolomé de Las Casas)
>
>   Madariaga (Salvador de Madariaga)
>
>   Rueda (Lope de Rueda)
>
>   Timoneda (Juan de Timoneda)

Spanish *del*, formed from the fusion of the preposition *de* and the definite article *el*, is capitalized and used with the last name alone.

>   Del Río (Angel Del Río)

A Spanish surname may include both the paternal name and the maternal name, with or without the conjunction *y*. The surname of a married woman usually includes her paternal surname and her husband's paternal surname, connected by *de*. Alphabetize Spanish names by the full surnames (consult your sources or a biographical dictionary for guidance in distinguishing surnames and given names).

>   Carreño de Miranda, Juan
>
>   Cervantes Saavedra, Miguel de
>
>   Díaz del Castillo, Bernal
>
>   García Márquez, Gabriel
>
>   Larra y Sánchez de Castro, Mariano José
>
>   López de Ayala, Pero
>
>   Matute, Ana María
>
>   Ortega y Gasset, José
>
>   Quevedo y Villegas, Francisco Gómez de
>
>   Sinues de Marco, María del Pilar
>
>   Zayas y Sotomayor, María de

Even the names of persons commonly known by the maternal portions of their surnames, such as Galdós and Lorca, should be alphabetized by the full surnames.

>   García Lorca, Federico
>
>   Pérez Galdós, Benito

LATIN NAMES

Roman male citizens generally had three names: a praenomen (given name), a nomen (clan name), and a cognomen (family or familiar name). Men in this category are usually referred to by nomen, cognomen, or both; your source or a standard reference book such as *The Oxford Classical Dictionary* will provide guidance.

> Brutus (Marcus Iunius Brutus)
>
> Calpurnius Siculus (Titus Calpurnius Siculus)
>
> Cicero (Marcus Tullius Cicero)
>
> Lucretius (Titus Lucretius Carus)
>
> Plautus (Titus Maccius Plautus)

Roman women usually had two names—a nomen (the clan name in the feminine form) and a cognomen (often derived from the father's cognomen): Livia Drusilla (daughter of Marcus Livius Drusus). Sometimes a woman's cognomen indicates her chronological order among the daughters of the family: Antonia Minor (younger daughter of Marcus Antonius). Most Roman women are referred to by nomen: Calpurnia, Clodia, Octavia, Sulpicia. Some, however, are better known by cognomen: Agrippina (Vipsania Agrippina).

When citing Roman names, use the forms most common in English.

> Horace (Quintus Horatius Flaccus)
>
> Julius Caesar (Gaius Iulius Caesar)
>
> Juvenal (Decimus Iunius Iuvenalis)
>
> Livy (Titus Livius)
>
> Ovid (Publius Ovidius Naso)
>
> Quintilian (Marcus Fabius Quintilianus)
>
> Terence (Publius Terentius Afer)
>
> Vergil (Publius Vergilius Maro)

Finally, some medieval and Renaissance figures are best known by their adopted or assigned Latin names.

> Albertus Magnus (Albert von Bollstädt)
>
> Comenius (Jan Amos Komenský)
>
> Copernicus (Niklas Koppernigk)
>
> Paracelsus (Theophrastus Bombast von Hohenheim)

3.6.12   ASIAN NAMES

In Chinese, Japanese, Korean, and Vietnamese, surnames precede given names.

CHINESE

Deng Nan

Deng Xiaoping

JAPANESE

Ueda Akinari

Ueda Makoto

KOREAN

Kim Jong-gil

Kim Nam-ju

VIETNAMESE

Nguyen Du

Nguyen Trai

Western authors should follow known preferences, however, even if the preferred forms do not accord with normal practice or standard romanization (Y. R. Chao, Syngman Rhee). (On romanization, see 3.11.)

In the older Wade-Giles system of romanizing Chinese, the given name appears in two syllables, separated by a hyphen (Huang Tso-lin, Mao Tse-tung); in the pinyin system, the given name appears without a hyphen (Huang Zuolin, Mao Zedong). Scholars presenting Chinese names need to balance the sometimes conflicting goals of consistency and clarity. In general, if you use the pinyin system, add the Wade-Giles spelling, in parentheses, for the names of persons who died before 1950 or who are better known by the older spelling. This practice allows a reader unfamiliar with the systems of romanization to become acquainted with the differences between them and to locate in other scholarly works information you cite. Many figures from the past are known by names of only two syllables, sometimes hyphenated: Lao-tzu, Han-shan, Li Po, Wang Wei.

For the names of persons in a language with which you are not familiar, consult relevant reference works or knowledgeable scholars for guidance on the order of names and on the use of prefixes (as in Arabic names). When a work you cite includes a romanization of the author's name on the title page, spell the author's name in your bibliography according to the system recommended in 3.11, and follow the name by the romanization (in parentheses) printed on the title page, if it is different.

------------------------------ **3.7** ------------------------------
CAPITALIZATION

3.7.1   ENGLISH

Capitalized in English are (1) the first word of a sentence, (2) the subject pronoun *I*, (3) the names and initials of persons (except for some particles), (4) the names of months and days of the week, (5) titles that immediately precede personal names (President Wilson) but not persons' titles used alone (*the president, a professor of English*), (6) other proper nouns, and (7) most adjectives derived from proper nouns.

In the title or subtitle of a work, capitalize the first word, the last word, and all principal words, including those that follow hyphens in compound terms. Therefore, capitalize the following parts of speech:

- Nouns (e.g., *flowers* and *Europe*, as in *The Flowers of Europe*)
- Pronouns (e.g., *our*, as in *Save Our Children*; *that*, as in *The Mouse That Roared*)
- Verbs (e.g., *watches*, as in *America Watches Television*; *is*, as in *What Is Literature?*)
- Adjectives (e.g., *more*, as in *No More Parades*; *that*, as in *Who Said That Phrase?*)
- Adverbs (e.g., *slightly*, as in *Only Slightly Corrupt*; *down*, as in *Go Down, Moses*)
- Subordinating conjunctions (e.g., *after, although, as if, as soon as, because, before, if, that, unless, until, when, where, while*, as in *One If by Land* and *Anywhere That Chance Leads*)

Do not capitalize the following parts of speech when they fall in the middle of a title:

- Articles (*a, an, the*, as in *Felix Holt, the Radical*)

- Prepositions (e.g., *against, as, between, in, of, to,* as in *The Merchant of Venice* and "A Dialogue between the Soul and Body")
- Coordinating conjunctions (*and, but, for, nor, or, so, yet,* as in *Romeo and Juliet*)
- The *to* in infinitives (as in *The Courage to Be*)

Use a colon and a space to separate a title from a subtitle, unless the title ends in a question mark, an exclamation point, or a dash. Include other punctuation only if it is part of the title.

The following examples illustrate how to capitalize and punctuate a variety of titles. For a discussion of which titles to italicize and which to place in quotation marks, see 3.8.2–3.

> *Death of a Salesman*
>
> *The Teaching of Spanish in English-Speaking Countries*
>
> *Storytelling and Mythmaking: Images from Film and Literature*
>
> *Life As I Find It*
>
> *The Artist as Critic*
>
> *What Are You Doing in My Universe?*
>
> *Whose Music? A Sociology of Musical Language*
>
> *Where Did You Go? Out. What Did You Do? Nothing.*
>
> "Ode to a Nightingale"
>
> "Italian Literature before Dante"
>
> "What Americans Stand For"
>
> "Why Fortinbras?"

When the first line of a poem serves as the title of the poem, reproduce the line exactly as it appears in the text.

> Dickinson's poem "I heard a Fly buzz—when I died—" contrasts the mundane and the momentous.

In the name of a periodical, an initial definite article is usually not treated as part of the title (the *Washington Post*). Capitalize the word *series* or *edition* only when it is part of a title (Norton Critical Edition, Twayne World Authors Series; but Penguin edition, *Oxford Companion* series). Do not capitalize the descriptive name for a part of a work—for example, *preface, introduction,* or *appendix*—unless it is a well-known title, such as Wordsworth's Preface to *Lyrical Ballads*.

Do not capitalize a noun, spelled out or abbreviated, followed by a numeral or letter indicating place in a sequence (*act 5, version A, ch. 3, no. 20, pl. 4, vol. 2*). Never capitalize entire words (i.e., every letter) in titles, even if the words are capitalized on the title page, except for terms composed of initials (*MLN*).

3.7.2   FRENCH

In prose and verse, French capitalization is the same as English except that the following terms are not capitalized in French unless they begin sentences or, sometimes, lines of verse: (1) the subject pronoun *je* 'I,' (2) the names of months and days of the week, (3) the names of languages, (4) adjectives derived from proper nouns, (5) titles preceding personal names, and (6) the words meaning "street," "square," "lake," "mountain," and so on, in most place-names.

> Un Français m'a parlé anglais près de la place de la Concorde.
>
> Hier j'ai vu le docteur Maurois qui conduisait une voiture Ford.
>
> Le capitaine Boutillier m'a dit qu'il partait pour Rouen le premier
> jeudi d'avril avec quelques amis normands.

There are two widely accepted methods of capitalizing French titles and subtitles of works. One method is to capitalize the first word in titles and subtitles and all proper nouns in them. This method is normally followed in publications of the Modern Language Association.

> *L'ami du peuple*
> *La chambre claire: Note sur la photographie*
> *Du côté de chez Swann*
> *Le grand Meaulnes*
> *La guerre de Troie n'aura pas lieu*
> *Nouvelle revue d'onomastique*

In the other method, when a title or subtitle begins with an article, the first noun and any preceding adjectives are also capitalized.

> *L'Ami du peuple*
> *La Chambre claire: Note sur la photographie*
> *Du côté de chez Swann*
> *Le Grand Meaulnes*
> *La Guerre de Troie n'aura pas lieu*

In this system, all major words in titles of series and periodicals are sometimes capitalized.

Nouvelle Revue d'Onomastique

Whichever practice you choose or your publisher requires, follow it consistently throughout your manuscript.

3.7.3   GERMAN

In prose and verse, German capitalization differs considerably from English. Always capitalized in German are all nouns—including adjectives, infinitives, pronouns, prepositions, and other parts of speech when used as nouns—as well as the pronoun *Sie* 'you' and its possessive, *Ihr* 'your,' and their inflected forms. Not capitalized unless they begin sentences or, usually, lines of verse are (1) the subject pronoun *ich* 'I,' (2) the names of languages and of days of the week used as adjectives, adverbs, or complements of prepositions, and (3) adjectives and adverbs formed from proper nouns, except when the proper nouns are names of persons and the adjectives and adverbs refer to the persons' works or deeds.

> Ich glaube an das Gute in der Welt.

> Er schreibt, nur um dem Auf und Ab der Buch-Nachfrage zu entsprechen.

> Fahren Sie mit Ihrer Frau zurück?

> Ein französischer Schriftsteller, den ich gut kenne, arbeitet sonntags immer an seinem neuen Buch über die platonische Liebe.

> *Der Staat* ist eine der bekanntesten Platonischen Schriften.

In letters and ceremonial writings, the pronouns *du* and *ihr* 'you' and their derivatives are capitalized.

In a title or subtitle, capitalize the first word and all words normally capitalized.

> *Thomas Mann und die Grenzen des Ich*
> *Ein treuer Diener seines Herrn*
> *Zeitschrift für vergleichende Sprachforschung*

3.7.4   ITALIAN

In prose and verse, Italian capitalization is the same as English except that in Italian centuries and other large divisions of time are capitalized (*il Seicento*) and the following terms are not capitalized unless they begin sentences or, usually, lines of verse: (1) the subject pronoun *io* 'I,' (2) the names of months and days of the week, (3) the names of languages and nationalities, (4) nouns, adjectives, and adverbs derived from proper nouns, (5) titles preceding personal names, and (6) the words meaning "street," "square," and so on, in most place-names.

> Un italiano parlava francese con uno svizzero in piazza di Spagna.
>
> Il dottor Bruno ritornerà dall'Italia giovedì otto agosto e io partirò il nove.

In a title or subtitle, capitalize only the first word and all words normally capitalized.

> *L'arte tipografica in Urbino*
> *Bibliografia della critica pirandelliana*
> *Collezione di classici italiani*
> *Dizionario letterario Bompiani*
> *Studi petrarcheschi*

3.7.5   PORTUGUESE

In prose and verse, Portuguese capitalization is the same as English except that the following terms are not capitalized in Portuguese unless they begin sentences or, sometimes, lines of verse: (1) the subject pronoun *eu* 'I,' (2) the names of days of the week, (3) the names of months in Brazil (they are capitalized in Portugal), (4) adjectives derived from proper nouns, (5) titles preceding personal names in Portugal (they are capitalized in Brazil), and (6) the words meaning "street," "square," and so on, in most place-names in Portugal (they are capitalized in Brazil). As in English, points of the compass are not capitalized when indicating direction (*ao norte da América*), but they are capitalized when indicating regions (*os americanos do Norte*). Brazilian Portuguese capitalizes nouns used to refer to abstract concepts, to institutions, or to branches of knowledge (*a Igreja, a Nação, a Matemática*).

PENINSULAR USAGE

Vi o doutor Silva na praça da República.

BRAZILIAN USAGE

O francês falava da História do Brasil na Praça Tiradentes, utilizando o inglês.

Ontem eu vi o Doutor Garcia, aquele que tem um carro Ford.

Então me disse Dona Teresa que pretendia sair para o Recife a primeira segunda-feira de abril com alguns amigos mineiros.

In a title or subtitle, capitalize only the first word and all words normally capitalized.

O bico da pena

O espírito das leis

Gabriela, cravo e canela

Problemas das linguagem e do estilo

Boletim de filologia

Revista lusitana

Correio da manhã

Some editors and presses, however, capitalize all major words: *Gabriela, Cravo e Canela* and *Boletim de Filologia*.

3.7.6   RUSSIAN

In prose and verse, Russian capitalization is the same as English except that the following terms are not capitalized in Russian unless they begin sentences or, sometimes, lines of verse: (1) the subject pronoun я 'I,' (2) the names of months and days of the week, (3) the names of languages, (4) adjectives derived from proper nouns, (5) titles preceding personal names, and (6) the words meaning "street," "square," and so on, in most place-names. Romanized Russian should follow the same usage (on romanization, see 3.11).

В субботу, тринадцатого апреля, празднуя свой день рождения, доктор Петухов вновь вспомнил о своей встрече с французом из Лиона на улице Марата.

В то время петербургская знать предпочитала говорить по-французски.

Напрасно я пытался уговорить его не делать этого.

In a title or subtitle and in the name of an organization or institution, capitalize the first word and all words normally capitalized.

«К истории образования восточнославянских языков: По данным Галицкого евангелия 1266-1301 гг.»

Общественные науки за рубежом: Литературоведение

Вопросы литературы

3.7.7   SPANISH

In prose and verse, Spanish capitalization is the same as English except that the following terms are not capitalized in Spanish unless they begin sentences or, sometimes, lines of verse: (1) the subject pronoun *yo* 'I,' (2) the names of months and days of the week, (3) the names of languages and nationalities, (4) nouns and adjectives derived from proper nouns, (5) titles preceding personal names, and (6) the words meaning "street," "square," and so on, in most place-names.

El francés hablaba inglés en la plaza Colón.

Ayer yo vi al doctor García en un coche Ford.

Me dijo don Jorge que iba a salir para Sevilla el primer martes de abril con unos amigos neoyorquinos.

In a title or subtitle, capitalize only the first word and words normally capitalized.

Breve historia del ensayo hispanoamericano

Extremos de América

La gloria de don Ramiro

Historia verdadera de la conquista de la Nueva España

Revista de filología española

Trasmundo de Goya

Some editors and presses follow other rules. In titles of series and periodicals, they capitalize all major words: *Revista de Filología Española*.

3.7.8   LATIN

Although practice varies, Latin most commonly follows the English rules for capitalization, except that *ego* 'I' is not capitalized.

> Semper ego auditor tantum? Numquamne reponam / Vexatus totiens rauci Theseide Cordi?

> Quidquid id est, timeo Danaos et dona ferentes.

> Nil desperandum.

> Quo usque tandem abutere, Catilina, patientia nostra?

In a title or subtitle, capitalize only the first word and all words normally capitalized.

> *De senectute*
>
> *Liber de senectute*
>
> *Pro Marcello*

3.7.9   OTHER LANGUAGES

In romanizing languages that do not have capital letters (e.g., Arabic, Chinese, Japanese), capitalize the first words of sentences and, sometimes, of lines of poetry and all names of persons and places. (On romanization, see 3.11.) In romanized Arabic, the article *al* (and its forms) is lowercase except when it begins a sentence. Capitalize romanized names of institutions, religions, movements, and the like if comparable names are capitalized in English. A lowercase romanized term appearing in English text is italicized; a capitalized romanized name (other than the titles listed in 3.8.2) in English text is not italicized, unless it is part of an expression that is otherwise lowercase. In a title or subtitle, capitalize only the first word and all words normally capitalized.

For additional information on capitalization in a variety of languages, consult *The Chicago Manual of Style* (15th ed.; Chicago: U of Chicago P, 2003; print, Web), the United States Government Printing Office's *Style Manual* (29th ed.; Washington: GPO, 2000; CD-ROM, print, Web), *ALA-LC Romanization Tables: Transliteration Schemes for Non-Roman Scripts* (comp. and ed. Randall K. Barry; Washington: Lib. of Cong., 1997; print, Web), and *Words into Type* (by Marjorie E. Skillin et al.; 3rd ed.; Englewood Cliffs: Prentice, 1974; print).

3.8
TITLES OF WORKS IN THE MANUSCRIPT

3.8.1   GENERAL GUIDELINES

Whenever you cite the title of a published work in your manuscript, take the title from the title page, not, for example, from the cover or from the top of a page. Do not reproduce any unusual typographic characteristics, such as special capitalization or lowercasing of letters (see 3.7.1). Place a colon between a title and a subtitle, unless the title ends in a question mark, an exclamation point, or a dash. A title page may present a title designed like one of the following examples:

> MODERNISM & NEGRITUDE

> **READING SITES**
> Social Difference and
> Reader Response

> Turner's early sketchbooks

These titles should appear in a manuscript as follows:

Modernism and Negritude

Reading Sites: Social Difference and Reader Response

Turner's Early Sketchbooks

To indicate titles in your manuscript, whether in English or in another language, either italicize them or enclose them in quotation marks. In general, italicize the titles of works published independently (see 3.8.2) and use quotation marks for titles of works published within larger works and for unpublished works (see 3.8.3).

3.8.2   ITALICIZED TITLES

Italicize the names of books, plays, poems published as books, pamphlets, periodicals (newspapers, magazines, and journals), Web sites, online databases, films, television and radio broadcasts, compact discs, audiocassettes, record albums, dance performances, operas and other long musical compositions (except those identified simply by form, number, and key; see 3.8.5), paintings, works of sculpture, ships, aircraft, and spacecraft.

The Awakening (book)

The Piano Lesson (play)

The Waste Land (poem published as a book)

New Jersey Driver Manual (pamphlet)

Wall Street Journal (newspaper)

Time (magazine)

PMLA (journal)

Stanford Encyclopedia of Philosophy (Web site)

LexisNexis Academic (online database)

Die bitteren Tränen der Petra von Kant (film)

Star Trek (television broadcast)

What's the Word? (radio broadcast)

Sgt. Pepper's Lonely Hearts Club Band (compact disc, audiocassette, record album)

Ailey's *Revelations* (dance performance)

Rigoletto (opera)

Berlioz's *Symphonie fantastique* (long musical composition identified by name)

Chagall's *I and My Village* (painting)

French's *The Minute Man* (sculpture)

HMS *Vanguard* (ship)

Spirit of St. Louis (aircraft)

Challenger (spacecraft)

3.8.3   TITLES IN QUOTATION MARKS

Enclose in quotation marks the titles of articles, essays, stories, and poems published within larger works; chapters of books; pages in Web sites; individual episodes of television and radio broadcasts; and short musical compositions (e.g., songs). Also use quotation marks for unpublished works, such as lectures, addresses delivered at conferences, manuscripts of any length, and dissertations.

"Literary History and Sociology" (journal article)

"Etruscan" (encyclopedia article)

"The Fiction of Langston Hughes" (essay in a book)

"The Lottery" (story)

"Kubla Khan" (poem)

"Contemporary Theory, the Academy, and Pedagogy" (chapter in a book)

"Philosophy of Economics" (page in a Web site)

"The Trouble with Tribbles" (episode of the television broadcast *Star Trek*)

"Lost Homelands" (episode of the radio broadcast *What's the Word?*)

"Mood Indigo" (song)

"Adapting to the Age of Information" (lecture)

"Cybernetic Constructivism" (address)

"Coffee at the Automat" (manuscript)

"Acts of Coercion: Father-Daughter Relationships and the Pressure to Confess in British Women's Fiction, 1778-1814" (dissertation)

3.8.4   TITLES AND QUOTATIONS WITHIN TITLES

Italicize a title normally indicated by italics when it appears within a title enclosed in quotation marks.

"*Romeo and Juliet* and Renaissance Politics" (an article about a play)

"Language and Childbirth in *The Awakening*" (an article about a novel)

Enclose in single quotation marks a title normally indicated by quotation marks when it appears within another title requiring quotation marks.

"Lines after Reading 'Sailing to Byzantium'" (a poem about a poem)

"The Uncanny Theology of 'A Good Man Is Hard to Find'" (an article about a story)

Also place single quotation marks around a quotation that appears within a title requiring quotation marks.

> "Emerson's Strategies against 'Foolish Consistency'" (an article with
> a quotation in its title)

Use quotation marks around a title normally indicated by quotation
marks when it appears within an italicized title.

> *"The Lottery" and Other Stories* (a book of stories)
>
> *New Perspectives on "The Eve of St. Agnes"* (a book about a poem)

If a period is required after an italicized title that ends with a quotation
mark, place the period before the quotation mark.

> The study appears in *New Perspectives on "The Eve of St. Agnes."*

There are two common methods for identifying a normally italicized title when it appears within an italicized title. In one practice,
the title within is neither italicized nor enclosed in quotation marks.
This method is preferred in publications of the Modern Language
Association.

> *Approaches to Teaching Murasaki Shikibu's* The Tale of Genji
> (a book about a novel)
>
> *From* The Lodger *to* The Lady Vanishes: *Hitchcock's Classic British*
> *Thrillers* (a book about films)

In the other method, all titles within italicized titles are placed in quotation marks and italicized.

> *Approaches to Teaching Murasaki Shikibu's "The Tale of Genji"*
>
> *From "The Lodger" to "The Lady Vanishes": Hitchcock's Classic British*
> *Thrillers*

Each approach has advantages and disadvantages. In the first method,
the titles of works published independently and the material containing them are always given opposite treatments. This practice has the
advantage of consistency, but it can lead to ambiguity: it is sometimes
hard to tell where a title like *Approaches to Teaching Murasaki Shikibu's*
The Tale of Genji ends and where the adjacent text begins.

The second method prevents confusion between titles and the adjacent text. However, it treats titles of works published independently two
ways: they receive quotation marks in italicized titles but nowhere else.
In addition, within italicized titles this method abandons the distinction
between works that are published independently and those that are not.

Whichever practice you choose or your publisher requires, follow it consistently throughout your manuscript.

EXCEPTIONS

The convention of using italics and quotation marks to indicate titles does not generally apply to the names of scriptural writings (including all books and versions of the Bible); of laws, acts, and similar political documents; of musical compositions identified by form, number, and key; of series, societies, buildings, and monuments; and of conferences, seminars, workshops, and courses. These terms all appear without italics or quotation marks.

SCRIPTURE

Bible	Talmud
Old Testament	Koran
Genesis	Upanishads
Gospels	

But italicize titles of individual published editions of scriptural writings (*The Interlinear Bible, The Talmud of the Land of Israel: A Preliminary Translation and Explanation, The Upanishads: A Selection for the Modern Reader*) and treat the editions in the works-cited list like any other published book.

LAWS, ACTS, AND SIMILAR POLITICAL DOCUMENTS

Magna Carta

Declaration of Independence

Bill of Rights

Treaty of Trianon

MUSICAL COMPOSITIONS IDENTIFIED BY FORM, NUMBER, AND KEY

Beethoven's Symphony no. 7 in A, op. 92

Vivaldi's Concerto for Two Trumpets and Strings in C, RV539

SERIES

Bollingen Series

University of North Carolina Studies in Comparative Literature

Masterpiece Theatre

SOCIETIES

American Historical Association

Renaissance Society of America

BUILDINGS AND MONUMENTS

Moscone Center

Sears Tower

Arch of Constantine

CONFERENCES, SEMINARS, WORKSHOPS, AND COURSES

The Social Poem: A Conference on Contemporary Poetry in the Public
  Sphere

Canadian Writers' Workshop

MLA Annual Convention

Introduction to Linguistics

Portuguese 102

Words designating the divisions of a work are also not italicized or put
within quotation marks, nor are they capitalized when used in the text
("The author says in her preface . . . ," "In canto 32 Ariosto writes . . .").

preface	bibliography	act 4
introduction	appendix	scene 7
list of works cited	index	stanza 20
chapter 2	canto 32	

3.8.6   SHORTENED TITLES

If you cite a title often in the text of your manuscript, you may, after stating the title in full at least once, use a shortened form, preferably a familiar or obvious one (e.g., "Nightingale" for "Ode to a Nightingale"), or an
abbreviation (for guidance on abbreviating titles of works, see 8.6).

─────────────── 3.9 ───────────────

QUOTATIONS

3.9.1   ACCURACY OF QUOTATIONS

The accuracy of quotations is extremely important. They must reproduce the original sources exactly. Unless indicated in square brackets or

parentheses (see 3.9.6), changes must not be made in the spelling, capitalization, or interior punctuation of the source. You must construct a clear, grammatically correct sentence that allows you to introduce or incorporate a quotation with complete accuracy. Alternatively, you may paraphrase the original and quote only fragments, which may be easier to integrate into the text. If you change a quotation in any way, make the alteration clear to the reader, following the rules and recommendations below.

3.9.2   PROSE

If a prose quotation runs no more than four lines and requires no special emphasis, put it in quotation marks and incorporate it into the text.

> "It was the best of times, it was the worst of times," wrote Charles Dickens about the eighteenth century.

You need not always reproduce complete sentences. Sometimes you may want to quote just a word or phrase as part of your sentence.

> For Charles Dickens the eighteenth century was both "the best of times" and "the worst of times."

You may put a quotation at the beginning, middle, or end of your sentence or, for the sake of variety or better style, divide it by your own words.

> Joseph Conrad writes of the company manager in *Heart of Darkness*, "He was obeyed, yet he inspired neither love nor fear, nor even respect."

or

> "He was obeyed," writes Joseph Conrad of the company manager in *Heart of Darkness*, "yet he inspired neither love nor fear, nor even respect."

If a quotation ending a sentence requires a parenthetical reference, place the sentence period after the reference. (For more information on punctuating quotations, see 3.9.7.)

> For Charles Dickens the eighteenth century was both "the best of times" and "the worst of times" (35).

"He was obeyed," writes Joseph Conrad of the company manager in *Heart of Darkness*, "yet he inspired neither love nor fear, nor even respect" (87).

If a quotation runs to more than four lines when run into the text, set it off from your text by beginning a new line, indenting one inch from the left margin, and typing it double-spaced, without adding quotation marks. A colon generally introduces a quotation displayed in this way, though sometimes the context may require a different mark of punctuation or none at all. If you quote only a single paragraph or part of one, do not indent the first line more than the rest. A parenthetical reference for a prose quotation set off from the text follows the last line of the quotation.

> At the conclusion of *Lord of the Flies*, Ralph and the other boys realize the horror of their actions:
>
> > The tears began to flow and sobs shook him. He gave himself up to them now for the first time on the island; great, shuddering spasms of grief that seemed to wrench his whole body. His voice rose under the black smoke before the burning wreckage of the island; and infected by that emotion, the other little boys began to shake and sob too. (186)

If you need to quote two or more paragraphs, indent the first line of each paragraph an additional quarter inch. If the first sentence quoted does not begin a paragraph in the source, however, do not indent it the additional amount. Indent only the first lines of the successive paragraphs.

> In *Moll Flanders* Defoe maintains the pseudoautobiographical narration typical of the picaresque tradition:
>
> > My true name is so well known in the records, or registers, at Newgate and in the Old Bailey, and there are some things of such consequence still depending there relating to my particular conduct, that it is not to be expected I should set my name or the account of my family to this work. . . .
> >
> > It is enough to tell you, that . . . some of my worst comrades, who are out of the way of doing me harm . . . know me by the name of Moll Flanders. . . . (1)

On omitting words within quotations, see 3.9.5. For translations of quotations, see 3.9.8.

POETRY

If you quote part or all of a single line of verse that does not require special emphasis, put it in quotation marks within your text. You may also incorporate two or three lines in this way, using a slash with a space on each side (/) to separate them.

> Bradstreet frames the poem with a sense of mortality: "All things within this fading world hath end" (1).

> Reflecting on the "incident" in Baltimore, Cullen concludes, "Of all the things that happened there / That's all that I remember" (11-12).

Verse quotations of more than three lines should begin on a new line. Unless the quotation involves unusual spacing, indent each line one inch from the left margin and double-space between lines, adding no quotation marks that do not appear in the original. A parenthetical reference for a verse quotation set off from the text follows the last line of the quotation (as in quotations of prose); a parenthetical reference that will not fit on the line should appear on a new line, flush with the right margin of the page.

> Elizabeth Bishop's "In the Waiting Room" is rich in evocative detail:
> > It was winter. It got dark
> > early. The waiting room
> > was full of grown-up people,
> > arctics and overcoats,
> > lamps and magazines. (6-10)

A line that is too long to fit within the right margin should be continued on the next line and the continuation indented an additional quarter inch. You may reduce the indention of the quotation to less than one inch from the left margin if doing so will eliminate the need for such continuations. If the spatial arrangement of the original lines, including indention and spacing within and between them, is unusual, reproduce it as accurately as possible.

E. E. Cummings concludes the poem with this vivid description of a carefree scene, reinforced by the carefree form of the lines themselves:

> it's
>
> spring
>
> and
>
>   the
>
>   goat-footed
>
> balloonMan   whistles
>
> far
>
> and
>
> wee (16-24)

When a verse quotation begins in the middle of a line, the partial line should be positioned where it is in the original and not shifted to the left margin.

In a poem on Thomas Hardy ("T. H."), Molly Holden recalls her encounter with a "young dog fox" one morning:

>   I remember
> he glanced at me in just that way, independent
> and unabashed, the handsome sidelong look
> that went round and about but never directly
> met my eyes, for that would betray his soul.
> He was not being sly, only careful. (43-48)

For translations of quotations, see 3.9.8.

3.9.4   DRAMA

If you quote dialogue between two or more characters in a play, set the quotation off from your text. Begin each part of the dialogue with the appropriate character's name indented one inch from the left margin and written in all capital letters: HAMLET. Follow the name with a period, and start the quotation. Indent all subsequent lines in that character's speech an additional quarter inch. When the dialogue shifts to another character, start a new line indented one inch from the left margin. Maintain this pattern throughout the entire quotation.

Marguerite Duras's screenplay for *Hiroshima mon amour* suggests at the outset the profound difference between observation and experience:

> HE. You saw nothing in Hiroshima. Nothing.
>
> SHE. I saw *everything. Everything.* . . . The hospital, for
>   instance, I saw it. I'm sure I did. There is a hospital in
>   Hiroshima. How could I help seeing it?
>
> HE. You did not see the hospital in Hiroshima. You saw
>   nothing in Hiroshima. (2505-06)

A short time later Lear loses the final symbol of his former power, the soldiers who make up his train:

> GONERIL.   Hear me, my lord.
>   What need you five-and-twenty, ten or five,
>   To follow in a house where twice so many
>   Have a command to tend you?
>
> REGAN.   What need one?
>
> LEAR. O, reason not the need! (2.4.254-58)

For the other aspects of formatting, follow the recommendations above for quoting prose and poetry (3.9.2–3). In general, stage directions are treated like other quoted text: they should be reproduced exactly as they appear in the original source (see 3.9.1). When stage directions interrupt the grammatical sense of your sentence, they may be replaced with an ellipsis (see 3.9.5).

3.9.5   ELLIPSIS

Whenever you wish to omit a word, a phrase, a sentence, or more from a quoted passage, you should be guided by two principles: fairness to the author quoted and the grammatical integrity of your writing. A quotation should never be presented in a way that could cause a reader to misunderstand the sentence structure of the original source. If you quote only a word or a phrase, it will be obvious that you left out some of the original sentence.

> In his inaugural address, John F. Kennedy spoke of a "new frontier."

But if omitting material from the original sentence or sentences leaves a quotation that appears to be a sentence or a series of sentences, you must use ellipsis points, or three spaced periods, to indicate that your quotation does not completely reproduce the original. Whenever you omit words from a quotation, the resulting passage—your prose and the quotation integrated into it—should be grammatically complete and correct.

For an ellipsis within a sentence, use three periods with a space before each and a space after the last (. . .).

ORIGINAL

Medical thinking, trapped in the theory of astral influences, stressed air as the communicator of disease, ignoring sanitation or visible carriers. (Barbara W. Tuchman, *A Distant Mirror: The Calamitous Fourteenth Century* [1978; New York: Ballantine, 1979; print; 101–02])

QUOTATION WITH AN ELLIPSIS IN THE MIDDLE

In surveying various responses to plagues in the Middle Ages, Barbara W. Tuchman writes, "Medical thinking . . . stressed air as the communicator of disease, ignoring sanitation or visible carriers" (101-02).

When the ellipsis coincides with the end of your sentence, use three periods with a space before each following a sentence period — that is, four periods, with no space before the first or after the last.

QUOTATION WITH AN ELLIPSIS AT THE END

In surveying various responses to plagues in the Middle Ages, Barbara W. Tuchman writes, "Medical thinking, trapped in the theory of astral influences, stressed air as the communicator of disease. . . ."

If a parenthetical reference follows the ellipsis at the end of your sentence, however, use three periods with a space before each, and place the sentence period after the final parenthesis.

QUOTATION WITH AN ELLIPSIS AT THE END
FOLLOWED BY A PARENTHETICAL REFERENCE

In surveying various responses to plagues in the Middle Ages, Barbara W. Tuchman writes, "Medical thinking, trapped in the theory of astral influences, stressed air as the communicator of disease . . ." (101-02).

In a quotation of more than one sentence, an ellipsis in the middle can indicate the omission of any amount of text.

ORIGINAL

Presidential control reached its zenith under Andrew Jackson, the extent of whose attention to the press even before he became a candidate is suggested by the fact that he subscribed to twenty newspapers. Jackson was never content to have only one organ grinding out his tune. For a time, the *United States Telegraph* and the *Washington Globe* were almost equally favored as party organs, and there were fifty-seven journalists on the government payroll. (William L. Rivers, *The Mass Media: Reporting, Writing, Editing* [2nd ed.; New York: Harper, 1975; print; 7])

QUOTATION OMITTING A SENTENCE

In discussing the historical relation between politics and the press, William L. Rivers notes:

> Presidential control reached its zenith under Andrew Jackson, the extent of whose attention to the press even before he became a candidate is suggested by the fact that he subscribed to twenty newspapers. . . . For a time, the *United States Telegraph* and the *Washington Globe* were almost equally favored as party organs, and there were fifty-seven journalists on the government payroll. (7)

QUOTATION WITH AN OMISSION FROM THE MIDDLE
OF ONE SENTENCE TO THE END OF ANOTHER

In discussing the historical relation between politics and the press, William L. Rivers notes, "Presidential control reached its zenith under Andrew Jackson. . . . For a time, the *United States Telegraph* and the *Washington Globe* were almost equally favored as party organs, and there were fifty-seven journalists on the government payroll" (7).

QUOTATION WITH AN OMISSION FROM THE MIDDLE
OF ONE SENTENCE TO THE MIDDLE OF ANOTHER

In discussing the historical relation between politics and the press, William L. Rivers notes that when presidential control "reached its zenith under Andrew Jackson . . . there were fifty-seven journalists on the government payroll" (7).

The omission of words and phrases from quotations of poetry is also indicated by three or four periods (as in quotations of prose).

ORIGINAL

In Worcester, Massachusetts,
I went with Aunt Consuelo
to keep her dentist's appointment
and sat and waited for her
in the dentist's waiting room.
It was winter. It got dark
early. The waiting room
was full of grown-up people,
arctics and overcoats,
lamps and magazines.
(Elizabeth Bishop, "In the Waiting Room," lines 1–10)

QUOTATION WITH AN ELLIPSIS AT THE END

Elizabeth Bishop's "In the Waiting Room" is rich in evocative detail:

> In Worcester, Massachusetts,
>
> I went with Aunt Consuelo
>
> to keep her dentist's appointment
>
> and sat and waited for her
>
> in the dentist's waiting room.
>
> It was winter. It got dark
>
> early. The waiting room
>
> was full of grown-up people. . . . (1-8)

The omission of a line or more in the middle of a poetry quotation that is set off from the text is indicated by a line of spaced periods approximately the length of a complete line of the quoted poem.

QUOTATION OMITTING A LINE OR MORE IN THE MIDDLE

Elizabeth Bishop's "In the Waiting Room" is rich in evocative detail:

> In Worcester, Massachusetts,
>
> I went with Aunt Consuelo
>
> to keep her dentist's appointment
>
> . . . .
>
> It was winter. It got dark
>
> early. (1-3, 6-7)

If the author you are quoting uses ellipsis points, you should distinguish them from your ellipses by putting square brackets around the ones you add or by including an explanatory phrase in parentheses after the quotation.

ORIGINAL

"We live in California, my husband and I, Los Angeles. . . . This is beautiful country; I have never been here before." (N. Scott Momaday, *House Made of Dawn* [1968; New York: Perennial-Harper, 1977; print; 29])

QUOTATION WITH AN ADDED ELLIPSIS

In N. Scott Momaday's *House Made of Dawn*, when Mrs. St. John arrives at the rectory, she tells Father Olguin, "We live in California, my husband and I, Los Angeles. . . . This is beautiful country [. . .]" (29).

or

In N. Scott Momaday's *House Made of Dawn*, when Mrs. St. John arrives at the rectory, she tells Father Olguin, "We live in California, my husband and I, Los Angeles. . . . This is beautiful country . . ." (29; 1st ellipsis in orig.).

Some publishers prefer that square brackets always be placed around ellipsis points inserted into quotations, so that all alterations in quotations are indicated by brackets (cf. 3.9.6).

3.9.6   OTHER ALTERATIONS OF SOURCES

Occasionally, you may decide that a quotation will be unclear or confusing to your reader unless you provide supplementary information. For example, you may need to insert material missing from the original, to add *sic* ("thus," "so") to assure readers that the quotation is accurate even though the spelling or logic might make them think otherwise, or to italicize words for emphasis. While such contributions to a quotation are permissible, you should keep them to a minimum and make sure to distinguish them from the original, usually by explaining them in parentheses after the quotation or by putting them in square brackets within the quotation.

A comment or an explanation that immediately follows the closing quotation mark appears in parentheses.

> Shaw admitted, "Nothing can extinguish my interest in Shakespear" (sic).

> Lincoln specifically advocated a government "*for* the people" (emphasis added).

A comment or an explanation that goes inside the quotation must appear within square brackets, not parentheses.

> He claimed he could provide "hundreds of examples [of court decisions] to illustrate the historical tension between church and state."

> Milton's Satan speaks of his "study [pursuit] of revenge."

Similarly, if a pronoun in a quotation seems unclear, you may add an identification in square brackets.

> In the first act he soliloquizes, "Why she would hang on him [Hamlet's father] / As if increase of appetite had grown / By what it fed on. . . ."

3.9.7   PUNCTUATION WITH QUOTATIONS

Whether set off from the text or run into it, quoted material is usually preceded by a colon if the quotation is formally introduced and by a comma or no punctuation if the quotation is an integral part of the sentence structure.

> Shelley held a bold view: "Poets are the unacknowledged legislators of the World" (794).

> Shelley thought poets "the unacknowledged legislators of the World" (794).

> "Poets," according to Shelley, "are the unacknowledged legislators of the World" (794).

Do not use opening and closing quotation marks to enclose quotations set off from the text, but reproduce any quotation marks that are in the passage quoted.

In "Memories of West Street and Lepke," Robert Lowell, a

conscientious objector (or "C.O."), recounts meeting a Jehovah's

Witness in prison:

> I was so out of things, I'd never heard
> of the Jehovah's Witnesses.
> "Are you a C.O.?" I asked a fellow jailbird.
> "No," he answered, "I'm a J.W." (36-39)

Use double quotation marks around quotations incorporated into the
text, single quotation marks around quotations within those quotations.

In "Memories of West Street and Lepke," Robert Lowell, a

conscientious objector (or "C.O."), recounts meeting a Jehovah's

Witness in prison: "'Are you a C.O.?' I asked a fellow jailbird. / 'No,' he

answered, 'I'm a J.W.'" (38-39).

When a quotation consists entirely of material enclosed by quotation
marks in the source work, usually one pair of double quotation marks
is sufficient, provided that the introductory wording makes clear the
special character of the quoted material.

Meeting a fellow prisoner, Lowell asks, "Are you a C.O.?" (38).

Except for changing internal double quotation marks to single ones
when you incorporate quotations into your text, you should reproduce
internal punctuation exactly as in the original. The closing punctuation, though, depends on where the quoted material appears in your
sentence. Suppose, for example, that you want to quote the following sentence: "You've got to be carefully taught." If you begin your
sentence with this line, you have to replace the closing period with a
punctuation mark appropriate to the new context.

"You've got to be carefully taught," wrote Oscar Hammerstein II about

how racial prejudice is perpetuated.

If the quotation ends with a question mark or an exclamation point, however, the original punctuation is retained, and no comma is required.

"How can I describe my emotions at this catastrophe, or how delineate

the wretch whom with such infinite pains and care I had endeavoured

to form?" wonders the doctor in Mary Shelley's *Frankenstein* (42).

"What a wonderful little almanac you are, Celia!" Dorothea Brooke
responds to her sister (7).

By convention, commas and periods that directly follow quotations
go inside the closing quotation marks, but a parenthetical reference
should intervene between the quotation and the required punctuation.
Thus, if a quotation ends with a period, the period appears after the
reference.

N. Scott Momaday's *House Made of Dawn* begins with an image that
also concludes the novel: "Abel was running" (7).

If a quotation ends with both single and double quotation marks, the
comma or period precedes both.

"The poem alludes to Stevens's 'Sunday Morning,'" notes Miller.

All other punctuation marks—such as semicolons, colons, question
marks, and exclamation points—go outside a closing quotation mark,
except when they are part of the quoted material.

ORIGINAL

I believe taxation without representation is tyranny!

QUOTATIONS

He attacked "taxation without representation" (32).

Did he attack "taxation without representation"?

What dramatic events followed his attack on "taxation without
representation"!

but

He declared, "I believe taxation without representation is tyranny!"

If a quotation ending with a question mark or an exclamation point
concludes your sentence and requires a parenthetical reference, retain
the original punctuation within the quotation mark and follow with
the reference and the sentence period outside the quotation mark.

In Mary Shelley's *Frankenstein*, the doctor wonders, "How can I
describe my emotions at this catastrophe, or how delineate the wretch
whom with such infinite pains and care I had endeavoured to form?"
(42).

Dorothea Brooke responds to her sister, "What a wonderful little almanac you are, Celia!" (7).

TRANSLATIONS OF QUOTATIONS

If you believe that a significant portion of your audience will not be familiar with the language of a quotation you present, you should add a translation. If the translation is not yours, give its source in addition to the source of the quotation. In general, the translation should immediately follow the quotation whether they are run into or set off from the text, although their order may be reversed if most readers will not likely be able to read the original. If the quotation is run into the text, use double quotation marks around a translation placed in parentheses following the quotation but single quotation marks around a translation that immediately follows without intervening punctuation.

> At the opening of Dante's *Inferno*, the poet finds himself in "una selva oscura" ("a dark wood"; 1.2; Ciardi 28).

> At the opening of Dante's *Inferno*, the poet finds himself in "una selva oscura" 'a dark wood' (1.2; Ciardi 28).

Do not use quotation marks around quotations and translations set off from the text.

> Dante's *Inferno* begins literally in the middle of things:
> Nel mezzo del cammin di nostra vita
> mi ritrovai per una selva oscura,
> ché la diritta via era smarrita.
> Ahi quanto a dir qual era è cosa dura
> esta selva selvaggia e aspra e forte
> che nel pensier rinova la paura! (1.1-6)
> Midway in our life's journey, I went astray
> from the straight road and woke to find myself
> alone in a dark wood. How shall I say
> what wood that was! I never saw so drear,
> so rank, so arduous a wilderness!
> Its very memory gives a shape to fear. (Ciardi 28)

See also 3.4.8b for guidelines on translating a foreign word or phrase within a sentence.

3.10
NUMBERS

3.10.1   ARABIC NUMERALS

Although there are still a few well-established uses for roman numerals (see 3.10.7), virtually all numbers not spelled out are commonly represented today by arabic numerals.

3.10.2   USE OF WORDS OR NUMERALS

In discussions that require few numbers, you may spell out numbers written in a word or two and represent other numbers by numerals (*one, thirty-six, ninety-nine, one hundred, fifteen hundred, two thousand, three million,* but *2½, 101, 137, 1,275*). To form the plural of a spelled-out number, treat the word like an ordinary noun (*sixes, sevens*).

If your project is one that calls for frequent use of numbers — say, an analysis of printing practices or a study of statistical findings — use numerals for all numbers that precede technical units of measurement (*30 inches, 5 kilograms*). In such a project, also use numerals for numbers that are presented together and that refer to similar things, such as in comparisons or reports of experimental data. Spell out other numbers if they can be written in one or two words. In the following example of statistical writing, neither "ten years" nor "six-state region" is presented with related figures, so the numbers are spelled out, unlike the other numbers in the sentence.

> In the ten years covered by the study, the number of participating institutions in the United States doubled, reaching 90, and membership in the six-state region rose from 4 to 15.

But do not begin a sentence with a numeral.

> Two thousand four was an election year in the United States.

Except at the beginning of a sentence, always use numerals in the following instances:

WITH ABBREVIATIONS OR SYMBOLS

6 lbs.	4:20 p.m.	3%
8 KB	$9	2″

IN ADDRESSES

4401 13th Avenue

IN DATES

1 April 2006

April 1, 2006

IN DECIMAL FRACTIONS

8.3

IN DIVISIONS

page 7

chapter 12

year 3 of the study

For large numbers, you may use a combination of numerals and words.

4.5 million

Express related numbers in the same style.

only 5 of the 250 delegates

exactly 3 automobiles and 129 trucks

from 1 billion to 1.2 billion

3.10.3   COMMAS IN NUMBERS

Commas are usually placed between the third and fourth digits from the right, the sixth and seventh, and so on.

1,000

20,000

7,654,321

Following are some of the exceptions to this practice:

PAGE AND LINE NUMBERS

on page 1014

ADDRESSES

at 4132 Broadway

FOUR-DIGIT YEAR NUMBERS

in 1999

But commas are added in year numbers of five or more figures.

in 20,000 BC

3.10.4   PERCENTAGES AND AMOUNTS OF MONEY

Treat percentages and amounts of money like other numbers: use numerals with the appropriate symbols.

1%	$5.35	68¢
45%	$35	
100%	$2,000	

In discussions involving infrequent use of numbers, you may spell out a percentage or an amount of money if you can do so in three words or fewer (*five dollars, forty-five percent, two thousand dollars, sixty-eight cents*). Do not combine spelled forms of numbers with symbols.

3.10.5   DATES AND TIMES OF THE DAY

Be consistent in writing dates: use either the day-month-year style (*22 July 2006*) or the month-day-year style (*July 22, 2006*) but not both. If you begin with the month, be sure to add a comma after the day and also after the year, unless another punctuation mark goes there, such as a period or a question mark.

April 15, 2007, was the sixtieth anniversary of the racial integration of baseball.

Do not use a comma between month and year (*August 2006*). European usage gives all dates in day-month-year order. In abbreviated dates, the intended order is sometimes ambiguous (e.g., in *7-3-56*). To give a date in two systems, put one set in parentheses.

> 3 November 1693 (K'ang hsi 32/10/6)

Spell out centuries in lowercase letters.

> the twentieth century

Hyphenate centuries when they are used as adjectives before nouns.

> eighteenth-century thought
>
> nineteenth- and twentieth-century literature

Decades are usually written out without capitalization (*the nineties*), but it is acceptable to express them in figures (*the 1990s, the '60s*). Whichever form you use, be consistent.

The abbreviation *BC* follows the year, but *AD* precedes it.

> 19 BC
>
> AD 565

Instead of *BC* and *AD*, some writers prefer to use *BCE*, "before the common era," and *CE*, "common era," both of which follow the year.

Numerals are used for most times of the day (*2:00 p.m., the 6:20 flight*). Exceptions include time expressed in quarter and half hours and in hours followed by *o'clock*.

> a quarter to twelve
>
> half past ten
>
> five o'clock

3.10.6   INCLUSIVE NUMBERS

In a range of numbers, give the second number in full for numbers through ninety-nine.

> 2-3   21-48
>
> 10-12   89-99

For larger numbers, give only the last two digits of the second number, unless more are necessary.

96-101	923-1,003
103-04	1,003-05
395-401	1,608-774

In a range of years beginning in AD 1000 or later, omit the first two digits of the second year if they are the same as the first two digits of the first year. Otherwise, write both years in full.

2000-03

1898-1901

In a range of years beginning from AD 1 through 999, follow the rules for inclusive numbers in general.

73-76

600-62

Do not abbreviate ranges of years that begin before AD 1.

748-742 BC

143 BC-AD 149

On the use of commas in numbers, see 3.10.3.

3.10.7   ROMAN NUMERALS

Use capital roman numerals for the primary divisions of an outline and after the names of individuals in a series.

Elizabeth II

John D. Rockefeller IV

John Paul II

Use lowercase roman numerals for citing pages of a book that are so numbered (e.g., the pages in a preface). Write out inclusive roman numerals in full: *xxv–xxvi, xlvi–xlix*. Some scholars, editors, and presses prefer to use roman numerals to designate acts and scenes of plays (see 7.4.8).

—————————— **3.11** ——————————
ROMANIZATION

In most general studies, quotations and documentation in languages that do not use the Latin alphabet are transliterated into that alphabet, or romanized. In specialized studies with extensive quotations in languages that do not use the Latin alphabet, some publishers allow quotations in the writing systems of the sources.

The most comprehensive single source for the systems of romanization commonly used in general scholarly studies is *ALA-LC Romanization Tables: Transliteration Schemes for Non-Roman Scripts* (comp. and ed. Randall K. Barry; Washington: Lib. of Cong., 1997; print, Web). Approved by the Library of Congress and the American Library Association, this work supersedes all previous ALA-LC romanization tables. The Library of Congress provides the scanned text with updates on its Web site. Over fifty languages are covered by the tables. The system for Arabic followed by the *International Journal of Middle East Studies* is widely recognized. The Modern Language Association romanizes Russian according to J. Thomas Shaw's *The Transliteration of Modern Russian for English-Language Publications* (1967; New York: MLA, 1979; print).

—————————— **3.12** ——————————
FURTHER GUIDANCE

Dictionaries of Usage

Bernstein, Theodore M. *The Careful Writer: A Modern Guide to English Usage.* 1965. New York: Free, 1998. Print.

Bryant, Margaret M. *Current American Usage: How Americans Say It and Write It.* New York: Funk, 1962. Print.

Copperud, Roy H. *American Usage and Style: The Consensus.* New York: Van Nostrand, 1980. Print.

Evans, Bergen, and Cornelia Evans. *A Dictionary of Contemporary American Usage.* New York: Random, 1957. Print.

Follett, Wilson. *Modern American Usage: A Guide.* Ed. Jacques Barzun. New York: Hill, 1966. Print.

———. *Modern American Usage: A Guide.* Rev. Erik Wensberg. Rev. ed. New York: Hill-Farrar, 1998. Print.

Fowler, H[enry] W. *A Dictionary of Modern English Usage.* Oxford: Clarendon, 1926. Print.

———. *A Dictionary of Modern English Usage.* Ed. Ernest Gowers. 2nd ed.
New York: Oxford UP, 1965. Print.

———. *The New Fowler's Modern English Usage.* Ed. R. W. Burchfield. Rev.
3rd ed. 1998. New York: Oxford UP, 2000. Print.

Garner, Bryan A. *Garner's Modern American Usage.* New York: Oxford UP,
2003. Print.

Lovinger, Paul W. *The Penguin Dictionary of American English Usage and
Style.* New York: Penguin, 2002. Print.

Mager, Nathan H., and Sylvia K. Mager. *Prentice Hall Encyclopedic Dictionary of English Usage.* 2nd ed. Englewood Cliffs: Prentice, 1992. Print.

Morris, William, and Mary Morris. *Harper Dictionary of Contemporary Usage.* 2nd ed. 1985. New York: Harper, 1992. Print.

Nicholson, Margaret. *A Dictionary of American-English Usage Based on Fowler's* Modern English Usage. New York: Oxford UP, 1957. Print.

Waite, Maurice, E. S. C. Weiner, and Andrew Delahunty, eds. *The Oxford
Dictionary and Usage Guide to the English Language.* New York: Oxford
UP, 1995. Print.

Weiner, E. S. C., and Andrew Delahunty, comps. *The Oxford Guide to English Usage.* 2nd ed. Oxford: Oxford UP, 1993. Print.

Wilson, Kenneth G. *The Columbia Guide to Standard American English.* New
York: Columbia UP, 1993. Print.

Guides to Nondiscriminatory Language

American Psychological Association. "Guidelines to Reduce Bias in Language." *Publication Manual of the American Psychological Association.*
5th ed. Washington: Amer. Psychological Assn., 2001. 61–76. Print.

Frank, Francine Wattman, and Paula A. Treichler. *Language, Gender, and
Professional Writing: Theoretical Approaches and Guidelines for Nonsexist Usage.* New York: MLA, 1989. Print.

International Association of Business Communication. *Without Bias: A
Guidebook for Nondiscriminatory Communication.* Ed. Judy E. Pickens,
Patricia W. Rao, and Linda C. Roberts. 2nd ed. New York: Wiley,
1982. Print.

Maggio, Rosalie. *The Bias-Free Word Finder: A Dictionary of Nondiscriminatory Language.* Boston: Beacon, 1992. Print.

———. *The Dictionary of Bias-Free Usage: A Guide to Nondiscriminatory Language.* Phoenix: Oryx, 1991. Print.

———. *The Nonsexist Word Finder: A Dictionary of Gender-Free Usage.* 1987.
Boston: Beacon, 1989. Print.

———. *Talking about People: A Guide to Fair and Accurate Language*. Phoenix: Oryx, 1997. Print.

Miller, Casey, and Kate Swift. *The Handbook of Nonsexist Writing*. 2nd ed. New York: Harper, 1988. Print.

———. *Words and Women*. Rev. ed. New York: Harper, 1991. Print.

Schwartz, Marilyn, and the Task Force of the Association of American University Presses. *Guidelines for Bias-Free Writing*. Bloomington: Indiana UP, 1995. Print.

Sorrells, Bobbye D. *The Nonsexist Communicator: Solving the Problem of Gender and Awkwardness in Modern English*. Englewood Cliffs: Prentice, 1983. Print.

Warren, Virginia L. "Guidelines for the Nonsexist Use of Language." *Proceedings and Addresses of the American Philosophical Association* 59.3 (1986): 471–84. Print.

Books on Style

Barzun, Jacques. *Simple and Direct: A Rhetoric for Writers*. 4th ed. New York: Harper, 2001. Print.

Beardsley, Monroe C. *Thinking Straight: Principles of Reasoning for Readers and Writers*. 4th ed. Englewood Cliffs: Prentice, 1975. Print.

Cook, Claire Kehrwald. *Line by Line: How to Edit Your Own Writing*. Boston: Houghton, 1985. Print.

Eastman, Richard M. *Style: Writing and Reading as the Discovery of Outlook*. 3rd ed. New York: Oxford UP, 1984. Print.

Elbow, Peter. *Writing without Teachers*. 2nd ed. New York: Oxford UP, 1998. Print.

———. *Writing with Power: Techniques for Mastering the Writing Process*. 2nd ed. New York: Oxford UP, 1998. Print.

Gibson, Walker. *Tough, Sweet, and Stuffy: An Essay on Modern American Prose Styles*. Westport: Greenwood, 1984. Print.

Gowers, Ernest. *The Complete Plain Words*. Ed. Sidney Greenbaum and Janet Whitcut. Rev. ed. 1990. Boston: Godine, 2002. Print.

Lanham, Richard A. *Style: An Anti-textbook*. Rev. 2nd ed. Philadelphia: Dry, 2007. Print.

Smith, Charles K. *Styles and Structures: Alternative Approaches to College Writing*. New York: Norton, 1974. Print.

Strunk, William, Jr., and E. B. White. *The Elements of Style*. 4th ed. New York: Longman-Allyn, 2000. Print.

Williams, Joseph M. *Style: Lessons in Clarity and Grace*. 9th ed. New York: Longman-Allyn, 2007. Print.

———. *Style: Toward Clarity and Grace*. 1990. Chicago: U of Chicago P, 1995. Print.

4

PREPARATION OF SCHOLARLY MANUSCRIPTS

4.1
INTRODUCTION

Your manuscript will likely go through several stages of review and revision before publication. From the beginning, you should keep the formatting of the text as simple as possible. When requesting a manuscript for review, most publishers prefer to receive one or more printed copies; publishers do not want to be burdened with printing out the manuscript from electronic files. A publisher does not usually request copies of electronic files until a manuscript has been accepted for publication. After acceptance of your manuscript, you will probably be asked to provide the publisher with a printed copy and electronic files that match it exactly. Follow any formatting requirements your editor or publisher supplies. Be sure to keep a printout of the manuscript, as well as electronic copies in at least two places. The recommendations in this chapter are common in the United States and Canada. (See ch. 5 for preparing theses and dissertations.)

4.2

PHYSICAL CHARACTERISTICS OF THE PRINTED MANUSCRIPT

4.2.1   DIVISIONS OF THE TEXT

Articles and Essays. Scholarly articles and essays in the humanities often have no formal divisions. Sometimes an author inserts extra space (a blank line) at one point or more to divide the text into groups of related paragraphs. Since such a break may be overlooked in a printout if it falls at the bottom or top of a page, mark it by typing "[extra space]," flush left, or three asterisks, centered, in the blank line.

If an article or essay is made up of unified sections of thought, they may be labeled with numbers, headings, or both. When creating such designations, always use arabic numerals, and do not add extra spacing above or below the line containing the number or heading. A number alone is usually centered, but type a heading or combined number and heading flush left. Separate a heading from a preceding number by a period and a space.

2. From 1900 to 1940

To facilitate documentation in scholarly research, your text when published should incorporate reference markers that enable other scholars to cite a specific portion of your work and direct their readers to it. Page numbers usually serve this purpose, but other reference markers are needed for some works published electronically. Paragraphs are sometimes numbered in electronic publications. The appropriate number in square brackets — "[12]" — is usually placed at the beginning of each paragraph.

Books. The major divisions of a book usually appear in the order listed below. Each division should begin on a new page. Although only the words not given in brackets serve as formal titles, you can aid your editor by typing the others, in square brackets as shown, flush left and one inch from the tops of the first pages of the appropriate divisions.

[title page]
[copyright page]
[dedication] (optional)
[epigraph] (optional)
Contents (the table of contents)
Illustrations (a list of the illustrations, if applicable)
Tables (a list of the tables, if applicable)
Foreword (optional)
Preface (optional)
Acknowledgments (optional)
Introduction (optional)
[text]
Appendix (optional)
Notes (optional)
Glossary (optional)
Contributors (notes on the contributors, if applicable)
Works Cited (the list of the works cited)
Index (optional)

Chapters are the most common divisions in the text of a book. Sometimes chapters are subdivided into unified sections of thought (see "Articles and Essays," above). Some books are also divided into "parts," each of which contains related chapters. Chapters should be numbered consecutively throughout the text, whether or not they are grouped into parts, and are normally given titles. Parts should also be numbered consecutively and may be given titles.

Consistency of Headings.   Titles of parts, of chapters, and of sections in a chapter or essay are generally referred to as headings or heads. Insofar as possible, make parallel heads grammatically similar (e.g., avoid shifting from sentences to single words for parallel heads in a chapter). If you adopt number and letter designations for heads, be consistent, and do not use a "1" unless there is a "2" or use an "a" unless there is a "b."

If your manuscript has a complex organization with many levels of heads, you might assist your editor by not only carefully working out the organizational system and clearly distinguishing the levels of heads in the manuscript but also supplying a list of all heads in outline form to establish their coordination and subordination. Some publishers allow the use of typographic features (e.g., boldface, italics) to distinguish levels of heads in the manuscript, while others discourage it.

4.2.2   MARGINS

Except for running heads (containing, e.g., your last name and the page number), leave margins of one inch at the top and bottom and on both sides of the text. (For running heads, see 4.2.5.) If you lack 8½-by-11-inch paper and use a larger size, do not print the text in an area greater than 6½ by 9 inches.

Indent the first word of a paragraph one-half inch from the left margin. Indent set-off quotations one inch from the left margin. Most publishers prefer that you indent first lines of paragraphs by using the tab key and indent set-off quotations by changing the paragraph settings. Do not use the space bar when you format indents.

4.2.3   TEXT FORMATTING

Always choose a standard, easily readable typeface — one in which the regular type style contrasts clearly with the italic. Do not justify the lines of the manuscript at the right margin; turn off your word processor's automatic hyphenation feature.

Set your word processor to double-space the entire manuscript, including title, table of contents, quotations, notes, and list of works cited. Do not single-space any part of a manuscript intended for editing or typesetting.

4.2.4   TITLE AND AUTHOR'S NAME

If you are preparing a manuscript for a particular journal or publisher, follow any given instructions or, in the absence of instructions, the relevant recommendations below. If you plan to submit a manuscript seriatim to journals or publishers until it is accepted, prepare it in accordance with the instructions for anonymous submission.

A manuscript for a journal with a policy of anonymous submission should include a separate, unnumbered page giving the title and your full name, postal and e-mail addresses, and telephone and fax numbers. Repeat the title, without author's name, on the first page of the manuscript proper, centered and one inch from the top of the page (see fig. 3). Ensure that your word processor double-spaces between the lines of the title and between the title and the first line of the text. There is no need to add other space between the lines.

A separate title page is not needed for an article manuscript submitted to a journal that does not require anonymity or for a chapter or

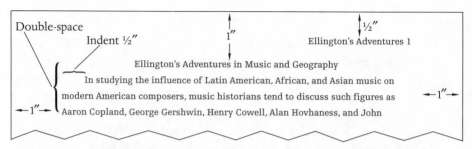

Fig. 3. The top of the first numbered page of a manuscript submitted anonymously.

an essay in a collection by more than one author. Instead, beginning one inch from the top of the first page and flush with the left margin, type on separate lines your name, postal and e-mail addresses, and telephone and fax numbers. Then, on separate lines, center the title and your name, as you wish them to appear in the publication. The beginning of the text follows your name on a new line (see fig. 4). Your word processor should double-space all these lines. Do not add any extra space between them.

A manuscript for a book should have a separate title page with the same information given to a journal requiring anonymous submission—title, name, postal and e-mail addresses, telephone and fax numbers. Individual chapters should not have separate title pages, but each should begin

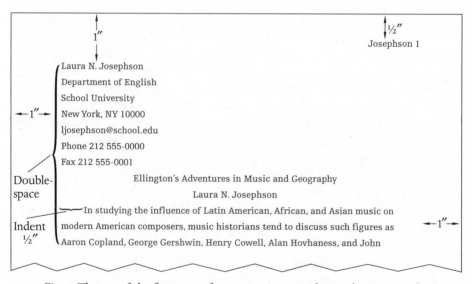

Fig. 4. The top of the first page of a manuscript not submitted anonymously.

on a new page. Starting one inch from the top of the page, type flush left the word *Chapter* followed by the chapter number and, on the next line, the title of the chapter. The text starts on the following line. Your word processor should double-space these lines; do not add extra space.

Do not italicize the title of your manuscript, put it in quotation marks, type it in all capital letters, or print it in any special font. Follow the rules for capitalization in 3.7, and italicize only the words that you would italicize in the text (see 3.5 and 3.8.2).

> Violence in Burgess's *A Clockwork Orange*
>
> The Words *Fair* and *Foul* in *Macbeth*
>
> Romanticism in England and the *Scapigliatura* in Italy

Do not use a period after the title or after any heading, including numerals used alone as section heads (see 4.2.1). A title ordinarily does not carry a symbol or number referring to a note; if the work was previously published, the editor may add a note to the title that cites the source.

4.2.5   PAGE NUMBERS

Number all pages consecutively throughout the manuscript. In the upper right-hand corner, one-half inch from the top and flush with the right margin, create a running head that consists of your last name followed by a space and the page number (see fig. 5) or, for a publication with an anonymous-submission policy, a shortened title of the work followed by a space and the page number. Do not use the abbreviation *p.* before a page number or add a period, a hyphen, or any other mark or symbol. Position the first line of the text one inch from the top of the page.

Although in writing the chapters of a book or separate essays for a collection you may paginate each chapter or essay separately, the final version of the manuscript submitted for production should be numbered consecutively from beginning to end. In a work with several authors, the name preceding each page number should be that of the author who is to receive the copyedited manuscript or proof of that page.

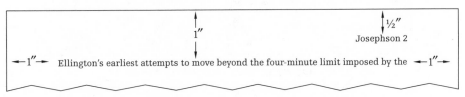

Fig. 5. The running head of a manuscript not submitted anonymously.

TABLES AND ILLUSTRATIONS

Illustrative visual materials should not be embedded in the text files for the manuscript. Instead, prepare a separate file for each table or illustration and indicate in the text approximately where the item should appear in the published work. Placement may be indicated with a bracketed instruction typed flush left on a line by itself (e.g., "[fig. 1 here]"). Consult your editor on the file formats needed. Files for tables include labels and captions as outlined below. Captions for other kinds of illustrative material should be gathered at the end of the text file for the article or chapter (see fig. 6). If the caption of a table or illustration provides complete information about the source and the source is not cited in the text, no entry for the source in the works-cited list is necessary.

A table is usually labeled *Table*, given an arabic numeral, and captioned. Type both label and caption flush left on separate lines above the table, and capitalize them as you would a title (do not use all capital letters). Give the source of the table and any notes immediately below the table. To avoid confusion between notes to the text and notes to the table, designate notes to the table with superscript lowercase letters rather than with numerals. Make dividing lines as needed, and ensure that your word processor double-spaces all lines (see fig. 7).

Any other type of illustrative visual material—for example, a photograph, map, line drawing, graph, or chart—should be labeled *Figure* (usually abbreviated *Fig.*), assigned an arabic numeral, and given a title or caption: "Fig. 1. Mary Cassatt, *Mother and Child*, Wichita Museum, Wichita." A label and title or caption ordinarily appear directly below the illustration in the published work.

Fig. 1. A sample of the copyedited manuscript of this manual, which was copyedited on paper.

Fig. 2. A sample of the manuscript of this manual copyedited electronically. Underlined passages are insertions.

Fig. 6. Captions gathered at the end of a chapter.

Table 1

Degrees in Modern Foreign Languages and Literatures Conferred by
Degree-Granting Institutions of Higher Education in the United States[a]

Year	Bachelor's Degrees	Master's Degrees	Doctor's Degrees
1995-96	13,337	2,562	746
1996-97	13,053	2,470	793
1997-98	13,618	2,367	819
1998-99	14,163	2,267	757
1999-2000	14,186	2,228	804
2000-01	14,292	2,244	818
2001-02	14,236	2,284	780
2002-03	14,843	2,256	749
2003-04	15,408	2,307	743
2004-05	16,008	2,517	762

Source: United States, Dept. of Educ., Inst. of Educ. Sciences, Natl. Center
for Educ. Statistics; *Digest of Education Statistics*; US Dept. of Educ.,
July 2006; Web; 7 Dec. 2007; table 290.

a. These figures include degrees conferred in a single language or a
combination of modern foreign languages and exclude degrees in linguistics,
Latin, classics, ancient and Middle and Near Eastern biblical and Semitic
languages, ancient and classical Greek, Sanskrit and classical Indian
languages, and sign language and sign language interpretation.

Fig. 7. A table in a manuscript.

Musical illustrations are labeled *Example* (usually abbreviated *Ex.*),
assigned an arabic numeral, and given a title or caption: "Ex. 1. Pyotr
Ilich Tchaikovsky, Symphony no. 6 in B, op. 74 (*Pathétique*), finale." A
label and caption ordinarily appear directly below the example in the
published work.

4.2.7   PAPER AND PRINTING

Use only white, 8½-by-11-inch paper of good quality. If you cannot obtain 8½-by-11-inch paper, use the closest size available. Print on only one side of the paper, with a high-quality printer.

4.2.8   CORRECTIONS AND REVISIONS

Proofread and correct your manuscript carefully before submitting it to a publisher. Software spelling and usage checkers can be helpful, but they should be used with caution. On the one hand, a spelling checker will call attention to words that are correctly spelled if they are not in its dictionary. On the other, it will not point out misspellings that match words in the dictionary (e.g., *their* used for *there*). Recommendations by usage checkers have to be evaluated critically. If you find a mistake in the final copy or decide to make a last-minute revision, reopen the file, make the change, and reprint the corrected page or pages. Be sure to save the changed file.

If you are working with a copyeditor or if a journal editor or publisher has accepted your manuscript but requests revisions before copyediting, it may be convenient to make changes by hand on the printed manuscript until there is complete agreement on the revisions. Make all handwritten changes legible and unambiguous. Insert corrections and revisions directly above the lines involved, using carets ($\wedge$) to indicate where they go; do not write a change below the line it affects. If the revised version will not fit on the page, continue it on a separate page identified with the same page number followed by the letter *A* (e.g., "32A," to follow page 32). Indicate at the bottom of the original page that a specially numbered page follows (e.g., write, "Page 32A follows"). You may also write an insertion entirely on a separate page (labeled, e.g., "Insert to page 32") and clearly mark the manuscript to show where the addition goes. When all revisions are accepted, follow the directions of your editor, who may ask you to enter the changes in the file and produce a new printout of the complete corrected version or a copy of the new version of the file or both.

4.2.9   BINDING

Secure manuscripts of articles and essays by paper or binder clips—never by staples. Use a rubber band around a book-length manuscript, and do not secure individual chapters in any way.

4.3

MANUSCRIPTS FOR PUBLICATION

Most scholarly journals and books are produced directly from computer files supplied by their authors. Although editors, consultant readers, and editorial boards usually evaluate a manuscript in printed form, once the manuscript is accepted for publication, the editor commonly asks for the final version of the manuscript in both print and electronic form. The editor usually provides guidelines for preparing the manuscript and its electronic files.

After receiving the manuscript, the publisher usually modifies the electronic files, correcting any technical problems in the files and formatting them to its specifications. Some journals and presses copyedit the manuscript electronically, and some copyedit a printout and transfer changes to the electronic files.

The publisher subsequently incorporates the design specifications for typefaces, type sizes, margins, and so forth, and transforms the files into proofs that the author reads and corrects. From the corrected proofs, the publisher prepares a final version from which the printer produces the published book or journal. If there is an electronic publication of the manuscript, the publisher usually generates it from the same set of files.

In the absence of guidelines provided by your publisher, follow the general principles below for preparing electronic files.

Do not add any formatting that is not essential to the manuscript. For example, do not engage your word processor's hyphenation feature or justify right margins, and use only one font. Material that would be italicized in a publication should be set in italics, not underlined (see 3.5). Delete any running head you create for the printed manuscript.

Type only the spaces and hyphens that are to appear in print—for example, the spaces between words and the hyphens in certain compound words. Use one space after a period or colon. To create a dash, type two hyphens, which your word processor may convert automatically into a dash. Both forms are acceptable in the preparation of a manuscript, but you should choose one and use it consistently throughout the manuscript. To indent first lines of paragraphs, use the tab key, not the space bar; for quotations set off from the text, specify a left-margin indention in the paragraph settings.

Each key must have only one meaning: the letter *l* cannot serve as the numeral one; the letter *O* cannot be used as a zero; any special characters must have a single purpose. For titles and headings in the manuscript, use the standard combination of capital and lowercase letters—not all capital letters.

You should ordinarily use a single file for an article or essay, but create a new file for each chapter or other major division of a book and for each computer-generated table and illustration. Create a single file for all endnotes. Use the tab key to indent the first line of each note. In a single file of notes for a book, carefully indicate the chapters to which the notes belong, and begin each chapter with note 1 unless the book has few notes. Do not use footnotes.

Name related files sequentially (*ch1, ch2; table 1, table 2; appA, appB*), and transmit them to the publisher. Ask your publisher the preferred method of delivery: on disk, by attachment to an e-mail message, or through a Web interface provided by the publisher. Whatever the method, you should provide documentation that indicates the author's name, the title of the manuscript, the name and release number of your word-processing software, your computer's operating system (e.g., Windows, Macintosh, Unix), and the date you completed work on the files. The editor of a collection with more than one author must submit all contributions in the format of one software program, adding authors' last names to the file names. Supply your editor with a list of the file names when you submit the electronic version of the manuscript. If your manuscript has accents or special characters not available on your computer, give your editor a list of them, pointing out how you indicated them on the printout and in the electronic files.

The printed copy and the electronic version you send to your editor must be identical. Inform your publisher of any subsequent revisions you wish to make, and the publisher will make the necessary changes to the files.

The guidelines above address the most common forms of print and electronic publication in the humanities. For complex electronic publications, such as scholarly editions, authors and editors will need additional resources. The MLA's Committee on Scholarly Editions has collaborated with the Text Encoding Initiative (TEI) on a book that provides guidance in this area (see Lou Burnard, Katherine O'Brien O'Keeffe, and John Unsworth, eds., *Electronic Textual Editing* [New York: MLA, 2006; CD-ROM, print]). The TEI has developed an application of XML especially for humanities texts and scholarship. TEI guidelines provide a set of tags, or textual markers, to delineate the overall structure of a document as well as its internal elements. The tags are most suitable for texts with strict hierarchical formats. TEI-XML tagging is increasingly accepted in humanities electronic texts. Yet it is a rigorous and complex procedure, even with the aid of tagging software. Once a document has been correctly tagged, users can sort, search, and analyze the text in a variety of ways.

5

PREPARATION OF THESES AND DISSERTATIONS

5.1
STUDENT WORKS AS PROFESSIONAL DOCUMENTS

Student works—such as class presentations, research and interpretive papers, the master's thesis, the doctoral dissertation—share elements with postdoctoral scholarly communications (e.g., teaching, conference lectures, articles, books; see 1.1). Student work and professional scholarly work have common concerns: conceptualization, investigation, organization, and presentation. Writing a thesis or dissertation especially embraces many activities, practices, and conventions common to subsequent professional publishing; the experience provides training for a career as a publishing scholar, even as the written outcome documents the author's ability and accomplishment. This chapter discusses similarities as well as differences between preparing manuscripts for publishers (see ch. 4) and preparing theses and dissertations to fulfill requirements for advanced degrees.

5.2
PRESCRIBED GUIDELINES

Professors and publishers usually permit authors to prepare their manuscripts according to style authorities that are standard in their fields. Authors of theses and dissertations, however, must often follow specific guidelines prescribed by their departments, schools, or universities. Before you begin work on a thesis or dissertation, therefore, it is essential to inquire about and obtain any such set of guidelines, which may be available on a campus Web site or distributed from a campus office in the form of a simple photocopied handout or an elaborately designed handbook.

In addition to supplying information like degree requirements, deadlines, administrative procedures, and fees, such guidelines usually also prescribe formal aspects of the work—for example, documentation style, size of type, and margins. The guidelines normally indicate whether the thesis or dissertation should be submitted on paper, as an electronic file, or both; they will also specify the number of print copies and the format for electronic files. The following sections describe common, but by no means universal, practices in the preparing of theses and dissertations. Consult the earlier chapters for information applicable to all scholarly writing. But should you find conflicting recommendations, follow those issued at your school.

5.3
SELECTING A TOPIC

Innovative in subject matter or method, your thesis or dissertation should make a substantial contribution to scholarship and learning. The courses you have taken will doubtless suggest potential topics.

Further reading in areas of interest and preliminary discussions with instructors will probably prove invaluable as you make your selection. While the topic should be broad enough to produce significant conclusions, it should also be narrow enough to produce a focused work. You should take care to choose a topic that will yield a completed thesis or dissertation within a reasonable period of time. Just as you will seek an adviser with whom you are compatible, try to choose a topic you think will engage you for the considerable time it will take to complete the work.

Before presenting the topic for formal approval, verify its originality by identifying previous studies in the area. Consult all relevant print and electronic sources for this information, including library catalogs, bibliographies in the field, the *MLA International Bibliography*, and *Dissertation Abstracts International* (which is available in multiple print and electronic formats from ProQuest). This search will help you not only to modify and redefine the topic but also to compile the basic bibliography for the project. Your thesis or dissertation adviser and other professors can assist you in defining objectives, setting the limits of research, testing the soundness of arguments and conclusions, and improving the bibliography.

5.4
PREPARING A PROSPECTUS

The preparation of a prospectus is an important stage between the selection and approval of a topic and the writing of the thesis or dissertation (cf. 1.5.4, on book prospectuses). Consult the school guidelines for directions concerning length, content, and format of the prospectus. Expected length varies widely, but most guidelines ask that the prospectus address the following aspects of the project: its main focus and the basic questions addressed; its significance, contribution, and place within the larger scholarly context; and its methodological foundation. The prospectus also typically contains an annotated projected table of contents and may offer a preliminary bibliography of primary and secondary sources. Your school guidelines will describe the process by which your prospectus must be approved. If your project involves human subjects, you will likely be asked to receive certification from an institutional review board or similar campus body. Research activities that may be subject to oversight include interviews, surveys, and analysis of student writing.

---------------------------------- 5.5 ----------------------------------
SPECIAL FORMAT REQUIREMENTS

5.5.1   THESES AND DISSERTATIONS AS PUBLISHED WORKS

Modern scholarship considers theses and dissertations forms of publication. Most schools archive copies of all theses and dissertations prepared in partial fulfillment of their degree requirements. Nearly all doctoral dissertations are recorded microphotographically by ProQuest and are readily accessible to other scholars through microfilm, on-demand printing, and digital files (see 5.6). Some schools archive paper copies, while others require students to contribute their theses or dissertations to an electronic institutional repository or the Networked Digital Library of Theses and Dissertations.

Graduate school guidelines generally require that the pages of these works be more similar to the pages of a printed book than to those of a manuscript. Consequently, authors of theses and dissertations are responsible for many formatting procedures that a professional publishing staff usually performs during the copyediting, design, typesetting, and production of a printed book. Guidelines for print copies often prescribe, for example, the quality of paper, kind of printer, and type style and size and require that the work be free of typing errors and handwritten corrections. Guidelines for electronic copies also govern the physical appearance of the work, as well as instructing authors on the formatting and submission of electronic files. The sections that follow discuss a number of other special format requirements for theses and dissertations.

5.5.2   DIVISIONS OF THE TEXT

The major divisions of the thesis or dissertation are similar to those of a book (see 4.2.1), with a few important differences. Both types of works contain a title page, but the title page of a thesis or dissertation includes not only the title and the author's name but also such information as the names of the faculty adviser and committee members, a statement indicating that the work has been submitted in partial fulfillment of degree requirements, and the date (e.g., the month and year the work is submitted or the degree is conferred).

Some guidelines require the inclusion of components that have no parallel in book manuscripts, such as an approval page, an abstract page, and a page offering a short biography of the candidate. The approval (or signature) page contains the names and signatures of all members of the thesis or dissertation committee accepting the work; this page usually follows and is sometimes combined with the title page (ProQuest discourages submission of the signature page so as to prevent the dissemination of signatures through its electronic databases [see 5.6]). The abstract, occasionally preceded by an abstract title page, reproduces the summary usually submitted for publication in *Dissertation Abstracts International* (see 5.6.2). The desired placement of the abstract and the biography varies according to individual guidelines; these pages typically appear among either the front matter (e.g., before the table of contents) or the back matter (e.g., after the bibliography or works-cited list).

Graduate school guidelines for print copies sometimes prescribe the insertion of blank sheets between certain divisions, in emulation of a printed book. Theses and dissertations, however, usually do not include indexes.

5.5.3   PAGE NUMBERS

Your guidelines will probably require you to number pages according to the system common in published books. Lowercase roman numerals appear on most of the pages containing the front matter or preliminary parts of the work: dedication (optional), epigraph (optional), table of contents, lists of illustrations and tables (if applicable), preface, and acknowledgments (often combined with the preface). Arabic numerals are used in the rest of the work, including the text and the bibliography as well as any endnotes, appendix, glossary, and index.

Page numbers do not usually appear on the title page and copyright page and sometimes do not appear on the first pages of chapters, the endnotes section, the bibliography, and other major divisions, although all are considered in the page count of the work. Numbers normally appear on all other pages, with the occasional exception of the approval page, abstract page, and biography page, which are sometimes neither numbered nor counted in the pagination.

The required position of the page numbers varies. Guidelines commonly prescribe that they appear centered at the bottom or the top or in the upper right-hand corner of the page.

5.5.4   MARGINS

Nearly all guidelines ask for a margin of at least one and a half inches from the left side of each page to allow for binding of paper copies (see 5.5.6). The other margins — at the top, bottom, and right side of the page — are normally one inch or slightly more (e.g., one and a quarter inches) to ensure successful photographing of the work (see 5.6.1). Most guidelines specify marginal limits for page numbers. The numbers are separated from the text by approximately one-half inch or three lines.

5.5.5   SPACING

Your guidelines will usually ask you to double-space the text of the thesis or dissertation but may request the use of single-spacing in one or more of the following types of material: a quotation set off from the text, an entry in the bibliography or list of works cited, an endnote or a footnote, a caption for a table or an illustration, and an item in the table of contents or in a list of tables or illustrations. Always skip a line, however, after each set-off quotation, bibliographic entry, note, caption, and listed item.

5.5.6   BINDING OF PRINT COPIES

Whereas authors normally use no more than paper or binder clips and rubber bands to secure manuscripts submitted to journals and book publishers, graduate schools that require deposit of a print copy usually require more formal binding of copies of theses and dissertations. Yet requirements differ considerably, from a simple black spring binder purchased at a bookstore to a professional library binding. Universities that, for a fee, have the work bound for the candidate usually ask that each copy be submitted only in a box or other protective container.

5.5.7   SUBMISSION OF ELECTRONIC FILES

Graduate schools that require deposit of electronic theses and dissertations (ETDs) provide detailed instructions on the preparation or conversion of electronic files. A typical method requires the student to convert word-processing files to a PDF file and then upload it to a university-sponsored Internet site.

Increasingly, graduate students are able to use other types of files in the preparation and presentation of theses and dissertations. Students may wish to include audio, image, video, and tabular files in their

ETDs. Before preparing multimedia works, students should determine which file formats are supported by their institutions and depositories. They should also be well versed in fair use (see 2.2.13).

5.6
PUBLISHING THE DISSERTATION
THROUGH PROQUEST

5.6.1   TERMS OF AGREEMENT

Most graduate schools require doctoral candidates to have their dissertations published by ProQuest (through UMI [University Microfilms International] Dissertation Publishing). The author signs a publishing agreement with ProQuest, which in turn lists the work in its bibliographic databases, publishes an abstract of it (see 5.6.2), photographs it for archival purposes, and can make it available on demand in a variety of formats. The agreement with ProQuest does not preclude your subsequently publishing the dissertation with a press.

Late in 2006 ProQuest introduced a new form of agreement with authors that provides two publishing options, *open access* and *traditional*. The open-access option allows anyone worldwide to read an electronic copy of the dissertation on the Internet without charge; ProQuest may also sell copies in multiple formats (e.g., microform, print) but will not pay royalties to the author for those sales. The traditional option makes copies of the dissertation available for purchase, and ProQuest pays royalties to the author on those sales. Both options allow authors to place restrictions on ProQuest's publication of the dissertation, such as embargoes, an exemption from search-engine access, and a limitation on third-party sales. In choosing a publishing option, you should consider the content of your dissertation and your plans for future publication on the topic. If your dissertation research involves human subjects, you may be bound by nondisclosure agreements from distributing the results beyond the academic community. If you plan to revise your dissertation for publication by a press or scholarly journal, ProQuest recommends that you choose the traditional option; publishers may not want to publish a work that has been freely available on the Internet. In any case, check to see if your institution has an explicit policy governing the choice of a publishing option, and consult your dissertation adviser before completing the agreement.

5.6.2   ABSTRACT

ProQuest requires the candidate to submit with the agreement an abstract, or summary, of the dissertation. The abstract is published in *Dissertation Abstracts International*, in print, CD-ROM, microform, and online formats. The abstract generally describes the problem studied, the materials and methods used, and the conclusions reached. Although there is no limit on the length of the abstract, ProQuest truncates abstracts included in the print version of *Dissertation Abstracts International*. Abstracts in the print version run no longer than 350 words for dissertations and no longer than 150 for master's theses.

5.6.3   COPYRIGHT

Most graduate school guidelines make it optional whether the copyright in theses and dissertations is registered with the Copyright Office at the Library of Congress (see 2.2.8) but strongly recommend registration for the dissertation. For a fee, ProQuest will have the dissertation copyright registered for you, or you may submit the application on your own. MA candidates are generally responsible for registering their copyrights themselves. Whether or not your copyright is registered, place a copyright notice on the copyright page (see 2.2.9).

5.6.4   PERMISSIONS

Since theses and dissertations are considered published works, their authors must seek necessary permission to reproduce material taken from others. The agreement with ProQuest requires authors to certify that permission has been obtained in writing from copyright holders when unpublished material is borrowed or when fair use has been exceeded (see 2.2.13–14). Permission letters must be attached to the ProQuest agreement form.

For each permission you obtain, you must insert a statement at an appropriate place in the thesis or dissertation. The typical statement consists of a full bibliographic reference (i.e., author, title, city of publication, publisher, year of publication), followed by a standard credit line (e.g., "Reprinted by permission of . . .") or wording stipulated by the copyright holder in the permission letter. Permission statements may appear individually in the text where the reprinted materials occur, or, especially if numerous, they may be given collectively in the acknowledgments section or on the copyright page.

6

DOCUMENTATION: PREPARING THE LIST OF WORKS CITED

6.1
THE PURPOSES OF DOCUMENTATION

Scholarly authors include documentation in their works to fulfill several aims. The first is to acknowledge the sources considered in the preparation of the work. Scholarly authors generously acknowledge their debts to predecessors by giving credit to each source. Whenever scholars draw on another's work, they specify what they borrowed—whether facts, ideas, opinions, or quotations—and where they borrowed it from. A second aim is to provide readers with a description of key features of each source; such qualities as authorship, medium of publication, date of publication, and the identity of the publisher are important for understanding the nature of a source and how the author encountered it. Finally, authors aim to invite the reader to locate and examine the sources they use.

As you conduct your research, you should establish an accurate record of your experience with sources. Assess the authority of each source (i.e., the identity of its author or authors and the editorial oversight performed by its publisher); understand how the medium of delivery shapes your encounter with a source, and cite only the sources you have consulted directly; and record sufficient information to allow readers to find the source, when possible.

6.2
DOCUMENTATION AND ETHICS

Using another person's ideas or expressions in your writing without acknowledging the source constitutes plagiarism. Derived from the Latin word *plagiarius* ("kidnapper"), *to plagiarize* means "to commit literary theft" and to "present as new and original an idea or product derived from an existing source" (*Merriam-Webster's Collegiate Dictionary* [11th ed.; 2003; print]). In short, the act of plagiarism gives the impression that you wrote or thought something that you in fact borrowed from someone, and to do so is a violation of professional ethics.

Forms of plagiarism include the failure to give appropriate acknowledgment when repeating another's wording or particularly apt phrase, paraphrasing another's argument, and presenting another's line of thinking. You may certainly use other persons' words and thoughts, but the borrowed material must not appear to be your creation.

In your writing, then, you must document nearly everything that you borrow. In addition to documenting direct quotations and paraphrases, you should consider the status of the information and ideas you glean from sources in relation to your audience and to the scholarly consensus on your topic. In general, information and ideas you deem broadly known by your readers and widely accepted by scholars, such as the basic biography of an author or the dates of a historical event, can be used without documentation. But where readers are likely to seek more guidance or where the facts are in significant dispute among scholars, documentation is needed; you could attribute a disputed fact to the source with which you agree or could document the entire controversy. While direct quotations and paraphrases are always documented, scholars seldom document proverbs, sayings, and clichés. You must indicate the source of any appropriated material that readers might otherwise mistake for yours.

Plagiarism is a moral and ethical offense rather than a legal one. Most instances of plagiarism fall outside the scope of copyright infringement, a legal offense. Plagiarism remains an offense even if the plagiarized work is not covered by copyright law or if the amount of material used and the nature of the use fall within the scope of fair use; copyright infringement remains a legal offense even if the violator acknowledges the source (see 2.2.13–15). The penalties for plagiarism can be severe, ranging from loss of respect to loss of degrees, tenure, or even employment. At all stages of research and writing, guard against the possibility of inadvertent plagiarism by keeping careful notes that distinguish between your musings and thoughts and the material you gather from others.

Another issue related to plagiarism concerns not outside sources but the author's own earlier writing. Whereas reprinting one's published work, such as having a journal article appear in a subsequent book of essays, is professionally acceptable—as long as appropriate permission is secured and complete bibliographic information about the original publication accompanies the reprint—professionals generally disapprove if previously published work is reissued, whether verbatim or slightly revised, under another title or in some other manner that gives the impression it is a new work. Although not the same as plagiarizing someone else's writing, self-plagiarism is another type of unethical activity. If your current work draws on your own previously published work, you must give full bibliographic information about the earlier publication.

6.3

MLA STYLE

Although all fields of research agree on the need to document scholarly borrowings, they do not all agree on the form documentation should take, and different fields generally follow different documentation conventions. MLA style is widely used in the humanities, especially in the field of language and literature. Generally simpler and more economical than other styles, MLA style shares with most others its central feature: brief parenthetical citations in the text keyed to an alphabetical list of works cited that appears at the end of the work.

Unlike documentation in other systems, a citation in MLA style contains only enough information to enable readers to find the source in the works-cited list, so that interruptions in the reading are kept to a minimum. A typical citation consists of an author's last name and a page reference: "(Marcuse 197)." If the author's name is mentioned in the text, only the page number appears in the citation: "(197)." If more than one work by the author is in the list of works cited, a shortened version of the title is given, but this too may be omitted from the citation if the title appears in the text. (See ch. 7 for a fuller discussion of parenthetical citations in MLA style.)

As you conduct your research, you should note the provenance of the sources you use. What are the available editions of a work? If a work is available in several media, which version did you choose to consult and why? What are the differences between a live performance and a recording? Attention to such questions will assist you in creating a persuasive and authoritative publication. Key features of sources should be recorded in the entries in the list of works cited. Sometimes you may wish to expand your description of sources in your text or in a note.

Chapters 6 and 7 offer an authoritative and comprehensive presentation of MLA style. For a list of guides to other citation styles, see the appendix.

6.4

THE LIST OF WORKS CITED

6.4.1   INTRODUCTION

MLA style provides a flexible, modular format for recording key features of works cited or consulted in the preparation of a scholarly publication. This chapter describes several sequences of elements that can be combined to form entries in the list of works cited. In building an entry, you should know which elements to look for in the source. Not all elements will be present in a given source. Moreover, since MLA style is flexible about the inclusion of some information and even about the ordering of the elements, you should understand how your choice relates to your research project. For example, as noted in 6.8.3, a publication on the work of a film director may list the director's name first, while a publication on the work of a film actor may list the performer's name first (the guidelines for citing editions [6.6.10] and translations [6.6.11] are similarly flexible). While it is tempting to think that every source has only one complete and correct format for its entry in the list of works cited, in truth there are often several options for recording key features of a work. For this reason, software programs that generate entries are not likely to be useful. You may need to improvise when the type of scholarly project or the publication medium of a source is not anticipated by this manual. Be consistent in your formatting throughout your work. Choose the format that is appropriate to your project and that will satisfy your readers' needs.

Although the list of works cited appears at the end of your text, you need to draft the section in advance, so that you will know what information to give in parenthetical references as you write—for example, whether you need to add a shortened title if you cite two or more works by the same author or to give an initial or first name if two of the cited authors have the same last name: "(K. Roemer 123–24)," "(M. Roemer 67)." This chapter explains how to prepare a list of works cited, and the next chapter demonstrates how to document sources as you use them in your text.

As the heading *Works Cited* indicates, this list contains all the works that you will cite in your text. The list simplifies documentation by permitting you to make only brief references to these works in the text. Other names for such a listing are *Bibliography* (literally, "description of books") and *Literature Cited*. Usually, however, the broader title

Works Cited is most appropriate, since scholarly work draws on not only printed books and articles but also nonprint sources.

Titles used for other kinds of source lists include *Annotated Bibliography*, *Works Consulted*, and *Selected Bibliography*. An annotated bibliography, also called *Annotated List of Works Cited*, contains descriptive or evaluative comments on the sources. (For more information on such listings, see James L. Harner, *On Compiling an Annotated Bibliography* [2nd ed.; New York: MLA, 2000; print].)

The title *Works Consulted* indicates that the list is not confined to works cited. The headings *Selected Bibliography*, *Selected List of Works Consulted*, and *Suggestions for Further Reading* are appropriate for lists that suggest readings.

6.4.2   PLACEMENT OF THE LIST OF WORKS CITED

The list of works cited appears at the end of the scholarly work; in a book or dissertation the list precedes only the index. Occasionally, as in textbooks or collections of pieces by different authors, each chapter or essay ends with its own list.

Begin the list of works cited on a new page and number each page, continuing the page numbers of the text (see fig. 8). Center the title, *Works Cited*, an inch from the top of the page. Double-space between the title and the first entry. Begin each entry flush with the left margin; if an entry runs more than one line, indent the subsequent line or lines one-half inch from the left margin. This format is sometimes called *hanging indention*, and you can set your word processor to create it automatically for a group of paragraphs. Hanging indention makes alphabetical lists easier to use. Double-space the entire list,

Fig. 8. The top of the first page of a works-cited list.

both between and within entries. Continue the list on as many pages as necessary.

6.4.3   ARRANGEMENT OF ENTRIES

Entries in a works-cited list are arranged in alphabetical order, which helps the reader to find the entry corresponding to a citation in the text. In general, alphabetize entries by the author's last name, using the letter-by-letter system. In this system, the order of names is determined by the letters before the commas that separate last names and first names. Spaces and other punctuation marks are ignored. The letters following the commas are considered only when two or more last names are identical. The following examples are alphabetized letter by letter. (For more information on alphabetizing names, see 3.6.4–13.)

> Descartes, René
>
> De Sica, Vittorio
>
> MacDonald, George
>
> McCullers, Carson
>
> Morris, Robert
>
> Morris, William
>
> Morrison, Toni
>
> Saint-Exupéry, Antoine de
>
> St. Denis, Ruth

If two or more entries citing coauthors begin with the same name, alphabetize by the last names of the second authors listed.

> Scholes, Robert, and Robert Kellogg
>
> Scholes, Robert, Carl H. Klaus, and Michael Silverman
>
> Scholes, Robert, and Eric S. Rabkin

If the author's name is unknown, alphabetize by the title, ignoring any initial *A*, *An*, or *The* or the equivalent in another language. For example, the title *An Encyclopedia of the Latin American Novel* would be alphabetized under the letter *e* rather than *a*, the title *Le théâtre en France au Moyen Âge* under *t* rather than *l*. If the title begins with a numeral, alphabetize the title as if the numeral were spelled out. For instance, *1914: The Coming of the First World War* should be alphabetized as if it began "Nineteen-Fourteen. . . ." (But see 6.8.14 on alphabetizing titles from the United States Code.)

If the name of an author whose works you used appears in various spellings in the works (e.g., Virgil, Vergil), consolidate all the entries for the sources under the preferred variant in your works-cited list. If your sources include works published under both an author's real name and a pseudonym, either consolidate the entries under the better-known name or list them separately, with a cross-reference at the real name and with the real name in square brackets after the pseudonym. If works by a woman are published under both her natal and her married names, list them separately, with cross-references at both names.

> Bakhtin, M. M. (*see also* Vološinov, V. N.). *The Dialogic Imagination: Four Essays*. Ed. Michael Holquist. Trans. Caryl Emerson and Holquist. Austin: U of Texas P, 1981. *Google Book Search*. Web. 3 Dec. 2007.
>
> Penelope, Julia (*see also* Stanley, Julia P.). "John Simon and the 'Dragons of Eden.'" *College English* 44.8 (1982): 848-54. *JSTOR*. Web. 3 Dec. 2007.
>
> Stanley, Julia P. (*see also* Penelope, Julia). "'Correctness,' 'Appropriateness,' and the Uses of English." *College English* 41.3 (1979): 330-35. *JSTOR*. Web. 3 Dec. 2007.
>
> Vološinov, V. N. [M. M. Bakhtin]. *Marxism and the Philosophy of Language*. Trans. Ladislav Matejka and I. R. Titunik. Cambridge: Harvard UP, 1986. *Google Book Search*. Web. 3 Dec. 2007.

Other kinds of bibliographies may be arranged differently. An annotated list, a list of works consulted, or a list of selected readings for a historical study, for example, may be organized chronologically by publication date. Some bibliographies are divided into sections and the items alphabetized in each section. A list may be broken down into primary and secondary sources or into different research media or genres (books, articles, films). Alternatively, it may be arranged by subject matter (literature and law, law in literature, law as literature), by period (classical utopia, Renaissance utopia), or by area (Egyptian mythology, Greek mythology, Norse mythology).

6.4.4   TWO OR MORE WORKS BY THE SAME AUTHOR

To cite two or more works by the same author, give the name in the first entry only. Thereafter, in place of the name, type three hyphens, followed by a period and the title. The three hyphens stand for exactly the same name as in the preceding entry. If the person named edited, translated, or compiled the work, place a comma (not a period) after the three hyphens, and write the appropriate abbreviation (*ed.*, *trans.*, or *comp.*) before giving the title. If the same person served as, say, the editor of two or more works listed consecutively, the abbreviation *ed.* must be repeated with each entry. This sort of label does not affect the order in which entries appear; works listed under the same name are alphabetized by title.

> Borroff, Marie. *Language and the Poet: Verbal Artistry in Frost,*
> *Stevens, and Moore.* Chicago: U of Chicago P, 1979. Print.
>
> ---, trans. *Pearl.* New York: Norton, 1977. Print.
>
> ---. "Sound Symbolism as Drama in the Poetry of Robert Frost." *PMLA*
> 107.1 (1992): 131-44. Print.
>
> ---, ed. *Wallace Stevens: A Collection of Critical Essays.* Englewood
> Cliffs: Prentice, 1963. Print.
>
> Frye, Northrop. *Anatomy of Criticism: Four Essays.* Princeton: Princeton
> UP, 1957. Print.
>
> ---, ed. *Design for Learning: Reports Submitted to the Joint*
> *Committee of the Toronto Board of Education and the University*
> *of Toronto.* Toronto: U of Toronto P, 1962. Print.
>
> ---. *The Double Vision: Language and Meaning in Religion.* Toronto:
> U of Toronto P, 1991. Print.
>
> ---, ed. *Sound and Poetry.* New York: Columbia UP, 1957. Print.
>
> ---. "Varieties of Eighteenth-Century Sensibility." *Eighteenth-*
> *Century Studies* 24.2 (1990-91): 157-72. *JSTOR.* Web. 17 Jan. 2007.

If a single author cited in an entry is also the first of multiple authors in the following entry, repeat the name in full; do not substitute three hyphens. Repeat the name in full whenever you cite the same person as part of a different authorship. The three hyphens are never used in combination with persons' names.

> Scholes, Robert. *Protocols of Reading.* New Haven: Yale UP, 1989. Print.
>
> ---. "Toward a Semiotics of Literature." *Critical Inquiry* 4.1 (1977):
> 105-20. *JSTOR.* Web. 2 Feb. 2007.
>
> Scholes, Robert, and Robert Kellogg. *The Nature of Narrative.* New
> York: Oxford UP, 1966. Print.

Scholes, Robert, and Eric S. Rabkin. *Science Fiction: History, Science, Vision*. New York: Oxford UP, 1977. Print.

Tannen, Deborah, ed. *Gender and Conversational Interaction*. New York: Oxford UP, 1993. Print.

---. *You Just Don't Understand: Women and Men in Conversation*. New York: Morrow, 1990. Print.

Tannen, Deborah, and Roy O. Freedle, eds. *Linguistics in Context: Connecting Observation and Understanding*. Norwood: Ablex, 1988. Print.

Tannen, Deborah, and Muriel Saville-Troike, eds. *Perspectives on Silence*. Norwood: Ablex, 1985. Print.

6.4.5   TWO OR MORE WORKS BY THE SAME AUTHORS

To cite two or more works by the same authors, give the names in the first entry only. Thereafter, in place of the names, type three hyphens, followed by a period and the title. The three hyphens stand for exactly the same names, in the same order, as in the preceding entry. Authors' names whose order in the source work is different from that of the previously listed names should be listed in the same order as in the work and alphabetized appropriately.

Durant, Will, and Ariel Durant. *The Age of Voltaire*. New York: Simon, 1965. Print.

---. *A Dual Autobiography*. New York: Simon, 1977. Print.

Gilbert, Sandra M., and Susan Gubar, eds. *The Female Imagination and the Modernist Aesthetic*. New York: Gordon, 1986. Print.

---. "Sexual Linguistics: Gender, Language, Sexuality." *New Literary History* 16.3 (1985): 515-43. *JSTOR*. Web. 26 June 2007.

6.4.6   CROSS-REFERENCES

To avoid unnecessary repetition in citing two or more works from the same collection, you may create a complete entry for the collection and cross-reference individual pieces to the entry. In a cross-reference, state the author and the title of the piece, the last name of the editor of the collection, and the inclusive page or reference numbers. If the piece is a translation, add the name of the translator after the title, unless one person translated the entire collection.

Hamill, Pete. Introduction. Sexton and Powers xi-xiv.

Mayakovsky, Vladimir. "Brooklyn Bridge." Trans. Max Hayward and
George Reavey. Sexton and Powers 136-41.

McCullers, Carson. "Brooklyn Is My Neighborhood." Sexton and
Powers 143-47.

Sexton, Andrea Wyatt, and Alice Leccese Powers, eds. *The Brooklyn
Reader: Thirty Writers Celebrate America's Favorite Borough.*
New York: Harmony, 1994. Print.

Walcott, Derek. "A Letter from Brooklyn." Sexton and Powers 264-65.

Whitman, Walt. "Crossing Brooklyn Ferry." Sexton and Powers 267-74.

If you list two or more works under the editor's name, however, add
the title (or a shortened version of it) to the cross-reference.

Angelou, Maya. "Pickin Em Up and Layin Em Down." Baker, *Norton
Book* 276-78.

Baker, Russell, ed. *The Norton Book of Light Verse.* New York: Norton,
1986. Print.

---, ed. *Russell Baker's Book of American Humor.* New York: Norton,
1993. Print.

Hurston, Zora Neale. "Squinch Owl Story." Baker, *Russell Baker's Book*
458-59.

Lebowitz, Fran. "Manners." Baker, *Russell Baker's Book* 556-59.

Lennon, John. "The Fat Budgie." Baker, *Norton Book* 357-58.

6.5

CITING PERIODICAL PRINT PUBLICATIONS

6.5.1   INTRODUCTION

Print periodicals—newspapers, magazines, journals—appear regularly
at fixed intervals. Unlike newspapers and magazines, which typically
appear daily, weekly, or monthly and include varied forms of writing on
diverse topics, journals are usually issued no more than four times a year
and address a discrete domain of scholarly, professional, or aesthetic
concern through critical or creative writing. Also unlike newspapers
and magazines, most journals are paginated continuously throughout
each annual volume—that is, if the first issue for a year ends on page
130, the second issue begins on page 131 and so forth. Some scholarly

journals do not number pages continuously throughout an annual volume but begin each issue on page 1. Include the issue number, whenever available, along with the volume number in a citation for any journal, since the issue number is essential for identifying issues paginated separately in annual volumes and is useful even for specifying consecutively paginated issues (e.g., in retrievals by interlibrary loan or from online databases). The volume and issue numbers of newspapers and magazines are not cited.

Entries for publications in print periodicals consist of several elements in a prescribed sequence. This list shows most of the possible components of an entry for an article in a print periodical and the order in which they are normally arranged:

1. Author's name (for more than one author, see 6.6.4; for a corporate author, see 6.6.5; for an anonymous work, see 6.5.9)
2. Title of the article (in quotation marks)
3. Name of the periodical (italicized)
4. Series number or name (if relevant; see 6.5.4)
5. Volume number (for a scholarly journal)
6. Issue number (if available, for a scholarly journal)
7. Date of publication (for a scholarly journal, the year; for other periodicals, the day, month, and year, as available)
8. Inclusive page numbers
9. Medium of publication consulted (*Print*)
10. Supplementary information (see esp. 6.5.12)

Section 6.5.2 explains how to formulate the most common entry for a periodical publication, an article in a scholarly journal. The rest of 6.5 explains how to cite additional items. For information on citing periodical publications accessed through the Web, see 6.7.3–4.

6.5.2   AN ARTICLE IN A SCHOLARLY JOURNAL

The works-cited-list entry for an article in a printed scholarly journal has three main divisions:

Author's name. "Title of the article." Publication information.

Here is an example:

Piper, Andrew. "Rethinking the Print Object: Goethe and the Book of Everything." *PMLA* 121.1 (2006): 124-38. Print.

Author's Name.   Take the author's name from the beginning or the end of the article. Reverse the name for alphabetizing, adding a comma after the last name. Put a period after the complete name.

> Piper, Andrew.

Apart from reversing the order, give the author's name as it appears in the article. Never abbreviate a name given in full. If, for example, the journal lists the author as "Carleton Brown," do not enter the name as "Brown, C." But use initials if the journal does. For additional advice on this topic, see 6.6.2.

Title of the Article.   In general, follow the recommendations for titles given in 3.8. State the full title of the article, enclosed in quotation marks (not italicized). Unless the title has its own concluding punctuation (e.g., a question mark), put a period before the closing quotation mark.

> Piper, Andrew. "Rethinking the Print Object: Goethe and the Book of
> Everything."

Publication Information.   In general, after the title of the article, give the journal title (italicized), the volume number, the issue number, the year of publication (in parentheses), a colon, the inclusive page numbers, a period, the medium of publication consulted, and a period.

> Piper, Andrew. "Rethinking the Print Object: Goethe and the Book of
> Everything." *PMLA* 121.1 (2006): 124-38. Print.

Take these facts directly from the journal, not from a source such as a bibliography. Publication information usually appears on the cover or title page of a journal. Omit any introductory article in the title of an English-language journal (*William and Mary Quarterly*, not *The William and Mary Quarterly*), but retain articles before titles of non-English-language journals (*La rivista dalmatica*). For newspaper titles, see 6.5.5. Do not precede the volume number with the word *volume* or the abbreviation *vol.*

In addition to the volume number, the journal's cover or title page may include an issue number ("Number 3") or a month or season before the year ("January 1998," "Fall 2006"). In general, the issues of a journal published in a single year compose one volume. Volumes are usually numbered in continuous sequence—each new volume is numbered one higher than its predecessor—while the numbering of issues starts over with 1 in each new volume. Add a period and the issue number directly after the volume number, without any intervening space: "14.2" signifies volume 14, issue 2; "10.3–4," volume 10, issues 3 and 4 combined. Some scholarly journals use issue numbers alone, without volume numbers; on citing articles in such journals, see 6.5.3. Annuals, which are published only once a year, are usually numbered in sequence. Some annuals, such as *Profession*, are not numbered; instead, each issue's place in the series is identified by the year of publication. Use the information available to complete your citation.

The inclusive page numbers cited should encompass the complete article, not just the portion you used. (Specific page references appear parenthetically at appropriate places in your text; see ch. 7.) Follow the rules for writing inclusive numbers in 3.10.6. Write the page reference for the first page exactly as shown in the source ("198–232," "A32–34," "lxii–lxv"). If an article is not printed on consecutive pages—if, for example, after beginning on page 6 it skips to page 10—write only the first page number and a plus sign, leaving no intervening space: "6+." (See examples in 6.5.5–6.)

Here are some additional examples of the basic entry for an article printed in a scholarly journal:

> Barthelme, Frederick. "Architecture." *Kansas Quarterly* 13.3-4 (1981): 77-80. Print.
>
> Brueggeman, Brenda Jo, and Debra A. Moddelmog. "Coming-Out Pedagogy: Risking Identity in Language and Literature Classrooms." *Pedagogy* 2.3 (2002): 311-35. Print.
>
> Forti-Lewis, Angelica. "Virginia Woolf, Dacia Maraini e *Una stanza per noi*: L'autocoscienza politica e il testo." *Rivista di studi italiani* 12.2 (1994): 29-47. Print.
>
> Hernández-Reguant, Ariana. "Copyrighting Che: Art and Authorship under Cuban Late Socialism." *Public Culture* 16.1 (2004): 1-29. Print.
>
> MLA Committee on the Status of Women in the Profession. "Women in the Profession, 2000." *Profession* (2000): 191-217. Print.
>
> Tibullus, Albius. "How to Be Tibullus." Trans. David Wray. *Chicago Review* 48.4 (2002-03): 102-06. Print.
>
> Vickeroy, Laurie. "The Politics of Abuse: The Traumatized Child in Toni Morrison and Marguerite Duras." *Mosaic* 29.2 (1996): 91-109. Print.
>
> Williams, Linda. "Of Kisses and Ellipses: The Long Adolescence of American Movies." *Critical Inquiry* 32.2 (2006): 288-340. Print.

6.5.3   AN ARTICLE IN A SCHOLARLY JOURNAL
                   THAT USES ONLY ISSUE NUMBERS

Some scholarly journals do not use volume numbers at all, numbering issues only. Cite the issue numbers of such journals alone.

> Chauí, Marilena. "Política cultural, cultura política." *Brasil* 13 (1995): 9-24. Print.
>
> Litvak, Lily. "La Buena Nueva: Cultura y prensa anarquista (1880-1913)." *Revista de Occidente* 304 (2006): 5-18. Print.
>
> Stein, Karen. "Margaret Atwood's Modest Proposal: *The Handmaid's Tale*." *Canadian Literature* 148 (1996): 57-73. Print.

6.5.4   AN ARTICLE IN A SCHOLARLY JOURNAL
                   WITH MORE THAN ONE SERIES

Some scholarly journals have been published in more than one series. In citing a journal with numbered series, write the number (an arabic digit with the appropriate ordinal suffix: *2nd*, *3rd*, *4th*, etc.) and the abbreviation *ser.* between the journal title and the volume number.

> Striner, Richard. "Political Newtonism: The Cosmic Model of Politics in Europe and America." *William and Mary Quarterly* 3rd ser. 52.4 (1995): 583-608. Print.

For a journal divided into a new series and an original series, indicate the series with *ns* or *os* before the volume number.

> Helmling, Steven. "A Martyr to Happiness: Why Adorno Matters." *Kenyon Review* ns 28.4 (2006): 156-72. Print.

6.5.5   AN ARTICLE IN A NEWSPAPER

To cite an English-language newspaper, give the name as it appears on the masthead but omit any introductory article (*New York Times*, not *The New York Times*). Retain articles before the names of non-English-language newspapers (*Le monde*). If the city of publication is not included in the name of a locally published newspaper, add the city in square brackets, not italicized, after the name: "*Star-Ledger* [Newark]." For nationally published newspapers (e.g., *Wall Street Journal, Chronicle of Higher Education*), you need not add the city of publication. Next give the complete date — day, month, and year. Abbreviate the names of all months except May, June, and July (see 8.2). Do not give the volume and issue numbers even if they are listed. If an edition is named on the masthead, add a comma after the date and specify the edition (e.g., *natl. ed.*, *late ed.*), because different editions of the same issue of a newspaper contain different material. Follow the edition — or the date if there is no edition — with a colon and the page number or numbers. Then state the medium of publication consulted. Here are examples illustrating how an article appeared in different sections of two editions of the *New York Times* on the same day:

> Rosenberg, Geanne. "Electronic Discovery Proves an Effective Legal Weapon." *New York Times* 31 Mar. 1997, late ed.: D5. Print.

> Rosenberg, Geanne. "Electronic Discovery Proves an Effective Legal Weapon." *New York Times* 31 Mar. 1997, natl. ed.: C5. Print.

If each section is paginated separately, include the appropriate section number or letter. Determining how to indicate a section can sometimes be complicated. The *New York Times*, for example, is currently divided in two distinct ways, depending on the day of the week, and each system calls for a different method of indicating section and page. On Monday through Saturday, there are normally several sections, labeled *A*, *B*, *C*, *D*, and so forth and paginated separately, and the section letter is part of each page number: "A1," "B1," "C5," "D3." Whenever the pagination of a newspaper includes a section designation, copy the page number or numbers exactly.

DAILY *NEW YORK TIMES*

> Barbaro, Michael. "Early Holiday Sales Are Strong at Department Stores." *New York Times* 1 Dec. 2006, late ed.: C4. Print.

The Sunday edition contains numerous individually paged sections (covering the arts and entertainment, business, sports, travel, and so on) designated not by letters but by numbers ("Section 4," "Section 7"), which do not appear as parts of the page numbers. Whenever the section designation of a newspaper is not part of the pagination, put a comma after the date (or after the edition, if any) and add the abbreviation *sec.*, the appropriate letter or number, a colon, the page number or numbers, and the medium of publication.

SUNDAY *NEW YORK TIMES*

> Haughney, Christine. "Women Unafraid of Condo Commitment." *New York Times* 10 Dec. 2006, late ed., sec. 11: 1+. Print.

Newspaper articles are often not printed on consecutive pages — for example, an article might begin on page 1, then skip to page 16. For such articles, write only the first page number and a plus sign, leaving no intervening space: "6+," "C3+." The parenthetical reference in the text tells readers the exact page from which material was used.

Here are some additional examples from different newspapers:

> McKay, Peter A. "Stocks Feel the Dollar's Weight." *Wall Street Journal* 4 Dec. 2006: C1+. Print.
>
> Melikian, Souren. "Fading Charms of 1700s Decor." *International Herald Tribune* 24-25 May 1997: 8. Print.
>
> Perrier, Jean-Louis. "La vie artistique de Budapest perturbée par la loi du marché." *Le monde* 26 Feb. 1997: 28. Print.
>
> Taylor, Paul. "Keyboard Grief: Coping with Computer-Caused Injuries." *Globe and Mail* [Toronto] 27 Dec. 1993: A1+. Print.
>
> Van der Werf, Martin. "Brown U. Documents Ties to Slavery, but Does Not Apologize." *Chronicle of Higher Education* 27 Oct. 2006: A27. Print.

6.5.6   AN ARTICLE IN A MAGAZINE

To cite a magazine published every week or every two weeks, give the complete date (beginning with the day and abbreviating the month, except for May, June, and July; see 8.2), followed by a colon, the inclusive page numbers of the article, and the medium of publication consulted. If the article is not printed on consecutive pages, write only the first page number and a plus sign, leaving no intervening space. Do not give the volume and issue numbers even if they are listed.

> Kaminer, Wendy. "The Last Taboo." *New Republic* 14 Oct. 1996: 24+. Print.
>
> McEvoy, Dermot. "Little Books, Big Success." *Publishers Weekly* 30 Oct. 2006: 26-28. Print.

To cite a magazine published every month or every two months, give the month or months and year. If the article is not printed on consecutive pages, write only the first page number and a plus sign, leaving no intervening space. Do not give the volume and issue numbers even if they are listed.

> Csikszentmihalyi, Mihaly. "The Creative Personality." *Psychology Today* July-Aug. 1996: 36-40. Print.
>
> Laskin, Sheldon H. "Jena: A Missed Opportunity for Healing." *Tikkun* Nov.-Dec. 2007: 29+. Print.
>
> Wood, Jason. "Spellbound." *Sight and Sound* Dec. 2005: 28-30. Print.

6.5.7   A REVIEW

To cite a review, give the reviewer's name and the title of the review (if there is one); then write *Rev. of* (neither italicized nor enclosed in quotation marks), the title of the work reviewed, a comma, the word *by*, and the name of the author. If the work of someone other than an author—say, an editor, a translator, or a director—is under review, use the appropriate abbreviation, such as *ed.*, *trans.*, or *dir.*, instead of *by*. For a review of a performance, add pertinent information about the production (see the sample entry for Tommasini). If more than one work is under review, list titles and authors in the order given at the beginning of the review (see the entry for Bordewich). Conclude the entry with the name of the periodical and the rest of the publication information.

If the review is titled but unsigned, begin the entry with the title of the review and alphabetize by that title (see the entry for "The Cooling of an Admiration"). If the review is neither titled nor signed, begin the entry with *Rev. of* and alphabetize it under the title of the work reviewed (see the entry for *Anthology of Danish Literature*).

> Rev. of *Anthology of Danish Literature*, ed. F. J. Billeskov Jansen and P. M. Mitchell. *Times Literary Supplement* 7 July 1972: 785. Print.
>
> Bordewich, Fergus M. Rev. of *Once They Moved like the Wind: Cochise, Geronimo, and the Apache Wars*, by David Roberts, and *Brave Are My People: Indian Heroes Not Forgotten*, by Frank Waters. *Smithsonian* Mar. 1994: 125-31. Print.
>
> "The Cooling of an Admiration." Rev. of *Pound/Joyce: The Letters of Ezra Pound to James Joyce, with Pound's Essays on Joyce*, ed. Forrest Read. *Times Literary Supplement* 6 Mar. 1969: 239-40. Print.

Koestenbaum, Wayne. "Call It Hollywood." Rev. of *Dark Lover: The Life and Death of Rudolf Valentino*, by Emily Leider. *London Review of Books* 16 Dec. 2004: 31-32. Print.

Mendelsohn, Daniel. "September 11 at the Movies." Rev. of *United 93*, dir. Paul Greengrass, and *World Trade Center*, dir. Oliver Stone. *New York Review of Books* 21 Sept. 2006: 43-46. Print.

Strandberg, Victor. Rev. of *Dangerous Intimacy: The Untold Story of Mark Twain's Final Years*, by Karen Lystra. *American Literature* 77.1 (2005): 186-87. Print.

Tommasini, Anthony. "In G. and S., Better to Have More Words, Less Voice." Rev. of *The Mikado*, by William S. Gilbert and Arthur Sullivan. New York City Opera. New York State Theater, New York. *New York Times* 10 Mar. 1997, late ed.: C22. Print.

Updike, John. "Fine Points." Rev. of *The New Fowler's Modern English Usage*, ed. R. W. Burchfield. *New Yorker* 23-30 Dec. 1996: 142-49. Print.

6.5.8   AN ABSTRACT IN AN ABSTRACTS JOURNAL

An abstracts journal publishes summaries of journal articles and of other literature. If you are citing an abstract, begin the entry with the publication information for the original work. Then add the relevant information for the journal from which you derived the abstract—title (italicized), volume number, issue number, year (in parentheses), item number or, when the abstract is not numbered, inclusive page numbers, and medium of publication for the abstracts journal. Precede an item number with the word *item*. If the title of the journal does not make clear that you are citing an abstract, add the word *Abstract*, neither italicized nor in quotation marks, immediately after the original publication information.

Dissertation Abstracts International (*DAI*) has a long and complex history that might affect the way you cite an abstract in it. Before volume 30 (1969), *Dissertation Abstracts International* was titled *Dissertation Abstracts* (*DA*). From volume 27 to volume 36, *DA* and *DAI* were paginated in two series: A, for humanities and social sciences, and B, for sciences and engineering. With volume 37, *DAI* added a third separately paginated section, C, for abstracts of European dissertations; in 1989 this section expanded its coverage to include institutions throughout the world. The abstracts in *DAI* are available electronically from ProQuest.

(For recommendations on citing dissertations themselves, see 6.6.25–26 and 6.7.2. On citing dissertation abstracts in an online database, see 6.7.4.)

> Pineda, Marcela. "Desire in Postmodern Discourse: An Analysis of the Poetry of Cristina Peri Rossi." Diss. Indiana U, 2004. *DAI* 65.12 (2005): item DA3156288. Print.

6.5.9   AN ANONYMOUS ARTICLE

If no author's name is given for the article you are citing, begin the entry with the title. Ignore any initial *A*, *An*, or *The* when you alphabetize the entry. Do not include the name of a wire service or news bureau.

> "The Decade of the Spy." *Newsweek* 7 Mar. 1994: 26-27. Print.
>
> "Dubious Venture." *Time* 3 Jan. 1994: 64-65. Print.

6.5.10   AN EDITORIAL

If you are citing a signed editorial, begin with the author's name, give the title, and then add the descriptive label *Editorial*, neither italicized nor enclosed in quotation marks. Conclude with the appropriate publication information. If the editorial is unsigned, begin with the title and continue in the same way.

> "It's Subpoena Time." Editorial. *New York Times* 8 June 2007, late ed.: A28. Print.
>
> Zuckerman, Mortimer B. "Are Order and Liberty at Odds?" Editorial. *US News and World Report* 5 Aug. 1996: 64. Print.

6.5.11   A LETTER TO THE EDITOR

To identify a letter to the editor, add the descriptive label *Letter* after the name of the author, but do not italicize the word or place it in quotation marks.

> Carlos, Sabarimuthu. Letter. *PMLA* 119.3 (2004): 555. Print.
>
> Safer, Morley. Letter. *New York Times* 31 Oct. 1993, late ed., sec. 2: 4. Print.

Identify a published response to a letter as "Reply to letter of . . . ," adding the name of the writer of the initial letter. Do not italicize this phrase or place it in quotation marks.

Shih, Shu-mei. Reply to letter of Sabarimuthu Carlos. *PMLA* 119.3
(2004): 555-56. Print.

6.5.12   A SERIALIZED ARTICLE

To cite a serialized article or a series of related articles published in
more than one issue of a periodical, include all bibliographic information in one entry if each installment has the same author and title.

Meserole, Harrison T., and James M. Rambeau. "Articles on American
Literature Appearing in Current Periodicals." *American Literature*
52.4 (1981): 688-705; 53.1 (1981): 164-80; 53.2 (1981): 348-59. Print.
Sedgwick, Eve Kosofsky. "Epistemology of the Closet." *Raritan* 7.4
(1988): 39-69; 8.1 (1988): 102-30. Print.

If the installments bear different titles, list each one separately. You
may include a brief supplementary description at the end of the entry
to indicate that the article is part of a series.

Dillon, Sam. "Special Education Absorbs School Resources." *New York
Times* 7 Apr. 1994, late ed.: A1+. Print. Pt. 2 of a series, A Class
Apart: Special Education in New York City, begun 6 Apr. 1994.
Richardson, Lynda. "Minority Students Languish in Special Education
System." *New York Times* 6 Apr. 1994, late ed.: A1+. Print. Pt. 1 of
a series, A Class Apart: Special Education in New York City.
Winerip, Michael. "A Disabilities Program That 'Got out of Hand.'" *New
York Times* 8 Apr. 1994, late ed.: A1+. Print. Pt. 3 of a series, A Class
Apart: Special Education in New York City, begun 6 Apr. 1994.

6.5.13   A SPECIAL ISSUE

To cite an entire special issue of a journal, begin the entry with the
name of the person who edited the issue (if given on the title page),
followed by a comma and the abbreviation *ed.* (or *eds.* if there are multiple editors). Next give the title of the special issue (italicized), followed
by *Spec. issue of* and the name of the journal (the name is italicized).
Conclude the entry with the journal's volume and issue numbers (separated by a period: "9.1"), the year of publication (in parentheses), a
colon, a space, the complete pagination of the issue, a period, the me-

dium of publication consulted, and a period. (To cite a book that is a reprint of a special issue of a journal, see 6.6.16.)

> Appiah, Kwame Anthony, and Henry Louis Gates, Jr., eds. *Identities.* Spec. issue of *Critical Inquiry* 18.4 (1992): 625-884. Print.
>
> Perret, Delphine, and Marie-Denise Shelton, eds. *Maryse Condé.* Spec. issue of *Callaloo* 18.3 (1995): 535-711. Print.
>
> *Symposium Issue: Race, Ethnicity, and Civic Identity in the Americas.* Spec. issue of *American Literary History* 17.3 (2005): 419-644. Print.

If you are citing one article from a special issue and wish to indicate complete publication information about the issue, use the following form:

> Makward, Christiane. "Reading Maryse Condé's Theater." *Maryse Condé.* Ed. Delphine Perret and Marie-Denise Shelton. Spec. issue of *Callaloo* 18.3 (1995): 681-89. Print.

6.6
CITING NONPERIODICAL PRINT PUBLICATIONS

6.6.1   INTRODUCTION

Entries for nonperiodical print publications, such as books and pamphlets, consist of several elements in a prescribed sequence. This list shows most of the possible components of a book entry and the order in which they are normally arranged:

1. Name of the author, editor, compiler, or translator (for more than one author, see 6.6.4; for a corporate author, see 6.6.5; for an anonymous work, see 6.6.9)
2. Title of the book (italicized)
3. Edition used (see 6.6.13)
4. Number(s) of the volume(s) used (see 6.6.14)
5. City of publication, name of the publisher, and year of publication
6. Medium of publication consulted (*Print*)
7. Supplementary bibliographic information and annotation (see esp. 6.6.11, 6.6.14–15)

Section 6.6.2 explains how to formulate the most common entry for a nonperiodical print publication, a book by a single author. The rest of 6.6 explains how to cite additional items.

6.6.2   A BOOK BY A SINGLE AUTHOR

One of the most common items in works-cited lists is the entry for a book by a single author. Such an entry characteristically has three main divisions:

> Author's name. *Title of the book.* Publication information.

Here is an example:

> Spacks, Patricia Meyer. *Privacy: Concealing the Eighteenth-Century Self.* Chicago: U of Chicago P, 2003. Print.

Author's Name. Reverse the author's name for alphabetizing, adding a comma after the last name. Put a period after the complete name.

> Spacks, Patricia Meyer.

Apart from reversing the order, give the author's name as it appears on the title page. Never abbreviate a name given in full. If, for example, the title page lists the author as "Carleton Brown," do not enter the name as "Brown, C." But use initials if the title page does.

> Mitchell, W. J. T.
> Rowling, J. K.

You may spell out a name abbreviated on the title page if you think the additional information would be helpful to readers. Put square brackets around the material you add.

> Lewis, C[live] S[taples].
> Nesbit, E[dith].
> Tolkien, J[ohn] R[onald] R[euel].

Similarly, you may give the real name of an author listed under a pseudonym, enclosing the added name in square brackets (see 6.4.3).

> Eliot, George [Mary Ann Evans].
> Novalis [Friedrich von Hardenberg].

If the name of the author is known but not stated on the title page, give the name in brackets. Add a question mark if the authorship is not universally accepted.

> [Medici, Lorenzo de'?].

In general, omit titles, affiliations, and degrees that precede or follow names.

ON TITLE PAGE	IN WORKS-CITED LIST
Anthony T. Boyle, PhD	Boyle, Anthony T.
Sister Jean Daniel	Daniel, Jean.
Gerard Manley Hopkins, SJ	Hopkins, Gerard Manley.
Lady Mary Wortley Montagu	Montagu, Mary Wortley.
Sir Philip Sidney	Sidney, Philip.
Saint Teresa de Jesús	Teresa de Jesús.

A suffix that is an essential part of the name—like *Jr.* or a roman numeral—appears after the given name, preceded by a comma.

Rockefeller, John D., IV.

Rust, Arthur George, Jr.

Title of the Book. In general, follow the recommendations for titles given in 3.8. State the full title of the book, including any subtitle. If the book has a subtitle, put a colon directly after the main title, unless the main title ends in a question mark, an exclamation point, or a dash. Place a period after the entire title (including any subtitle), unless it ends in another punctuation mark. Italicize the entire title, including any colon, subtitle, and punctuation in the title.

Spacks, Patricia Meyer. *Privacy: Concealing the Eighteenth-Century Self.*

Extremely long titles or titles usually condensed may be shortened. In shortening a title, include the beginning words of the title up to the first noun and the words by which the work is customarily known. Indicate any omissions by three spaced periods or by four periods if the omission is at the end of the title (see 3.9.5, on ellipsis). For example, *Some Thoughts concerning the Present Revival of Religion in New-England, and the Way in Which It Ought to Be Acknowledged and Promoted, Humbly Offered to the Publick, in a Treatise on That Subject, in Five Parts* may be cited as

Some Thoughts concerning the Present Revival of Religion in New-England. . . .

Publication Information. In general, give the city of publication, the publisher's name, the year of publication, and the medium of publication.

Take these facts directly from the book, not from a source such as a bibliography or a library catalog. The publisher's name that appears on the title page is generally the name to cite. The name may be accompanied there by the city and date. Any publication information not available on the title page can usually be found on the copyright page (i.e., the reverse of the title page) or, particularly in books published outside the United States, in the colophon, at the back of the book. Use a colon between the city of publication and the publisher, a comma between the publisher and the date, and a period after the date. Add the medium of publication consulted, followed by a period.

> Spacks, Patricia Meyer. *Privacy: Concealing the Eighteenth-Century Self*. Chicago: U of Chicago P, 2003. Print.

If several cities are listed in the book, give only the first. It is not necessary to identify a state, province, or country after the city name. Shorten the publisher's name, following the guidelines in 8.5. If the year of publication is not recorded on the title page, use the latest copyright date.

Additional examples of the basic book entry follow. (For citing books in languages other than English, see 6.6.22.)

> Burgess, Anthony [John Burgess Wilson]. *A Dead Man in Deptford*. New York: Carroll, 1995. Print.
>
> Johnson, Roberta. *Gender and Nation in the Spanish Modernist Novel*. Nashville: Vanderbilt UP, 2003. Print.
>
> Mathy, Jean-Philippe. *French Resistance: The French-American Culture Wars*. Minneapolis: U of Minnesota P, 2000. Print.
>
> Metcalf, John. *What Is a Canadian Literature?* Guelph: Red Kite, 1988. Print.
>
> Mitchell, William J. *City of Bits: Space, Place, and the Informationbahn*. Cambridge: MIT P, 1995. Print.
>
> Yousef, Nancy. *Isolated Cases: The Anxieties of Autonomy in Enlightenment Philosophy and Romantic Literature*. Ithaca: Cornell UP, 2004. Print.

6.6.3   AN ANTHOLOGY OR A COMPILATION

To cite an anthology or a compilation (e.g., a bibliography) that was edited or compiled by someone whose name appears on the title page, begin your entry with the name of the editor or compiler, followed by a comma and the abbreviation *ed.* or *comp.* If the person named performed more than one function—serving, say, as editor and translator—give both roles in the order in which they appear on the title page.

> Kepner, Susan Fulop, ed. and trans. *The Lioness in Bloom: Modern Thai Fiction about Women.* Berkeley: U of California P, 1996. Print.
>
> Sevillano, Mando, comp. *The Hopi Way: Tales from a Vanishing Culture.* Flagstaff: Northland, 1986. Print.
>
> Shell, Marc, ed. *American Babel: Literatures of the United States from Abnaki to Zuni.* Cambridge: Harvard UP, 2002. Print.
>
> Spafford, Peter, comp. and ed. *Interference: The Story of Czechoslovakia in the Words of Its Writers.* Cheltenham: New Clarion, 1992. Print.

See also the sections on works in an anthology (6.6.6); introductions, prefaces, and similar parts of books (6.6.8); editions (6.6.10); and translations (6.6.11).

6.6.4   A BOOK BY TWO OR MORE AUTHORS

To cite a book by two or three authors, give their names in the same order as on the title page—not necessarily in alphabetical order. Reverse only the name of the first author, add a comma, and give the other name or names in normal form (Deleuze, Gilles, and Félix Guattari). Place a period after the last name. Even if the authors have the same last name, state each name in full (Lee, Matt, and Ted Lee). If the persons listed on the title page are editors, translators, or compilers, place a comma (not a period) after the final name and add the appropriate abbreviation (*eds., trans.,* or *comps.* for "editors," "translators," or "compilers").

> Booth, Wayne C., Gregory G. Colomb, and Joseph M. Williams. *The Craft of Research.* 2nd ed. Chicago: U of Chicago P, 2003. Print.
>
> Broer, Lawrence R., and Gloria Holland. *Hemingway and Women: Female Critics and the Female Voice.* Tuscaloosa: U of Alabama P, 2002. Print.
>
> Welsch, Roger L., and Linda K. Welsch. *Cather's Kitchens: Foodways in Literature and Life.* Lincoln: U of Nebraska P, 1987. Print.

If there are more than three authors, you may name only the first and add *et al.* ("and others"), or you may give all names in full in the order in which they appear on the title page.

> Gilman, Sander, et al. *Hysteria beyond Freud.* Berkeley: U of California P, 1993. Print.
>
> Quirk, Randolph, et al. *A Comprehensive Grammar of the English Language.* London: Longman, 1985. Print.

or

> Gilman, Sander, Helen King, Roy Porter, George Rousseau, and Elaine Showalter. *Hysteria beyond Freud.* Berkeley: U of California P, 1993. Print.
>
> Quirk, Randolph, Sidney Greenbaum, Geoffrey Leech, and Jan Svartvik. *A Comprehensive Grammar of the English Language.* London: Longman, 1985. Print.

6.6.5   A BOOK BY A CORPORATE AUTHOR

A corporate author may be a commission, an association, a committee, or any other group whose individual members are not identified on the title page. Omit any initial article in the name of the corporate author, and do not abbreviate its name. Cite the book by the corporate author, even if the corporate author is the publisher. (On citing government publications, see 6.6.20.)

> American Council of Learned Societies. *Teaching the Humanities: Essays from the ACLS Elementary and Secondary Schools Teacher Curriculum Development Project.* New York: ACLS, 1994. Print.
>
> Carnegie Foundation for the Advancement of Teaching. *Campus Life: In Search of Community.* Princeton: Carnegie Foundation for the Advancement of Teaching, 1990. Print.

6.6.6   A WORK IN AN ANTHOLOGY

If you are citing an essay, a short story, a poem, or another work that appears in an anthology or some other book collection, you need to add the following information to the basic book entry (6.6.2).

Author, Title, and (If Relevant) Translator of the Part of the Book Being Cited.   Begin the entry with the author and title of the piece, normally enclosing the title in quotation marks.

> Allende, Isabel. "Toad's Mouth."

But if the work was originally published independently (as, e.g., auto-biographies, plays, and novels generally are), italicize its title instead (see the sample entries below for Hansberry and Sastre). Follow the title of the part of the book with a period. If the anthology contains the work of more than one translator, give the translator's name next, preceded by the abbreviation *Trans.* ("Translated by").

> Allende, Isabel. "Toad's Mouth." Trans. Margaret Sayers Peden.

Then state the title of the anthology (italicized).

> Allende, Isabel. "Toad's Mouth." Trans. Margaret Sayers Peden.
> *A Hammock beneath the Mangoes: Stories from Latin America.*

Name of the Editor, Translator, or Compiler of the Book Being Cited.   If all the works in the collection have the same translator or if the book has an editor or compiler, write *Trans., Ed.,* or *Comp.* ("Translated by," "Edited by," or "Compiled by"), as appropriate, after the book title and give that person's name. If the editor or compiler is also the person named earlier in the entry as the author of the work, use only the last name after *Ed.* or *Comp.*

> Allende, Isabel. "Toad's Mouth." Trans. Margaret Sayers Peden.
> *A Hammock beneath the Mangoes: Stories from Latin America.*
> Ed. Thomas Colchie.

If someone served in more than one role — say, as editor and translator — state the roles in the order in which they appear on the title page (e.g., "Ed. and trans."; see the entry below for Hanzlík). Similarly, if different persons performed different roles, give the names in the order in which they appear on the title page: "Trans. Jessie Coulson. Ed. George Gibian."

Page Numbers of the Cited Piece.   Give the inclusive page numbers of the piece you are citing. Be sure to provide the page numbers for the entire piece, not just for the material you used (on writing inclusive numbers, see 3.10.6). Inclusive page numbers follow the publication

date and a period. (If the book has no page numbers, see 6.6.24.) The
entry concludes with the medium of publication consulted.

> Allende, Isabel. "Toad's Mouth." Trans. Margaret Sayers Peden.
>
> *A Hammock beneath the Mangoes: Stories from Latin America.*
>
> Ed. Thomas Colchie. New York: Plume, 1992. 83-88. Print.

Here are additional sample entries for works in anthologies:

> Bordo, Susan. "The Moral Content of Nabokov's *Lolita." Aesthetic*
>
> *Subjects.* Ed. Pamela R. Matthews and David McWhirter.
>
> Minneapolis: U of Minnesota P, 2003. 125-52. Print.
>
> Hansberry, Lorraine. *A Raisin in the Sun. Black Theater: A Twentieth-*
>
> *Century Collection of the Work of Its Best Playwrights.* Ed. Lindsay
>
> Patterson. New York: Dodd, 1971. 221-76. Print.
>
> Hanzlík, Josef. "Vengeance." Trans. Ewald Osers. *Interference: The*
>
> *Story of Czechoslovakia in the Words of Its Writers.* Comp. and
>
> ed. Peter Spafford. Cheltenham: New Clarion, 1992. 54. Print.
>
> Sastre, Alfonso. *Sad Are the Eyes of William Tell.* Trans. Leonard
>
> Pronko. *The New Wave of Spanish Drama.* Ed. George E.
>
> Wellwarth. New York: New York UP, 1970. 165-321. Print.
>
> "A Witchcraft Story." *The Hopi Way: Tales from a Vanishing Culture.*
>
> Comp. Mando Sevillano. Flagstaff: Northland, 1986. 33-42. Print.

Often works in anthologies have been published before. If you wish
to inform your reader of the date when a previously published piece
other than a scholarly article first appeared, you may follow the title
of the piece with the year of original publication and a period. You do
not need to record the medium of the previous publication.

> Douglass, Frederick. *Narrative of the Life of Frederick Douglass, an*
>
> *American Slave, Written by Himself.* 1845. *Classic American*
>
> *Autobiographies.* Ed. William L. Andrews. New York: Mentor,
>
> 1992. 229-327. Print.
>
> Franklin, Benjamin. "Emigration to America." 1782. *The Faber Book*
>
> *of America.* Ed. Christopher Ricks and William L. Vance. Boston:
>
> Faber, 1992. 24-26. Print.

To cite a previously published scholarly article in a collection, give
the complete data for the earlier publication and then add *Rpt. in*

("Reprinted in"), the title of the collection, and the new publication facts. (On citing articles in print periodicals, see 6.5.2; on citing articles accessed through the Web, see 6.7.3–4.)

> Appadurai, Arjun. "Disjuncture and Difference in the Global Cultural Economy." *Public Culture* 2.2 (1990): 1-24. Rpt. in *Colonial Discourse and Post-colonial Theory: A Reader*. Ed. Patrick Williams and Laura Chrisman. New York: Columbia UP, 1994. 324-39. Print.

If the article was originally published under a different title, first state the new title and publication facts, followed by *Rpt. of* ("Reprint of"), the original title, and the original publication facts.

> Lewis, C. S. "Viewpoints: C. S. Lewis." *Twentieth-Century Interpretations of* Sir Gawain and the Green Knight. Ed. Denton Fox. Englewood Cliffs: Prentice, 1968. 100-01. Rpt. of "The Anthropological Approach." *English and Medieval Studies Presented to J. R. R. Tolkien on the Occasion of His Seventieth Birthday*. Ed. Norman Davis and C. L. Wrenn. London: Allen, 1962. 219-23. Print.

Some anthologies reprint excerpts from previously published material. If the work you are citing is an excerpt, use *Excerpt from* instead of *Rpt. of.*

If you refer to more than one piece from the same collection, you may wish to cross-reference each citation to a single entry for the book (see 6.4.6). On citing articles in reference books, see 6.6.7. On citing introductions, prefaces, and the like, see 6.6.8. On citing a piece in a multivolume anthology, see 6.6.14.

6.6.7 AN ARTICLE IN A REFERENCE BOOK

Treat an encyclopedia article or a dictionary entry as you would a piece in a collection (6.6.6), but do not cite the editor of the reference work. If the article is signed, give the author's name first (often articles in reference books are signed with initials identified elsewhere in the work); if it is unsigned, give the title first. If the encyclopedia or dictionary arranges articles alphabetically, you may omit volume and page numbers.

When citing widely used reference books, especially those that frequently appear in new editions, do not give full publication information. For such works, list only the edition (if stated), the year of publication, and the medium of publication consulted.

> "Azimuthal Equidistant Projection." *Merriam-Webster's Collegiate Dictionary*. 11th ed. 2003. Print.
>
> "Ginsburg, Ruth Bader." *Who's Who in America*. 62nd ed. 2008. Print.
>
> "Japan." *The Encyclopedia Americana*. 2004 ed. Print.
>
> Mohanty, Jitendra N. "Indian Philosophy." *The New Encyclopaedia Britannica: Macropaedia*. 15th ed. 1987. Print.
>
> "Noon." *The Oxford English Dictionary*. 2nd ed. 1989. Print.

If you are citing a specific entry among several for the same word, add *Entry* and the appropriate designation (e.g., number).

> "Manual." Entry 2. *Webster's Third New International Dictionary*. 1981. Print.

If you are citing a specific definition among several, add the abbreviation *Def.* ("Definition") and the appropriate designation (e.g., number, letter).

> "Noon." Def. 4b. *The Oxford English Dictionary*. 2nd ed. 1989. Print.

When citing specialized reference books, however, especially those that have appeared in only one edition, give full publication information.

> Bram, Jean Rhys. "Moon." *The Encyclopedia of Religion*. Ed. Mircea Eliade. 16 vols. New York: Macmillan, 1987. Print.
>
> Le Patourel, John. "Normans and Normandy." *Dictionary of the Middle Ages*. Ed. Joseph R. Strayer. 13 vols. New York: Scribner's, 1987. Print.

6.6.8   AN INTRODUCTION, A PREFACE, A FOREWORD,
OR AN AFTERWORD

To cite an introduction, a preface, a foreword, or an afterword, begin with the name of its author and then give the name of the part being cited, neither italicized nor enclosed in quotation marks (*Introduction, Preface, Foreword, Afterword*). If the writer of the piece is different from the author of the complete work, cite the author of the work after its title, giving the full name, in normal order, preceded by the word *By*. If the writer of the piece is also the author of the complete work, use only the last name after *By*. If the complete work is a translation, add the name of the translator next. Continue with full publication information, the inclusive page numbers, and, finally, the medium of publication consulted.

> Borges, Jorge Luis. Foreword. *Selected Poems, 1923-1967*. By Borges.
>
> Ed. Norman Thomas Di Giovanni. New York: Delta-Dell, 1973.
>
> xv-xvi. Print.
>
> Drabble, Margaret. Introduction. *Middlemarch*. By George Eliot. New
>
> York: Bantam, 1985. vii-xvii. Print.
>
> Elliott, Emory. Afterword. *The Jungle*. By Upton Sinclair. New York:
>
> Signet, 1990. 342-50. Print.
>
> Felstiner, John. Preface. *Paul Celan: Selected Poems and Prose*. By Paul
>
> Celan. Trans. Felstiner. New York: Norton, 2000. xvii-xxxi. Print.
>
> Knox, Bernard. Introduction. *The Odyssey*. By Homer. Trans. Robert
>
> Fagles. New York: Viking, 1996. 3-64. Print.

If the introduction, preface, foreword, or afterword has a title, give the title, enclosed in quotation marks, immediately before the name of the part.

> Brodsky, Joseph. "Poetry as a Form of Resistance to Reality."
>
> Foreword. *Winter Dialogue*. By Tomas Venclova. Trans. Diana
>
> Senechal. Evanston: Hydra-Northwestern UP, 1997. vii-xviii.
>
> Print.
>
> Wallach, Rick. "Cormac McCarthy's Canon as Accidental Artifact."
>
> Introduction. *Myth, Legend, Dust: Critical Responses to Cormac*
>
> *McCarthy*. Ed. Wallach. New York: Manchester UP, 2000. xiv-xvi.
>
> Print.

6.6.9   AN ANONYMOUS BOOK

If a book has no author's or editor's name on the title page, begin the entry with the title. Do not use either *Anonymous* or *Anon*. Alphabetize the entry by the title, ignoring any initial article regardless of the language of the title. (Note that the first two sample entries are alphabetized by *Chicago* and *Holy*.)

> *The Chicago Manual of Style.* 15th ed. Chicago: U of Chicago P, 2003.
> Print.
>
> *The Holy Bible.* Wheaton: Crossway-Good News, 2003. Print. Eng.
> Standard Vers.
>
> *New York Public Library American History Desk Reference.* New York:
> Macmillan, 1997. Print.

6.6.10   A SCHOLARLY EDITION

A scholarly edition (or edition, for short) is a work prepared for publication by someone other than the author—by an editor. For example, for a 2007 printing of Shakespeare's *Hamlet*, an editor would have selected a version of the play from the various versions available, decided on any changes in spelling or punctuation, and perhaps added explanatory notes or written an introduction. The editor's name would most likely appear on the title page along with Shakespeare's.

To cite a scholarly edition, begin with the author's name (or the title, for an anonymous work) if you refer primarily to the text itself; give the editor's name, preceded by the abbreviation *Ed.* ("Edited by"), after the title. If for clarity you wish to indicate the original date of publication, place the year directly after the title (see the entry for Crane).

> Crane, Stephen. *The Red Badge of Courage: An Episode of the
> American Civil War.* 1895. Ed. Fredson Bowers. Charlottesville:
> UP of Virginia, 1975. Print.
>
> Edgeworth, Maria. Castle Rackrent *and* Ennui. Ed. Marilyn Butler.
> London: Penguin, 1992. Print.
>
> Henderson, George Wylie. *Harlem Calling: The Collected Stories of
> George Wylie Henderson: An Alabama Writer of the Harlem
> Renaissance.* Ed. David G. Nicholls. Ann Arbor: U of Michigan P,
> 2006. Print.
>
> *Octovian.* Ed. Frances McSparran. London: Oxford UP, 1986. Print.
> Early English Text Soc. 289.
>
> Shakespeare, William. *Hamlet.* Ed. Barbara A. Mowat and Paul
> Werstine. New York: Washington Square-Pocket, 1992. Print.
>
> Twain, Mark. *Roughing It.* Ed. Harriet E. Smith and Edgar M. Branch.
> Berkeley: U of California P, 1993. Print.
>
> Wollstonecraft, Mary. *A Vindication of the Rights of Woman.* Ed.
> Carol H. Poston. New York: Norton, 1975. Print.

To cite a facsimile edition, follow the author's name and title with the original publication information (see 6.6.23 for a book published before 1900), the abbreviation *Facsim. ed.* ("Facsimile edition"), the new publication information, and the medium of publication.

> Milton, John. *Poems*. London, 1645. Facsim. ed. Oxford: Clarendon,
>
> 1924. Print.

If you are citing a specific work in a facsimile edition, treat it as you would a piece in a collection (see 6.6.6), giving inclusive page numbers at the end of the entry. If you wish to indicate the date of the specific work, place the year directly after the title of the piece.

> Milton, John. "Lycidas." 1638. *Poems*. London, 1645. Facsim. ed.
>
> Oxford: Clarendon, 1924. 57-65. Print.

If your citations are generally to the work of the editor (e.g., the introduction, the notes, or editorial decisions regarding the text), begin the entry with the editor's name, followed by a comma and the abbreviation *ed.* ("editor"), and give the author's name, preceded by the word *By*, after the title.

> Bowers, Fredson, ed. *The Red Badge of Courage: An Episode of the*
>
> *American Civil War*. By Stephen Crane. 1895. Charlottesville: UP
>
> of Virginia, 1975. Print.

If the edition is based on a named version of the text, as editions of the Bible usually are, then the name of the version can be recorded at the end of the entry, as supplementary bibliographic information.

> *The Bible*. Introd. and notes by Robert Carroll and Stephen Prickett.
>
> Oxford: Oxford UP, 1998. Print. Oxford World's Classics.
>
> Authorized King James Vers.

Consult 6.6.14 if you are citing more than one volume of a multivolume work or if the book is a part of a multivolume edition — say, *The Works of Mark Twain* — and you wish to give supplementary information about the entire project.

6.6.11   A TRANSLATION

To cite a translation, state the author's name first if you refer primarily to the work itself; give the translator's name, preceded by the abbreviation *Trans.* ("Translated by"), after the title. If the book has an editor as well as a translator, give the names, with appropriate abbreviations, in the order in which they appear on the title page (see the sample entry for Dostoevsky).

> Dostoevsky, Feodor. *Crime and Punishment.* Trans. Jessie Coulson.
> Ed. George Gibian. New York: Norton, 1964. Print.
> Homer. *The Odyssey.* Trans. Robert Fagles. New York: Viking, 1996. Print.
> Mankell, Henning. *Firewall.* Trans. Ebba Segerberg. New York:
> Vintage-Random, 2003. Print.
> Murasaki Shikibu. *The Tale of Genji.* Trans. Edward G. Seidensticker.
> New York: Knopf, 1976. Print.

If your citations are mostly to the translator's comments or choice of wording, begin the entry with the translator's name, followed by a comma and *trans.* ("translator"), and give the author's name, preceded by the word *By,* after the title. (On citing anthologies of translated works by different authors, see 6.6.6.)

> Coulson, Jessie, trans. *Crime and Punishment.* By Feodor Dostoevsky.
> Ed. George Gibian. New York: Norton, 1964. Print.

Although not required, some or all of the original publication facts may be added as supplementary information at the end of the entry, after the medium of publication.

> Genette, Gérard. *The Work of Art: Immanence and Transcendence.*
> Trans. G. M. Goshgarian. Ithaca: Cornell UP, 1997. Print. Trans.
> of *L'œuvre d'art: Immanence et transcendence.* Paris: Seuil,
> 1994.
> Levi, Primo. *Survival in Auschwitz: The Nazi Assault on Humanity.*
> Trans. Stuart Woolf. New York: Collier-Macmillan, 1987. Print.
> Trans. of *Se questo è un uomo.* Torino: Einaudi, 1958.

On citing a book in a language other than English, see 6.6.22.

6.6.12   AN ILLUSTRATED BOOK OR A GRAPHIC NARRATIVE

Illustrations serve a range of functions in nonperiodical print publications. For a volume in which illustrations supplement the written text, such as an illustrated edition of a literary work, give the illustrator's name, preceded by the abbreviation *Illus.* ("Illustrated by"), after the title. If an editor or a translator is also cited after the title, place the names in the order in which they appear on the title page.

> Baum, L. Frank. *The Wonderful Wizard of Oz*. Introd. Regina Barreca.
> Illus. W. W. Denslow. New York: Signet-Penguin, 2006. Print.

If you refer mainly to the illustrator's work instead of the author's, begin the entry with the illustrator's name, followed by *illus.* ("illustrator"), and give the author's name preceded by the word *By*, after the title.

> Denslow, W. W., illus. *The Wonderful Wizard of Oz*. By L. Frank Baum.
> Introd. Regina Barreca. New York: Signet-Penguin, 2006. Print.

In a graphic narrative, text and illustrations are intermingled. Format the works-cited-list entry for a graphic narrative entirely created by one person like that for any other nonperiodical print publication.

> Spiegelman, Art. *Maus: A Survivor's Tale*. 2 vols. New York: Pantheon-
> Random, 1986-91. Print.

Many graphic narratives are created through collaboration. Begin the entry for such a work with the name of the person whose contribution is most relevant to your research, following it with a label identifying the person's role. List other collaborators after the title in the order in which they appear on the title page, also with labels identifying their roles.

> Benoit, Ted, adapt. *Playback: A Graphic Novel*. By Raymond Chandler.
> Illus. François Ayroles. Introd. Philippe Garnier. New York:
> Arcade, 2006. Print.
> Pekar, Harvey, writer. *The Quitter*. Art by Dean Haspiel. Gray tones by
> Lee Loughridge. Letters by Pat Brosseau. New York: Vertigo-DC
> Comics, 2005. Print.

If the graphic narrative is part of a multivolume work, you may add information about the series following the medium of publication. (See 6.6.14 for more guidance on citing a multivolume work.)

> Yabuki, Kentaro, writer and artist. *Showdown at the Old Castle*. Eng.
> adapt. by Kelly Sue DeConnick. Trans. JN Productions. Touch-up
> art and lettering by Gia Cam Luc. San Francisco: Viz, 2007. Print.
> Vol. 9 of *Black Cat*.

For additional guidelines on citing visual art, see 6.8.6 and 6.8.9.

6.6.13   A BOOK PUBLISHED IN A SECOND OR
                              SUBSEQUENT EDITION

A book with no edition number or name on its title page is usually a
first edition. Unless informed otherwise, readers assume that bibliographic entries refer to first editions. When you use a later edition of
a work, identify the edition in your entry by number (*2nd ed.*, *3rd ed.*,
4th ed.), by name (*Rev. ed.*, for "Revised edition"; *Abr. ed.*, for "Abridged
edition"), or by year (*2006 ed.*) — whichever the title page indicates. The
specification of edition comes after the name of the editor, translator,
or compiler, if there is one, or otherwise after the title of the book. (On
citing encyclopedias, dictionaries, and similar works that are revised
regularly, see 6.6.7.)

> Baker, Nancy L., and Nancy Huling. *A Research Guide for*
>   *Undergraduate Students: English and American Literature.* 6th
>   ed. New York: MLA, 2006. Print.
>
> Cavafy, C. P. *Collected Poems.* Trans. Edmund Keeley and Philip
>   Sherrard. Ed. George Savidis. Rev. ed. Princeton: Princeton UP,
>   1992. Print.
>
> Chaucer, Geoffrey. *The Works of Geoffrey Chaucer.* Ed. F. N. Robinson.
>   2nd ed. Boston: Houghton, 1957. Print.
>
> Murasaki Shikibu. *The Tale of Genji.* Trans. Edward G. Seidensticker.
>   Abr. ed. New York: Vintage-Random, 1985. Print.
>
> Newcomb, Horace, ed. *Television: The Critical View.* 7th ed. New York:
>   Oxford UP, 2007. Print.

6.6.14   A MULTIVOLUME WORK

If you are using two or more volumes of a multivolume work, cite
the total number of volumes in the work ("5 vols."). This information
comes after the title — or after any editor's name or identification of
edition — and before the publication information. Specific references
to volume and page numbers ("3: 212–13") belong in the text. (See ch. 7
for parenthetical documentation.)

> Blanco, Richard L., ed. *The American Revolution, 1775-1783: An*
>   *Encyclopedia.* 2 vols. Hamden: Garland, 1993. Print.
>
> Doyle, Arthur Conan. *The Oxford Sherlock Holmes.* Ed. Owen Dudley
>   Edwards. 9 vols. New York: Oxford UP, 1993. Print.

Lauter, Paul, et al., eds. *The Heath Anthology of American Literature.*
5th ed. 5 vols. Boston: Houghton, 2006. Print.

Sadie, Stanley, ed. *The New Grove Dictionary of Music and Musicians.*
2nd ed. 29 vols. New York: Grove, 2001. Print.

Schlesinger, Arthur M., Jr., gen. ed. *History of U.S. Political Parties.*
4 vols. New York: Chelsea, 1973. Print.

Weinberg, Bernard. *A History of Literary Criticism in the Italian
Renaissance.* 2 vols. Chicago: U of Chicago P, 1961. Print.

If the volumes of the work were published over a period of years,
give the inclusive dates at the end of the citation ("1955–92"). If the
work is still in progress, write *to date* after the number of volumes
("3 vols. to date") and leave a space after the hyphen that follows the
beginning date ("1982– ").

Boswell, James. *The Life of Johnson.* Ed. George Birkbeck Hill and
L. F. Powell. 6 vols. Oxford: Clarendon, 1934-50. Print.

Cassidy, Frederic, and Joan Houston Hall, eds. *Dictionary of
American Regional English.* 4 vols. to date. Cambridge: Belknap-
Harvard UP, 1985- . Print.

Churchill, Winston S. *A History of the English-Speaking Peoples.*
4 vols. New York: Dodd, 1956-58. Print.

Crane, Stephen. *The University of Virginia Edition of the Works of
Stephen Crane.* Ed. Fredson Bowers. 10 vols. Charlottesville:
UP of Virginia, 1969-76. Print.

Wellek, René. *A History of Modern Criticism, 1750-1950.* 8 vols. New
Haven: Yale UP, 1955-92. Print.

If you are using only one volume of a multivolume work, state the
number of the volume in the bibliographic entry ("Vol. 2") and give
publication information for that volume alone; then you need give
only page numbers when you refer to that work in the text.

Doyle, Arthur Conan. *The Oxford Sherlock Holmes.* Ed. Owen Dudley
Edwards. Vol. 8. New York: Oxford UP, 1993. Print.

Parker, Hershel. *Melville: A Biography.* Vol. 1. Baltimore: Johns
Hopkins UP, 1996. Print.

Stowe, Harriet Beecher. "Sojourner Truth, the Libyan Sibyl." 1863. *The
Heath Anthology of American Literature.* Ed. Paul Lauter et al.
5th ed. Vol. B. Boston: Houghton, 2006. 2601-09. Print.

> Wellek, René. *A History of Modern Criticism, 1750-1950.* Vol. 5. New
> Haven: Yale UP, 1986. Print.

Although not required, the complete number of volumes may be added as supplementary information at the end of the listing, after the medium of publication, along with other relevant publication facts, such as inclusive dates of publication if the volumes were published over a period of years (see the sample entry for Wellek below).

> Doyle, Arthur Conan. *The Oxford Sherlock Holmes.* Ed. Owen Dudley
> Edwards. Vol. 8. New York: Oxford UP, 1993. Print. 9 vols.
>
> Stowe, Harriet Beecher. "Sojourner Truth, the Libyan Sibyl." 1863. *The
> Heath Anthology of American Literature.* Ed. Paul Lauter et al.
> 5th ed. Vol. B. Boston: Houghton, 2006. 2601-09. Print. 5 vols.
>
> Wellek, René. *A History of Modern Criticism, 1750-1950.* Vol. 5. New
> Haven: Yale UP, 1986. Print. 8 vols. 1955-92.

If you are using only one volume of a multivolume work and the volume has an individual title, you may cite the book without reference to the other volumes in the work.

> Churchill, Winston S. *The Age of Revolution.* New York: Dodd, 1957.
> Print.
>
> Durant, Will, and Ariel Durant. *The Age of Voltaire.* New York: Simon,
> 1965. Print.

Although not required, supplementary information about the complete multivolume work may follow the basic citation: the volume number, preceded by *Vol.* and followed by the word *of;* the title of the complete work; the total number of volumes; and, if the work appeared over a period of years, the inclusive publication dates.

> Churchill, Winston S. *The Age of Revolution.* New York: Dodd, 1957.
> Print. Vol. 3 of *A History of the English-Speaking Peoples.* 4 vols.
> 1956-58.
>
> Durant, Will, and Ariel Durant. *The Age of Voltaire.* New York: Simon,
> 1965. Print. Vol. 9 of *The Story of Civilization.* 11 vols. 1935-75.

If the volume you are citing is part of a multivolume scholarly edition (see 6.6.10), you may similarly give supplementary information about the entire edition. Follow the publication information for the volume with the appropriate volume number, preceded by *Vol.* and followed by the word *of;* the title of the complete work; the name of the general editor of the multivolume edition, followed by a comma and *gen. ed.*; the total number of volumes; and the inclusive publication dates for the edition (see the entry for Howells). If the entire edition was edited by one person, state the editor's name after the title of the edition rather than after the title of the volume (see the entry for Crane).

> Crane, Stephen. *The Red Badge of Courage: An Episode of the American Civil War.* 1895. Charlottesville: UP of Virginia, 1975. Print. Vol. 2 of *The University of Virginia Edition of the Works of Stephen Crane.* Ed. Fredson Bowers. 10 vols. 1969-76.
>
> Howells, W. D. *Their Wedding Journey.* Ed. John K. Reeves. Bloomington: Indiana UP, 1968. Print. Vol. 5 of *A Selected Edition of W. D. Howells.* Edwin H. Cady, gen. ed. 32 vols. 1968-83.

6.6.15   A BOOK IN A SERIES

If the title page or the preceding page (the half-title page) indicates that the book you are citing is part of a series, include the series name, neither italicized nor enclosed in quotation marks, and the series number (if any), followed by a period, at the end of the listing, after the medium of publication. Use common abbreviations for words in the series name (see 8.4), including *Ser.* if *Series* is part of the name.

> Anderson, Danny, and Jill S. Kuhnheim, eds. *Cultural Studies in the Curriculum: Teaching Latin America.* New York: MLA, 2003. Print. Teaching Langs., Lits., and Cultures.
>
> Bernstein, Elsa. *Twilight: A Drama in Five Acts.* Trans. Susanne Kord. New York: MLA, 2003. Print. Texts and Trans. 14.
>
> Neruda, Pablo. *Canto General.* Trans. Jack Schmitt. Berkeley: U of California P, 1991. Print. Latin Amer. Lit. and Culture 7.
>
> Pihl, Marshall R. *The Korean Singer of Tales.* Cambridge: Harvard UP, 1994. Print. Harvard-Yenching Inst. Monograph Ser. 37.

6.6.16   A REPUBLISHED BOOK OR JOURNAL ISSUE

To cite a republished book—for example, a paperback version of a book originally published in a clothbound version—give the original publication date, followed by a period, before the publication information for the book you are citing.

> García Márquez, Gabriel. *Love in the Time of Cholera.* Trans. Edith
>
> Grossman. 1988. New York: Penguin, 1989. Print.
>
> Holier, Denis, ed. *A New History of French Literature.* 1989. Cambridge:
>
> Harvard UP, 1994. Print.

New material added to the republication, such as an introduction, should be cited after the original publication facts.

> Dreiser, Theodore. *Sister Carrie.* 1900. Introd. E. L. Doctorow. New
>
> York: Bantam, 1982. Print.

To cite a republished book that was originally issued under a different title, first state the new title and publication facts, followed by *Rpt. of* ("Reprint of"), the original title, and the original date.

> *The WPA Guide to 1930s New Jersey.* New Brunswick: Rutgers UP,
>
> 1986. Print. Rpt. of *New Jersey: A Guide to Its Past and Present.*
>
> 1939.

To cite a book that is a reprint of a special issue of a journal, begin the entry with the name of the person who edited the book, followed by a comma and the abbreviation *ed.* (or *eds.* if there are multiple editors). Next give the title of the book (italicized), the publication information for the book, and the medium of publication. Conclude the entry with *Rpt. of spec. issue of,* the name of the journal (italicized), the journal's volume and issue numbers (separated by a period: "9.1"), the year of publication (in parentheses), a colon, a space, and the complete pagination of the issue.

> Appiah, Kwame Anthony, and Henry Louis Gates, Jr., eds. *Identities.*
>
> Chicago: U of Chicago P, 1995. Print. Rpt. of spec. issue of *Critical*
>
> *Inquiry* 18.4 (1992): 625-884.

6.6.17   A PUBLISHER'S IMPRINT

Publishers often group some of their books under imprints, or special names. If an imprint appears on a title page along with the publisher's name, state the imprint and follow it by a hyphen and the name of the publisher ("Anchor-Doubleday," "Collier-Macmillan," "Vintage-Random").

> Cassidy, Frederic, and Joan Houston Hall, eds. *Dictionary of*
>
> *American Regional English.* 4 vols. to date. Cambridge: Belknap-
>
> Harvard UP, 1985- . Print.

Findlater, Mary, and Jane Findlater. *Crossriggs*. 1908. Introd. Paul
    Binding. New York: Virago-Penguin, 1986. Print.

Lopate, Phillip, ed. *The Art of the Personal Essay: An Anthology from the
    Classical Era to the Present*. New York: Anchor-Doubleday, 1994. Print.

Rhodes, Dan. *Timoleon Vieta Come Home: A Sentimental Journey*.
    Orlando: Harvest-Harcourt, 2004. Print.

6.6.18   A BOOK WITH MULTIPLE PUBLISHERS

If the title page lists two or more publishers—not just two or more
offices of the same publisher—include all of them, in the order given,
as part of the publication information, putting a semicolon after the
name of each but the last.

Duff, J. Wight. *A Literary History of Rome: From the Origins to the
    Close of the Golden Age*. Ed. A. M. Duff. 3rd ed. 1953. London:
    Benn; New York: Barnes, 1967. Print.

Wells, H. G. *The Time Machine*. 1895. London: Dent; Rutland: Tuttle,
    1992. Print.

6.6.19   A BROCHURE, PAMPHLET, OR PRESS RELEASE

Treat a brochure or pamphlet as you would a book.

Evans, Grose. *French Painting of the Nineteenth Century in the
    National Gallery of Art*. Washington: Natl. Gallery of Art, 1980. Print.

Modern Language Association. *Language Study in the Age of
    Globalization: The College-Level Experience*. New York: MLA, n.d.
    Print.

Document a press release the same way, but cite the day and month of
the release, if available, along with the year.

Modern Language Association. *Modern Language Association
    Announces New and Improved MLA Language Map*. New York:
    MLA, 18 Apr. 2006. Print.

6.6.20   A GOVERNMENT PUBLICATION

Government publications emanate from many sources and so present special problems in bibliographic citation. In general, if you do

not know the writer of the document, cite as author the government agency that issued it — that is, state the name of the government first, followed by the name of the agency, using an abbreviation if the context makes it clear. (But see below for citing a document whose author is known.)

> California. Dept. of Industrial Relations.
>
> United States. Cong. House.

If you are citing two or more works issued by the same government, substitute three hyphens for the name in each entry after the first. If you also cite more than one work by the same government agency, use an additional three hyphens in place of the agency in the second entry and each subsequent one.

> United States. Cong. House.
>
> ---. ---. Senate.
>
> ---. Dept. of Health and Human Services.

The title of the publication, italicized, should follow immediately.

In citing the *Congressional Record* (abbreviated *Cong. Rec.*), give only the date, page numbers, and medium of publication.

> *Cong. Rec.* 7 Feb. 1973: 3831-51. Print.

In citing other congressional documents, include such information as the number and session of Congress, the house (*S* stands for Senate, *HR* for House of Representatives), and the type and number of the publication. Types of congressional publications include bills (*S* 33, *HR* 77), resolutions (S. Res. 20, H. Res. 50), reports (S. Rept. 9, H. Rept. 142), and documents (S. Doc. 333, H. Doc. 222, Misc. Doc. 67).

The usual publication information (i.e., place, publisher, and date) and the medium of publication consulted come next. Most federal publications, regardless of the branch of government issuing them, are published by the Government Printing Office (GPO), in Washington, DC; its British counterpart is Her (or His) Majesty's Stationery Office (HMSO), in London. Documents issued by the United Nations and most local governments, however, do not all emanate from a central office; give the publication information that appears on the title page.

> Great Britain. Ministry of Agriculture, Fisheries, and Food.
>
> > *Radionuclide Levels in Food, Animals, and Agricultural*
> > *Products: Post-Chernobyl Monitoring in England and Wales.*
> > London: HMSO, 1987. Print.

New York State. Commission on the Adirondacks in the Twenty-First
Century. *The Adirondack Park in the Twenty-First Century.*
Albany: State of New York, 1990. Print.

---. Committee on State Prisons. *Investigation of the New York State
Prisons.* 1883. New York: Arno, 1974. Print.

United Nations. *Consequences of Rapid Population Growth in
Developing Countries.* New York: Taylor, 1991. Print.

---. Centre on Transnational Corporations. *Foreign Direct Investment,
the Service Sector, and International Banking.* New York: United
Nations, 1987. Print.

---. Dept. of Economic and Social Affairs. *Industrial Development for
the Twenty-First Century: Sustainable Development Perspectives.*
New York: United Nations, 2007. Print.

United States. Cong. House. Permanent Select Committee on Intelligence.
Al-Qaeda: The Many Faces of an Islamist Extremist Threat. 109th
Cong., 2nd sess. H. Rept. 615. Washington: GPO, 2006. Print.

---. ---. Joint Committee on the Investigation of the Pearl Harbor
Attack. *Hearings.* 79th Cong., 1st and 2nd sess. 32 vols.
Washington: GPO, 1946. Print.

---. Dept. of Labor. *Child Care: A Workforce Issue.* Washington: GPO,
1988. Print.

---. Dept. of State. *U.S. Climate Action Report—2002: Third National
Communication of the United States of America under the
United Nations Framework Convention on Climate Change.*
Washington: GPO, 2002. Print.

If known, the name of the document's author may either begin the
entry or, if the agency comes first, follow the title and the word *By* or
an abbreviation (such as *Ed.* or *Comp.*).

Poore, Benjamin Perley, comp. *A Descriptive Catalogue of the
Government Publications of the United States, September 5,
1774-March 4, 1881.* US 48th Cong., 2nd sess. Misc. Doc. 67.
Washington: GPO, 1885. Print.

or

United States. Cong. *A Descriptive Catalogue of the Government
Publications of the United States, September 5, 1774-March 4,*

> *1881.* Comp. Benjamin Perley Poore. 48th Cong., 2nd sess. Misc.
> Doc. 67. Washington: GPO, 1885. Print.

To cite an online government document, see 6.7. To cite a legal source, see 6.8.14.

6.6.21   THE PUBLISHED PROCEEDINGS OF A CONFERENCE

Treat the published proceedings of a conference like a book, but add pertinent information about the conference (unless the book title includes such information).

> Brady, Brigid, and Patricia Verrone, eds. *Proceedings of the Northeast Region Annual Meeting, Conference on Christianity and Literature: Christ Plays in Ten-Thousand Places: The Christ-Figure in Text and Interpretation.* 22 Oct. 2005, Caldwell Coll. N.p.: Northeast Regional Conf. on Christianity and Lit., n.d. Print.
> Freed, Barbara F., ed. *Foreign Language Acquisition Research and the Classroom.* Proc. of Consortium for Lang. Teaching and Learning Conf., Oct. 1989, U of Pennsylvania. Lexington: Heath, 1991. Print.

Cite a presentation in the proceedings like a work in a collection of pieces by different authors (see 6.6.6).

> Mann, Jill. "Chaucer and the 'Woman Question.'" *This Noble Craft: Proceedings of the Tenth Research Symposium of the Dutch and Belgian University Teachers of Old and Middle English and Historical Linguistics, Utrecht, 19-20 January 1989.* Ed. Erik Kooper. Amsterdam: Rodopi, 1991. 173-88. Print.

6.6.22   A BOOK IN A LANGUAGE OTHER THAN ENGLISH

Cite a book published in a language other than English like any other book. Give the author's name, title, and publication information as they appear in the book, and conclude with the medium of publication. You may need to look in the colophon (a listing at the back of the book) for some or all of the publication information found on the title or copyright page of English-language books. If it seems necessary to clarify the title, provide a translation, in square brackets: *"Gengangere [Ghosts]."* Similarly, you may use square brackets to give the English name of a foreign city—"Wien [Vienna]"—or you may substitute the English name, depending on your readers' knowledge of the language. Shorten the publisher's name appropriately (see 8.5). For capitalization in languages other than English, see 3.7.2–9.

> Barthes, Roland. *O grau zero da escrita: Seguido de novos ensaios críticos*. Trans. Mario Laranjeira. São Paulo: Martins Fontes, 2004. Print.
>
> Dahlhaus, Carl. *Musikästhetik*. Köln: Gerig, 1967. Print.
>
> Eco, Umberto. *Il nome della rosa*. Milano: Bompiani, 1980. Print.
>
> Esquivel, Laura. *Como agua para chocolate: Novelas de entregas mensuales, con recetas, amores y remedios caseros*. Madrid: Mondadori, 1990. Print.
>
> Poche, Emanuel. *Prazské Palace*. Praha [Prague]: Odeon, 1977. Print.

6.6.23   A BOOK PUBLISHED BEFORE 1900

When citing a book published before 1900, you may omit the name of the publisher and use a comma, instead of a colon, after the place of publication.

> Brome, Richard. *The Dramatic Works of Richard Brome*. 3 vols. London, 1873. Print.
>
> Dewey, John. *The School and Society*. Chicago, 1899. Print.
>
> Segni, Bernardo, trans. *Rettorica et poetica d'Aristotile*. By Aristotle. Firenze, 1549. Print.

6.6.24   A BOOK WITHOUT STATED PUBLICATION INFORMATION OR PAGINATION

When a book does not indicate the publisher, the place or date of publication, or pagination, supply as much of the missing information as you can, using square brackets to show that it did not come from the source.

> New York: U of Gotham P, [2006].

If the date can only be approximated, put it after a *c.*, for *circa* ("around"): "[c. 2006]." If you are uncertain about the accuracy of the information you supply, add a question mark: "[2006?]." Use the following abbreviations for information you cannot supply.

n.p.	No place of publication given
n.p.	No publisher given
n.d.	No date of publication given
n. pag.	No pagination given

Inserted before the colon, the abbreviation *n.p.* indicates *no place*; after the colon, it indicates *no publisher*. *N. pag.* explains the absence of page references in citations of the work.

NO PLACE

N.p.: U of Gotham P, 2006.

NO PUBLISHER

New York: n.p., 2006.

NO DATE

New York: U of Gotham P, n.d.

NO PAGINATION

New York: U of Gotham P, 2006. N. pag.

The examples above are hypothetical; the following ones are entries for actual books.

Bauer, Johann. *Kafka und Prag*. [Stuttgart]: Belser, [1971?]. Print.

Malachi, Zvi, ed. *Proceedings of the International Conference on Literary and Linguistic Computing*. [Tel Aviv]: [Fac. of Humanities, Tel Aviv U], n.d. Print.

Michelangelo. *The Sistine Chapel*. New York: Wings, 1992. N. pag. Print.

Photographic View Album of Cambridge. [Eng.]: n.p., n.d. N. pag. Print.

Sendak, Maurice. *Where the Wild Things Are*. New York: Harper, 1963. N. pag. Print.

6.6.25   AN UNPUBLISHED DISSERTATION

Enclose the title of an unpublished dissertation in quotation marks; do not italicize it. Then write the descriptive label *Diss.*, and add the name of the degree-granting university, followed by a comma and the year. Conclude with the work's medium.

> Kane, Sonia. "Acts of Coercion: Father-Daughter Relationships and the Pressure to Confess in British Women's Fiction, 1778-1814." Diss. City U of New York, 2003. Print.
>
> Stephenson, Denise R. "Blurred Distinctions: Emerging Forms of Academic Writing." Diss. U of New Mexico, 1996. Print.

To cite a master's thesis, substitute the appropriate label (e.g., *MA thesis*, *MS thesis*) for *Diss*. On documenting other unpublished writing, see 6.8.12–13.

6.6.26   A PUBLISHED DISSERTATION

Cite a published dissertation as you would a book, but add pertinent dissertation information before the publication facts. If the dissertation was privately published, state *privately published* in place of the publisher's name.

> Dietze, Rudolf F. *Ralph Ellison: The Genesis of an Artist*. Diss. U Erlangen-Nürnberg, 1982. Nürnberg: Carl, 1982. Print. Erlanger Beiträge zur Sprach- und Kunstwissenschaft 70.
>
> Valentine, Mary-Blair Truesdell. *An Investigation of Gender-Based Leadership Styles of Male and Female Officers in the United States Army*. Diss. George Mason U, 1993. Ann Arbor: UMI, 1993. Print.
>
> Wendriner, Karl Georg. *Der Einfluss von Goethes* Wilhelm Meister *auf das Drama der Romantiker*. Diss. U Bonn, 1907. Leipzig: privately published, 1907. Print.

See 6.7.2 for dissertations on the Web, 6.5.8 for dissertation abstracts published in the print version of *Dissertation Abstracts* or *Dissertation Abstracts International*, and 6.7.4 for dissertation abstracts on the Web.

––––––––––––––––––– **6.7** –––––––––––––––––––

CITING WEB PUBLICATIONS

6.7.1   INTRODUCTION

On the World Wide Web, scholars access bibliographic databases, academic journals, archives of print publications, critical editions, reference

works, dissertations, and a wide variety of other documents and recordings. Citations of Web publications share some traits with those
of print publications and other traits with those of reprinted works,
broadcasts, and live performances. For example, most works on the
Web have an author, a title, and publication information and are thus
analogous to print publications. But while readers seeking a cited print
publication can be reasonably assured that a copy in a local library will
be identical to that consulted by the author, they can be less certain
that a Web publication will be so. Electronic texts can be updated easily and at irregular intervals. They may also be distributed in multiple
databases and accessed through a variety of interfaces displayed on
different kinds of equipment. Multiple versions of any work may be
available. In this sense, then, accessing a source on the Web is akin to
commissioning a performance. Any version of a Web source is potentially different from any past or future version and must be considered
unique. Scholars therefore need to record the date of access as well as
the publication data when citing sources on the Web.

Publications on the Web present special challenges for documentation. Because of the fluidity of the network and the many hypertextual
links between works accessed there, it is often difficult to determine
where one work stops and another begins. How, for instance, does one
define a Web site? One definition would consider all pages affiliated
with a particular domain name, like www.mla.org, to constitute a site.
Another view would consider all the pages organized by a particular
editor or project team as a site, even if the project is housed under a
larger body's domain name or distributed over several domains; the
Victorian Women Writers Project, for example, appears under Indiana
University's domain name (www.indiana.edu). Since both views have
merit, the guidelines presented here do not take one side but instead
offer a method to record the relation of works on the Web to the information hierarchies surrounding them.

In the past, the *MLA Style Manual and Guide to Scholarly Publishing*
recommended including URLs of Web sources in works-cited-list entries. Inclusion of URLs has proved to have limited value, however, for
they often change, can be specific to a subscriber or a session of use,
and can be so long and complex that typing them into a browser is
cumbersome and prone to transcription errors. Readers are now more
likely to find resources on the Web by searching for titles and authors'
names than by typing URLs. You should include a URL as supplementary information only when the reader probably cannot locate the
source without it or when your publisher requires it. If you present a

URL, give it immediately following the date of access, a period, and a space. Enclose the URL in angle brackets, and conclude with a period. If a URL must be divided between two lines, break it only after a slash; do not introduce a hyphen at the break or allow your word-processing program to do so. If possible, give the complete address, including the access-mode identifier (e.g., *http*, *ftp*), for the specific work you are citing.

> Eaves, Morris, Robert Essick, and Joseph Viscomi, eds. *The William*
>
> *Blake Archive*. Lib. of Cong., 28 Sept. 2007. Web. 20 Nov. 2007.
>
> <http://www.blakearchive.org/blake/>.

The recommendations in this section mostly treat peer-reviewed, scholarly sources and primary sources for which a considerable amount of relevant publication information is available. In truth, though, many sources do not supply all desired information—for instance, many texts do not include reference markers, such as page or paragraph numbers, so it is difficult if not impossible to direct a reader to the exact location of the material you are citing. Thus, while aiming for comprehensiveness, writers must often settle for citing whatever information is available to them. Since the Web can deliver sound and images as well as written text, you may want to describe your source in your text or endnotes when there is a risk that readers will not appreciate important aspects of the work. MLA style is flexible, and sometimes you must improvise to record features not anticipated by this manual. In some cases, citation formats devised to handle complex print publications may serve as a basis for improvisation; see in particular the sections on an article in a reference book (6.6.7), scholarly editions (6.6.10), translations (6.6.11), and government documents (6.6.20). Remember to be consistent in your formatting throughout your work. Since sites and other resources on the Web sometimes disappear altogether, you should consider downloading or printing the material you use during your research, so that you can verify it if it is inaccessible later.

Section 6.7.2 explains how to cite the vast majority of works found on the Web: nonperiodical publications. Section 6.7.3 covers works in scholarly journals. Section 6.7.4 explains how to cite works from periodical publications that are collected in online databases. Publishers well known for their periodical publications in media not online, such as newspapers, magazines, and regular news broadcasts, also publish works at nonperiodical, or irregular, intervals on the Web. Thus, it is important to look carefully at the work you are consulting and establish the context for its publication. Note that 6.7 addresses only sources accessed on the Web. For electronic publications you consult apart from a network, such as digital files stored on your computer and on CD-ROMs, see 6.8–9.

6.7.2   A NONPERIODICAL PUBLICATION

a. Introduction

Most works on the Web are nonperiodical — not released on a regular schedule. This section begins by describing the basic entry for nonperiodical works on the Web. Sometimes it is important to indicate that a work consulted on the Web also appeared in another medium. For example, you may want to give bibliographic data for a book that was scanned for viewing on the Web or the full description of a film that was digitized for viewing in your browser. Sections 6.7.2c–d provide guidelines for citing such works.

b. A Work Cited Only on the Web

An entry for a nonperiodical publication on the Web usually contains most of the following components, in sequence:

1. Name of the author, compiler, director, editor, narrator, performer, or translator of the work (for more than one author, see 6.6.4; for a corporate author, see 6.6.5; for an anonymous work, see 6.6.9)
2. Title of the work (italicized if the work is independent; in roman type and quotation marks if the work is part of a larger work [see 3.8.2–3])
3. Title of the overall Web site (italicized), if distinct from item 2
4. Version or edition used (see 6.6.13)
5. Publisher or sponsor of the site; if not available, use *N.p.*
6. Date of publication (day, month, and year, as available); if nothing is available, use *n.d.*
7. Medium of publication (*Web*)
8. Date of access (day, month, and year)

Each item is followed by a period except the publisher or sponsor, which is followed by a comma. Untitled works may be identified by a genre label (e.g., *Home page, Introduction, Online posting*), neither italicized nor enclosed in quotation marks, in the place where the title goes (see 6.6.8 and 6.8.7–10 for additional guidance). For inclusion of other information that may be pertinent (e.g., the name of the composer of a performed work), see the sample entries. If not otherwise recorded in the entry, the name of a creator of the overall Web site, such as its editor, may be listed following the title of the site (see the Yager example). If you cannot find some of this information, cite what is available.

Antin, David. Interview by Charles Bernstein. *Dalkey Archive Press.* Dalkey Archive P, n.d. Web. 21 Aug. 2007.

Committee on Scholarly Editions. "Guidelines for Editors of Scholarly Editions." *Modern Language Association.* MLA, 25 Sept. 2007. Web. 20 Nov. 2007.

Concerto Palatino, perf. "Canzon à 6 per l'Epistola." By Giovanni Priuli. *Boston Early Music Festival and Exhibition.* Boston Early Music Festival, 2003. Web. 20 July 2007.

"de Kooning, Willem." *Encyclopaedia Britannica Online.* Encyclopaedia Britannica, 2007. Web. 19 Mar. 2007.

Eaves, Morris, Robert Essick, and Joseph Viscomi, eds. *The William Blake Archive.* Lib. of Cong., 28 Sept. 2007. Web. 20 Nov. 2007.

Garcia Landa, José Ángel, comp. *A Bibliography of Literary Theory, Criticism and Philology.* 12th ed. U de Zaragoza, 2007. Web. 29 Nov. 2007.

Green, Joshua. "The Rove Presidency." *The Atlantic.com.* Atlantic Monthly Group, Sept. 2007. Web. 29 Nov. 2007.

"Hourly News Summary." *National Public Radio.* Natl. Public Radio, 20 July 2007. Web. 20 July 2007.

Lessig, Lawrence. "Free Debates: More Republicans Call on RNC." *Lessig 2.0.* N.p., 4 May 2007. Web. 20 Nov. 2007.

Liu, Alan, ed. Home page. *Voice of the Shuttle.* Dept. of English, U of California, Santa Barbara, n.d. Web. 21 Feb. 2007.

"Maplewood, New Jersey." Map. *Google Maps.* Google, 23 July 2007. Web. 23 July 2007.

Quade, Alex. "Elite Team Rescues Troops behind Enemy Lines." *CNN.com.* Cable News Network, 19 Mar. 2007. Web. 19 Mar. 2007.

Salda, Michael N., ed. *The Cinderella Project.* Vers. 1.2. U of Southern Mississippi, Oct. 2005. Web. 21 Nov. 2007.

"The Scientists Speak." Editorial. *New York Times*. New York Times,
20 Nov. 2007. Web. 20 Nov. 2007.

"Six Charged in Alleged N.J. Terror Plot." *WNBC.com*. WNBC, 8 May 2007.
Web. 9 May 2007.

Tyre, Peg. "Standardized Tests in College?" *Newsweek*. Newsweek, 16
Nov. 2007. Web. 21 Nov. 2007.

"Utah Mine Rescue Funeral." *CNN.com*. Cable News Network, 21 Aug.
2007. Web. 21 Aug. 2007.

"Verb Tenses." Chart. *The OWL at Purdue*. Purdue U Online Writing
Lab, 2001. Web. 23 July 2007.

Yager, Susan, narr. "The Former Age." By Geoffrey Chaucer. *Chaucer
Metapage*. Ed. Mark E. Allen et al. U of North Carolina, 13 Feb.
2007. Web. 30 Nov. 2007.

If you need to include a URL, follow the guidelines in 6.7.1.

c. A Work on the Web Cited with Print Publication Data

If the nonperiodical work you are citing also appeared in print, you
may determine that it is important to include the bibliographic data
for the print publication as part of your entry. A book that was scanned
for access in a database, for example, is usually cited in this way. Begin
the entry with the relevant facts about print publication as described in
6.6. See in particular the guidelines for a work in an anthology (6.6.6),
a translation (6.6.11), a multivolume work (6.6.14), a government publication (6.6.20), and an unpublished dissertation (6.6.25). Instead of
concluding with *Print* as the medium of publication, record the following information in sequence:

1. Title of the database or Web site (italicized)
2. Medium of publication consulted (*Web*)
3. Date of access (day, month, and year)

If the guidelines in 6.6 call for inclusive page numbers and they are
not present in the source, use *n. pag.* Supplementary bibliographic
information that in 6.6 follows the medium of publication should be
included immediately before item 1 above. Here are examples of entries for nonperiodical publications on the Web that have a previous or
concurrent publication in print:

Bierce, Ambrose. "Academy." *The Devil's Dictionary. The Collected Works of Ambrose Bierce.* Vol. 7. New York: Neale, 1911. N. pag. *The Ambrose Bierce Project.* Web. 12 Mar. 2007.

Bown, Jennifer M. "Going Solo: The Experience of Learning Russian in a Non-traditional Environment." Diss. Ohio State U, 2004. *OhioLINK.* Web. 8 May 2007.

Cascardi, Anthony J. *Ideologies of History in the Spanish Golden Age.* University Park: Pennsylvania State UP, 1997. *Penn State Romance Studies.* Web. 12 Mar. 2007.

Child, L. Maria, ed. *The Freedmen's Book.* Boston, 1866. *Google Book Search.* Web. 12 Mar. 2007.

Heim, Michael Henry, and Andrzej W. Tymowski. *Guidelines for the Translation of Social Science Texts.* New York: ACLS, 2006. *American Council of Learned Societies.* Web. 12 Mar. 2007.

United States. Dept. of Justice. Office of Juvenile Justice and Delinquency Prevention. *Law Enforcement and Juvenile Crime.* By Howard N. Snyder. 2001. *National Criminal Justice Reference Service.* Web. 21 Aug. 2007.

Whitman, Walt. Preface. *Leaves of Grass.* By Whitman. Brooklyn, 1855. iii-xii. *The Walt Whitman Archive.* Web. 12 Mar. 2007.

Whittier, John G. "A Prayer." *The Freedmen's Book.* Ed. L. Maria Child. Boston, 1866. 178. *Google Book Search.* Web. 15 Aug. 2007.

You may add supplementary information about the database or Web site (such as the name of its editor, sponsor, or publisher) following its name.

Ovid. *Metamorphoses.* Trans. Arthur Golding. London, 1567. *The Perseus Digital Library.* Ed. Gregory Crane. Tufts U. Web. 12 Mar. 2007.

If you need to include a URL, follow the guidelines in 6.7.1. See 6.7.4 for periodical print publications in online databases.

d. A Work on the Web Cited with Publication Data for Another Medium besides Print

The Web presents images (still and moving) and sound as well as written text. It is sometimes important to indicate that a source online is available in another medium besides print. If you viewed a digitized version of a film on the Web, for example, you may want to include in your entry the details usually cited for a film. To document sources such as these, begin the entry by following the recommendations in 6.8 but drop the medium of original publication (e.g, *Television, Photograph*). Conclude the entry with the following items:

1. Title of the database or Web site (italicized)
2. Medium of publication consulted (*Web*)
3. Date of access (day, month, and year)

Supplementary bibliographic information that in 6.8 follows the medium of publication should be included immediately before item 1 above. Be mindful of the distinction between sources accessed entirely on the Web and digital files used apart from an electronic network; for the latter, follow the directions in 6.8.18. Here are examples of entries for works available on the Web and in another medium besides print:

> Currin, John. *Blond Angel*. 2001. Indianapolis Museum of Art. *IMA: It's My Art*. Web. 9 May 2007.
>
> *The Great Train Robbery*. Dir. Edward Porter. Thomas Edison, 1903. *Internet Archive*. Web. 9 May 2007.
>
> Lange, Dorothea. *The Migrant Mother*. 1936. Prints and Photographs Div., Lib. of Cong. *Dorothea Lange: Photographer of the People*. Web. 9 May 2007.
>
> "Protest on Behalf of Southern Women." 1932. Mary Cornelia Barker Papers. Robert W. Woodruff Lib., Emory U. *Online Manuscript Resources in Southern Women's History*. Web. 23 July 2007.

If you need to include a URL, follow the guidelines in 6.7.1.

6.7.3   A SCHOLARLY JOURNAL

Some scholarly journals exist only in electronic form on the Web, while others appear both in print and on the Web. This section addresses journals published independently on the Web; periodicals collected in online databases are covered in 6.7.4. Following the legacy of print periodicals, most scholarly journals on the Web are organized by volume number (usually on an annual basis) and include issue numbers and the dates of publication. To cite a work from a scholarly journal on the Web, including an article, a review, an editorial, and a letter to the editor, begin the entry by following the recommendations in 6.5 for citing works in print periodicals, but drop the medium of publication (*Print*).

A periodical publication on the Web may not include page numbers. If pagination is not available, use *n. pag.* in place of inclusive page numbers. Conclude the entry with the following items:

1. Medium of publication consulted (*Web*)
2. Date of access (day, month, and year)

If the guidelines you are following in 6.5 call for supplementary bibliographic information after the medium of publication, this information should be included immediately before item 1 above. Here are examples of entries for scholarly journals on the Web:

Armstrong, Grace. Rev. of *Fortune's Faces: The* Roman de la Rose *and the Poetics of Contingency*, by Daniel Heller-Roazen. *Bryn Mawr Review of Comparative Literature* 6.1 (2007): n. pag. Web. 8 Nov. 2007.

Dionísio, João, and Antonio Cortijo Ocaña, eds. *Mais de pedras que de livros / More Rocks Than Books*. Spec. issue of *eHumanista* 8 (2007): 1-263. Web. 8 Nov. 2007.

Landauer, Michelle. "Images of Virtue: Reading, Reformation and the Visualization of Culture in Rousseau's *La nouvelle Héloïse*." *Romanticism on the Net* 46 (2007): n. pag. Web. 8 Nov. 2007.

Nater, Miguel. "El beso de la Esfinge: La poética de lo sublime en *La amada inmóvil* de Amado Nervo y en los *Nocturnos* de José Asunción Silva." *Romanitas* 1.1 (2006): n. pag. Web. 8 Nov. 2007.

Ouellette, Marc. "Theories, Memories, Bodies, and Artists." Editorial. *Reconstruction* 7.4 (2007): n. pag. Web. 28 Nov. 2007.

Raja, Masood Ashraf. Rev. of *Voices of Resistance: Muslim Women on War, Faith, and Sexuality*, ed. Sarah Husain. *Postcolonial Text* 3.2 (2007): n. pag. Web. 8 Nov. 2007.

Schmidt-Nieto, Jorge R. "The Political Side of Bilingual Education: The Undesirable Becomes Useful." *Arachne@Rutgers* 2.2 (2002): n. pag. Web. 12 Mar. 2007.

Shah, Parilah Mohd, and Fauziah Ahmad. "A Comparative Account of the Bilingual Education Programs in Malaysia and the United States." *GEMA Online Journal of Language Studies* 7.2 (2007): 63-77. Web. 8 Nov. 2007.

Shehan, Constance L., and Amanda B. Moras. "Deconstructing Laundry: Gendered Technologies and the Reluctant Redesign of Household Labor." *Michigan Family Review* 11 (2006): n. pag. Web. 8 Nov. 2007.

> Wood, Michael. "The Last Night of All." *PMLA* 122.5 (2008): 1394-402.
> Web. 22 Jan. 2008.

If you need to include a URL, follow the guidelines in 6.7.1.

6.7.4   A PERIODICAL PUBLICATION IN AN ONLINE DATABASE

Many databases include digital scans of entire periodicals that were previously published in print; often these scans present facsimiles of the printed works. Other databases aggregate articles from disparate periodicals, sometimes organizing the articles by subject. In some databases, typographic features and even the pagination found in print versions may be altered or lost. Sometimes copyrighted third-party materials (illustrations or text) in a print version may have been eliminated because permission for the electronic publication could not be cleared. Web presentations of periodicals may include enhancements, such as hypertextual links, sound recordings, and film clips, that are not present in their print counterparts.

To cite a work from a periodical in an online database, such as an article, a review, an editorial, or a letter to the editor, begin the entry by following the recommendations in 6.5 for citing works in print periodicals, but drop the medium of original publication (*Print*). A periodical article on the Web may not include page numbers. If possible, give the inclusive page numbers or, when pagination is not continuous, the first page number and a plus sign; if pagination is not available, use *n. pag.* Conclude the entry with the following items:

1. Title of the database (italicized)
2. Medium of publication consulted (*Web*)
3. Date of access (day, month, and year)

If the guidelines you are following in 6.5 call for supplementary bibliographic information after the medium of publication, this information should be included immediately before item 1 above (see the Richardson entry). Here are examples of entries for periodical publications collected in online databases:

> Chan, Evans. "Postmodernism and Hong Kong Cinema." *Postmodern Culture* 10.3 (2000): n. pag. *Project Muse.* Web. 20 May 2002.
> Evangelista, Stefano. Rev. of *Victorian and Edwardian Responses to the Italian Renaissance*, ed. John E. Law and Lene

Østermark-Johansen. *Victorian Studies* 46.4 (2006): 729-31. *Academic Search Premier*. Web. 12 Mar. 2007.

France, Anatole. "Pour la Paix, pour la Liberté." *New Age* 5 Sept. 1907: 297-98. *The Modernist Journals Project*. Web. 12 Mar. 2007.

Lal, Ananda. Letter. *TDR* 51.3 (2007): 17-18. *Project Muse*. Web. 30 Nov. 2007.

Miller, Steven, and Sara Guyer, eds. *Literature and the Right to Marriage*. Spec. issue of *Diacritics* 35.4 (2005): 1-120. *Project Muse*. Web. 30 Nov. 2007.

Mowitt, John. "Fictions of Security: (Re)Reading the Political Thriller in the Era of Globalization." Diss. U of Minnesota, 2007. *DAI* 69.8 (2008): item AAT3279708. *ProQuest Dissertations and Theses*. Web. 22 Jan. 2008.

Richardson, Lynda. "Minority Students Languish in Special Education System." *New York Times* 6 Apr. 1994, late ed.: A1+. Pt. 1 of a series, A Class Apart: Special Education in New York City. *LexisNexis*. Web. 15 Aug. 2007.

Rosenberg, Mark. "Something Old, Something New. . . ." Editorial. *Canadian Journal on Aging / La revue canadienne du vieillissement* 26.2 (2007): 81. *Project Muse*. Web. 30 Nov. 2007.

Tolson, Nancy. "Making Books Available: The Role of Libraries, Librarians, and Booksellers in the Promotion of African American Children's Literature." *African American Review* 32.1 (1998): 9-16. *JSTOR*. Web. 1 Oct. 2002.

If you need to include a URL, follow the guidelines in 6.7.1.

6.8

CITING ADDITIONAL COMMON SOURCES

6.8.1   A TELEVISION OR RADIO BROADCAST

The information in an entry for a television or radio broadcast usually appears in the following order:

1. Title of the episode or segment, if appropriate (in quotation marks)
2. Title of the program or series (italicized)
3. Name of the network (if any)

4. Call letters and city of the local station (if any)
5. Broadcast date
6. Medium of reception (e.g., *Radio, Television*)
7. Supplementary information

For instance, among the examples below, "Frederick Douglass" is an episode of the program *Civil War Journal*. Use a comma between the call letters and the city and between the city and the broadcast date ("KETC, Saint Louis, 13 Jan. 2006"). A period follows each of the other items. For the inclusion of other information that may be pertinent (e.g., performers, director, narrator, number of episodes), see the sample entries. In general, information relating to a particular episode follows the title of the episode, while information pertinent to a series follows the title of the series.

> *Don Giovanni.* By Wolfgang Amadeus Mozart. Perf. James Morris, Bryn Terfel, and Carol Vaness. Cond. Yakov Kreizberg. Lyric Opera of Chicago. Nuveen-Lyric Opera of Chicago Radio Network. WFMT, Chicago, 8 June 1996. Radio.
>
> "Frederick Douglass." *Civil War Journal.* Narr. Danny Glover. Dir. Craig Haffner. Arts and Entertainment Network. 6 Apr. 1993. Television.
>
> "The Phantom of Corleone." Narr. Steve Kroft. *Sixty Minutes.* CBS. WCBS, New York, 10 Dec. 2006. Television.
>
> "Shakespearean Putdowns." Narr. Robert Siegel and Linda Wertheimer. *All Things Considered.* Natl. Public Radio. WNYC, New York, 6 Apr. 1994. Radio.

If your reference is primarily to the work of a particular individual, cite that person's name before the title.

> Wadey, Maggie, adapt. "The Buccaneers." By Edith Wharton. Perf. Mira Sorvino, Alison Elliott, and Carla Gugino. 3 episodes. *Masterpiece Theatre.* Introd. Russell Baker. PBS. WGBH, Boston, 27 Apr.-11 May 1997. Television.
>
> Welles, Orson, dir. "The War of the Worlds." By H. G. Wells. Adapt. Howard Koch. *Mercury Theatre on the Air.* CBS Radio. WCBS, New York, 30 Oct. 1938. Radio.

If you are citing a transcript of a program, list its medium of publication and add the description *Transcript* at the end of the entry.

"Shakespearean Putdowns." Narr. Robert Siegel and Linda Wertheimer. *All Things Considered.* Natl. Public Radio. WNYC, New York, 6 Apr. 1994. Print. Transcript.

See 6.8.7 for interviews on television and radio broadcasts; see also 6.7.2d for television and radio broadcasts on the Web, 6.8.2–3 for sound, film, and video recordings, 6.8.4 for performances, and 6.8.17 for television and radio programs on CD-ROM.

6.8.2   A SOUND RECORDING

In an entry for a commercially available recording, which person or group is cited first (e.g., the composer, conductor, ensemble, or performer) depends on the desired emphasis. List the title of the recording (or the titles of the works included), the artist or artists (when distinct from a first-listed person or group), the manufacturer (*Capitol*), and the year of issue (if the year is unknown, write *n.d.*). Indicate the medium, neither italicized nor enclosed in quotation marks, after the date of publication: *Audiocassette, Audiotape* (reel-to-reel tape), *CD* (compact disc), or *LP* (long-playing record). Place a comma between the manufacturer and the date; periods follow the other items.

In general, italicize titles of recordings (*Romances for Saxophone*). You may wish to indicate, in addition to the year of issue, the date of recording (see the entries for Ellington and Holiday).

de Larrocha, Alicia, perf. *Mozart Piano Concertos Nos. 19 and 27.* By Wolfgang Amadeus Mozart. English Chamber Orch. Cond. Colin Davis. Red Seal-RCA Victor, 1997. CD.

Ellington, Duke, cond. *First Carnegie Hall Concert.* Duke Ellington Orch. Rec. 23 Jan. 1943. Prestige, 1977. LP.

The Mamas and the Papas. *Gold.* Comp. Andy McKaie. Geffen, 2005. CD.

Marsalis, Branford. *Romances for Saxophone.* English Chamber Orch. Cond. Andrew Litton. CBS, 1986. Audiocassette.

Sondheim, Stephen. *Passion.* Orch. Jonathan Tunick. Perf. Donna Murphy, Jere Shea, and Marin Mazzie. Cond. Paul Gemignani. Angel, 1994. CD.

If you are citing a specific song, place its title in quotation marks.

Bartoli, Cecilia, perf. "Les filles de Cadix." By Pauline Viardot. *Chant d'amour.* London, 1996. CD.

> Camper Van Beethoven. "Ambiguity Song." *Telephone Free Landslide Victory*. Rough Trade, n.d. LP.
>
> Gabriel, Peter. "A Different Drum." Perf. Gabriel, Shankar, and Youssou N'Dour. *Passion: Music for* The Last Temptation of Christ, *a Film by Martin Scorsese*. Geffen, 1989. CD.
>
> Holiday, Billie, perf. "God Bless the Child." Rec. 9 May 1941. *The Essence of Billie Holiday*. Columbia, 1991. CD.

Treat a spoken-word recording as you would a musical recording. Begin with the speaker, the writer, or the production director, depending on the desired emphasis. If relevant, you may add the date of the work's original publication immediately after the title.

> Burnett, Frances Hodgson. *The Secret Garden*. 1911. Narr. Helena Bonham Carter. Penguin-High Bridge, 1993. Audiocassette.
>
> Shakespeare, William. *Othello*. Dir. John Dexter. Perf. Laurence Olivier, Maggie Smith, Frank Finley, and Derek Jacobi. RCA Victor, 1964. LP.
>
> Welles, Orson, dir. *The War of the Worlds*. By H. G. Wells. Adapt. Howard Koch. Rec. 30 Oct. 1938. Evolution, 1969. LP.
>
> Whitman, Walt. "America." *In Their Own Voices: A Century of Recorded Poetry*. Rhino, 1996. CD.

Do not italicize or enclose in quotation marks the title of a private or archival recording or tape. Include the date recorded (if known) and the location and identifying number of the recording.

> Wilgus, D. K. Southern Folk Tales. Rec. 23-25 Mar. 1965. Audiotape. Archives of Folklore, U of California, Los Angeles. B.76.82.

In citing the libretto, the booklet, the liner notes, or other material accompanying a recording, give the author's name, the title of the material (if any), and a description of the material (*Libretto*). Then provide the usual bibliographic information for a recording.

> Boyd, Malcolm. Booklet. *The Bach Album*. Deutsche Grammophon, 1992. CD.
>
> Colette. Libretto. *L'enfant et les sortilèges*. Music by Maurice Ravel. Orch. National Bordeaux-Aquitaine. Cond. Alain Lombard. Valois, 1993. CD.

Lewiston, David. Liner notes. *The Balinese Gamelan: Music from the Morning of the World*. Nonesuch, n.d. LP.

See 6.7.2d for sound recordings on the Web.

6.8.3   A FILM OR A VIDEO RECORDING

An entry for a film usually begins with the title, italicized, and includes the director, the distributor, the year of release, and the medium. You may include other data that seem pertinent—such as the names of the screenwriter, performers, and producer—between the title and the distributor. For films dubbed or subtitled in English, you may give the English title and follow it with the original title, italicized, in square brackets.

It's a Wonderful Life. Dir. Frank Capra. Perf. James Stewart, Donna Reed, Lionel Barrymore, and Thomas Mitchell. RKO, 1946. Film.

Like Water for Chocolate [Como agua para chocolate]. Screenplay by Laura Esquivel. Dir. Alfonso Arau. Perf. Lumi Cavazos, Marco Lombardi, and Regina Torne. Miramax, 1993. Film.

If you are citing the contribution of a particular individual, begin with that person's name.

Chaplin, Charles, dir. *Modern Times*. Perf. Chaplin and Paulette Goddard. United Artists, 1936. Film.

Jhabvala, Ruth Prawer, adapt. *A Room with a View*. By E. M. Forster. Dir. James Ivory. Prod. Ismail Merchant. Perf. Maggie Smith, Denholm Eliot, Helena Bonham Carter, and Daniel Day-Lewis. Cinecom Intl., 1985. Film.

Mifune, Toshiro, perf. *Rashomon*. Dir. Akira Kurosawa. Daiei, 1950. Film.

Rota, Nino, composer. *Juliet of the Spirits* [*Giulietta degli spiriti*]. Dir. Federico Fellini. Perf. Giulietta Masina. Rizzoli, 1965. Film.

Cite a DVD (digital videodisc), videocassette, laser disc, slide program, or filmstrip as you would a film. Include the original release date when it is relevant.

Don Carlo. By Giuseppe Verdi. Dir. Franco Zeffirelli. Perf. Luciano Pavarotti and Samuel Ramey. La Scala Orch. and Chorus. Cond. Riccardo Muti. EMI, 1994. Videocassette.

> *It's a Wonderful Life*. Dir. Frank Capra. Perf. James Stewart, Donna Reed, Lionel Barrymore, and Thomas Mitchell. 1946. Republic, 2001. DVD.
>
> *Looking at Our Earth: A Visual Dictionary*. Natl. Geographic Educ. Services, 1992. Sound filmstrip.
>
> Mifune, Toshiro, perf. *Rashomon*. Dir. Akira Kurosawa. 1950. Home Vision, 2001. Videocassette.
>
> Noujaim, Jehane, dir. *Control Room*. Lions Gate, 2004. DVD.
>
> Renoir, Jean, dir. *Grand Illusion* [*La grande illusion*]. Perf. Jean Gabin and Erich von Stroheim. 1938. Voyager, 1987. Laser disc.

For television broadcasts of films, adapt the guidelines in 6.8.1; for films or film clips on CD-ROM, see 6.8.17; for films or film clips on the Web, see 6.7.2d.

6.8.4   A PERFORMANCE

An entry for a performance (play, opera, dance, concert) usually begins with the title, contains facts similar to those given for a film (see 6.8.3), and concludes with the site of the performance (usually the theater and city, separated by a comma and followed by a period), the date of the performance, and (in the place where the medium of publication is usually recorded) an indication that you are citing a performance.

> *Hamlet*. By William Shakespeare. Dir. John Gielgud. Perf. Richard Burton. Shubert Theatre, Boston. 4 Mar. 1964. Performance.
>
> *Heartbreak House*. By George Bernard Shaw. Dir. Robin Lefevre. Perf. Philip Bosco and Swoosie Kurtz. Roundabout Theatre Company. Amer. Airlines Theatre, New York. 1 Oct. 2006. Performance.
>
> *The River*. Chor. Alvin Ailey. Dance Theater of Harlem. New York State Theater, New York. 15 Mar. 1994. Performance.
>
> *The Siege of Paris*. Marionettes of the Cooperativa Teatroarte Cuticchio. Sylvia and Danny Kaye Playhouse, New York. 22 Mar. 1997. Performance.
>
> *Les vêpres siciliennes*. By Giuseppe Verdi. Libretto by Eugène Scribe and Charles Duveyrier. Dir. Federico Tiezzi. Cond. John Nelson. Perf. Daniela Dessì, David Kuebler, and Ferruccio Furlanetto. Teatro dell'Opera, Rome. 17 Jan. 1997. Performance.

If you are citing the contribution of a particular individual or group, begin with the appropriate name.

> Ars Musica Antiqua, perf. *In Praise of Women: Music by Women
> Composers from the Twelfth through the Eighteenth Centuries.*
> Scotch Plains Public Lib., NJ. 5 Apr. 1994. Performance.
>
> Culkin, Kieran, perf. *Suburbia.* By Eric Bogosian. Second Stage Theatre,
> New York. 16 Sept. 2006. Performance.
>
> Freni, Mirella, perf. *Fedora.* By Umberto Giordano. Cond. Roberto
> Abbado. Metropolitan Opera. Metropolitan Opera House, New
> York. 26 Apr. 1997. Performance.
>
> Joplin, Scott. *Treemonisha.* Dir. Frank Corsaro. Perf. Carmen Balthrop,
> Betty Allen, and Curtis Rayam. Houston Grand Opera Orch. and
> Chorus. Cond. Gunther Schuller. Miller Theatre, Houston. 18 May
> 1975. Performance.

For television and radio broadcasts of performances, see 6.8.1; for sound recordings of performances, see 6.8.2; for films and video recordings of performances, see 6.8.3.

6.8.5   A MUSICAL SCORE

Treat a published score like a book. Begin with the composer's name, and then give the title, italicized, as it appears on the title page, capitalizing the abbreviations *no.* and *op.* Continue with the date of composition (if the year is unknown, write *N.d.*), the place of publication, the name of the publisher, the date of publication, and the medium of publication consulted. If the score is part of a series, include the information about the series after the medium of publication.

> Donizetti, Gaetano. *Don Pasquale: An Opera in Three Acts with
> Italian-English Text.* 1842. New York: Belwin, 1969. Print.
> Kalmus Vocal Scores.

See 6.7.2 for scores on the Web, 6.8.1 for television and radio broadcasts of music, 6.8.2 for sound recordings of musical compositions, 6.8.3 for films and video recordings of musical performances, and 6.8.4 for musical performances.

6.8.6   A WORK OF VISUAL ART

To cite a painting, lithograph, sculpture, or similar work, state the artist's name first when available. In general, italicize the title and then list the date of composition (if the year is unknown, write *N.d.*). Indicate the medium of composition. Name the institution that houses the work (e.g., a museum); for a work in a private collection, give the name of the collection (*Collection of...*) or, if the collector is unknown or wishes to be anonymous, *Private collection.*

> Bearden, Romare. *The Train*. 1974. Photogravure and aquatint. Museum of Mod. Art, New York.
>
> Heckman, Albert. *Windblown Trees*. N.d. Lithograph on paper. Private collection.
>
> Perutz, Dolly Hellman. *Bird Flying Machine*. 1973. Bronze. Central Park, New York.
>
> Rembrandt Harmensz van Rijn. *Aristotle with a Bust of Homer*. 1653. Oil on canvas. Metropolitan Museum of Art, New York.
>
> Seurat, Georges. *Man Leaning on a Fence*. 1880-81? Graphite on paper. Collection of André Bromberg.

Cite a photograph in a museum or collection as you would a painting or sculpture.

> Evans, Walker. *Penny Picture Display*. 1936. Photograph. Museum of Mod. Art, New York.

If you use a reproduction of a painting, sculpture, or photograph, state not only the institution or private owner and the city (if available) but also the complete publication information for the source in which the reproduction appears, including the page, slide, figure, or plate number, whichever is relevant. Indicate the medium of reproduction.

> Eakins, Thomas. *Spinning*. 1881. Private collection. *Thomas Eakins*. Ed. Darrel Sewell. Philadelphia: Philadelphia Museum of Art in assn. with Yale UP, 2001. Plate 91. Print.
>
> Moholy-Nagy, Lászlò. *Photogram*. N.d. Museum of Mod. Art, New York. *The Contest of Meaning: Critical Histories of Photography*. Ed. Richard Bolton. Cambridge: MIT P, 1989. 94. Print.

See 6.7.2d for works of visual art on the Web; see 6.8.17 for works of visual art on CD-ROM.

6.8.7   AN INTERVIEW

For purposes of documentation, there are two kinds of interviews: those published or broadcast and those conducted by the researcher. Begin with the name of the person interviewed. If the interview is part of a publication, recording, or program, enclose the title of the interview, if any, in quotation marks; if the interview was published independently, italicize the title. If the interview is untitled, use the descriptive label *Interview*, neither italicized nor enclosed in quotation marks. The interviewer's name may be added if known and pertinent to your work (see the sample entries for Blackmun and Updike). Conclude with the appropriate bibliographic information and the medium of publication.

> Blackmun, Harry. Interview by Ted Koppel and Nina Totenberg.
>   *Nightline*. ABC. WABC, New York. 5 Apr. 1994. Television.
> Blanchett, Cate. "In Character with: Cate Blanchett." *Notes on a*
>   *Scandal*. Dir. Richard Eyre. Fox Searchlight, 2006. DVD.
> Fellini, Federico. "The Long Interview." *Juliet of the Spirits*. Ed. Tullio
>   Kezich. Trans. Howard Greenfield. New York: Ballantine, 1966.
>   17-64. Print.
> Gordimer, Nadine. Interview. *New York Times* 10 Oct. 1991, late ed.:
>   C25. Print.
> Lansbury, Angela. Interview. *Off-Camera: Conversations with the*
>   *Makers of Prime-Time Television*. By Richard Levinson and
>   William Link. New York: Plume-NAL, 1986. 72-86. Print.
> Updike, John. Interview by Scott Simon. *Weekend Edition*. Natl.
>   Public Radio. WBUR, Boston. 2 Apr. 1994. Radio.

To cite an interview that you conducted, give the name of the person interviewed, the kind of interview (*Personal interview, Telephone interview*), and the date.

> Pei, I. M. Personal interview. 22 July 1993.
> Reed, Ishmael. Telephone interview. 10 Dec. 2007.

See 6.7.2b for interviews on the Web.

6.8.8   A MAP OR CHART

In general, treat a map or chart like an article or a book, but add the appropriate descriptive label (*Map, Chart*).

> *Japanese Fundamentals*. Chart. Hauppauge: Barron, 1992. Print.
>
> *Michigan*. Map. Chicago: Rand, 2000. Print.
>
> "Western Boundaries of Brazil, 1600, 1780, and the Present." Map. *Brazilian Narrative Traditions in a Comparative Context*. By Earl E. Fitz. New York: MLA, 2005. 43. Print.

See 6.7.2b for maps and charts on the Web.

6.8.9   A CARTOON OR COMIC STRIP

To cite a cartoon or comic strip, state the artist's name; the title of the cartoon or comic strip (if any), in quotation marks; and the descriptive label *Cartoon* or *Comic Strip*, neither italicized nor enclosed in quotation marks. Conclude with the usual publication information and the medium of publication.

> Chast, Roz. Cartoon. *New Yorker* 4 Feb. 2002: 53. Print.
>
> Trudeau, Garry. "Doonesbury." Comic strip. *Star-Ledger* [Newark] 4 May 2002: 26. Print.

See 6.6.12 for graphic narratives.

6.8.10   AN ADVERTISEMENT

To cite an advertisement, state the name of the product, company, or institution that is the subject of the advertisement, followed by the descriptive label *Advertisement*, neither italicized nor enclosed in quotation marks. Conclude with the usual publication information and the medium of publication.

> Air Canada. Advertisement. CNN. 1 Apr. 1997. Television.
>
> Baccarat. Advertisement. *New York* Nov. 2007: 4. Print.

6.8.11   A LECTURE, A SPEECH, AN ADDRESS, OR A READING

In a citation of an oral presentation, give the speaker's name; the title of the presentation (if known), in quotation marks; the meeting and the sponsoring organization (if applicable); the location; and the date. Use an appropriate descriptive label (*Address, Lecture, Keynote speech, Reading*), neither italicized nor enclosed in quotation marks, to indicate the form of delivery.

> Alter, Robert, and Marilynne Robinson. "The Psalms: A Reading and
> Conversation." 92nd Street Y, New York. 17 Dec. 2007. Reading.
> Matuozzi, Robert. "Archive Trauma." Archive Trouble. MLA Annual
> Convention. Hyatt Regency, Chicago. 29 Dec. 2007. Address.
> Terkel, Studs. Conf. on Coll. Composition and Communication
> Convention. Palmer House, Chicago. 22 Mar. 1990. Address.

6.8.12   A MANUSCRIPT OR TYPESCRIPT

To cite a manuscript or typescript, state the author, the title or a description of the material (e.g., *Notebook*), the date of composition (at least the year; if the year is unknown, write *N.d.*), and the form of the material (*MS* for a manuscript, *TS* for a typescript). As appropriate, give the name and location of the library, research institution, or personal collection housing the material.

> Chaucer, Geoffrey. *The Canterbury Tales*. 1400-10. MS Harley 7334.
> British Lib., London.
> Dickinson, Emily. "Distance Is Not the Realm of Fox." 1870? MS.
> Pierpont Morgan Lib., New York.
> Henderson, George Wylie. *Baby Lou and the Angel Bud*. N.d. TS.
> Collection of Roslyn Kirkland Allen, New York.
> Jones, Celia. "Shakespeare's Dark Lady Illuminated." 1988. TS.

See 6.7.2d for manuscripts and typescripts on the Web.

6.8.13   A LETTER, A MEMO, OR AN E-MAIL MESSAGE

As bibliographic entries, letters fall into three general categories:

- Published letters
- Unpublished letters in archives
- Letters received by the researcher

Treat a published letter like a work in a collection (see 6.6.6), adding the date of the letter and the number (if the editor assigned one).

> Woolf, Virginia. "To T. S. Eliot." 28 July 1920. Letter 1138 of *The*
> *Letters of Virginia Woolf*. Ed. Nigel Nicolson and Joanne
> Trautmann. Vol. 2. New York: Harcourt, 1976. 437-38. Print.

If you use more than one letter in a published collection, however, provide a single entry for the entire work and cite the letters individually in the text, following the form recommended for cross-references in works-cited lists (see 6.4.6).

In citing an unpublished letter, follow the guidelines for manuscripts and typescripts (see 6.8.12).

> Benton, Thomas Hart. Letter to Charles Fremont. 22 June 1847. MS.
> John Charles Fremont Papers. Southwest Museum Lib., Los Angeles.

Cite a letter that you received as follows:

> Sorby, Angela. Letter to the author. 20 July 2003. MS.

Treat memos similarly: give the name of the writer of the memo, a description of the memo that includes the recipient, the date of the document, and the medium of delivery. Any title of the memo should be enclosed in quotation marks and placed immediately after the writer's name.

> Cahill, Daniel J. Memo to English dept. fac., Brooklyn Technical High
> School, New York. 1 June 2000. TS.

To cite e-mail, give the name of the writer; the title of the message (if any), taken from the subject line and enclosed in quotation marks; a description of the message that includes the recipient (e.g., *Message to the author*); the date of the message; and the medium of delivery.

> Boyle, Anthony T. "Re: Utopia." Message to Daniel J. Cahill. 21 June
> 1997. E-mail.
> Harner, James L. Message to the author. 20 Aug. 2002. E-mail.

6.8.14   A LEGAL SOURCE

The citation of legal documents and law cases may be complicated. If your work requires many such references, consult the most recent edition of *The Bluebook: A Uniform System of Citation* (Cambridge: Harvard Law Rev. Assn.; print), an indispensable guide in this field. *The*

Bluebook uses footnotes instead of parenthetical references keyed to a list of works cited, however, so its recommendations must be adapted to MLA style.

In general, do not italicize or enclose in quotation marks the titles of laws, acts, and similar documents in either the text or the list of works cited (Declaration of Independence, Constitution of the United States, Taft-Hartley Act). Such titles are usually abbreviated, and the works are cited by sections. The years are added if relevant. Although lawyers and legal scholars adopt many abbreviations in their citations, use only familiar abbreviations when writing for a more general audience (see ch. 8). References to the United States Code, which is often abbreviated *USC*, begin with the title number.

> 17 USC. Sec. 304. 2000. Print.

In the above entry, title 17 refers to laws concerned with copyrights. Alphabetize a USC entry as if it began *United States Code*. When including more than one reference to the code, list the entries in numerical order by title and, within titles, by section.

If you are citing an act in the works-cited list, state the name of the act, its Public Law number, its Statutes at Large volume number and inclusive page numbers, the date it was enacted, and its medium of publication. Use the abbreviations *Pub. L.* for Public Law and *Stat.* for Statutes at Large.

> Aviation and Transportation Security Act. Pub. L. 107-71. 115 Stat.
> 597-647. 19 Nov. 2001. Print.

Names of law cases are similarly abbreviated ("Brown v. Board of Educ.," for the case of Oliver Brown versus the Board of Education of Topeka, Kansas), but the first important word of each party's name is always spelled out. Names of cases, unlike those of laws, are italicized in the text but not in bibliographic entries. When you cite a case, include, in addition to the names of the first plaintiff and the first defendant, the volume, name (not italicized), and inclusive page or reference numbers of the law report cited; the name of the court that decided the case; the year of the decision; and appropriate publication information for the medium consulted. Once again, considerable abbreviation is the norm.

> Brown v. Board of Educ. 347 US 483-96. Supreme Court of the US.
> 1954. *Supreme Court Collection*. Legal Information Inst., Cornell
> U Law School, n.d. Web. 3 Aug. 2007.

It is common in legal scholarship to refer to a case by the first non-governmental party. Thus, for a case named *NLRB v. Yeshiva University*, scholars are likely to use *Yeshiva* as a short title. But in MLA style readers need the first part of the name (*NLRB*) to locate the full citation in the list of works cited. You should bear this in mind when formulating parenthetical references to legal sources.

To cite a government document, see 6.6.20.

6.8.15   AN ARTICLE IN A MICROFORM COLLECTION OF ARTICLES

If you are citing an article that was provided by a reference source such as NewsBank, which formerly selected periodical articles and made them available on microfiche, begin the entry with the original publication information, followed by the medium of publication. Then add the relevant information concerning the microform from which you derived the article—title of source (italicized), volume number, year (in parentheses), and appropriate identifying numbers ("fiche 42, grids 5–6").

> Chapman, Dan. "Panel Could Help Protect Children." *Winston-Salem*
> *Journal* 14 Jan. 1990: 14. Microform. *NewsBank: Welfare and*
> *Social Problems* 12 (1990): fiche 1, grids A8-11.

6.8.16   AN ARTICLE REPRINTED IN A LOOSE-LEAF
COLLECTION OF ARTICLES

If you are citing a reprinted article that was provided by an information service such as the Social Issues Resources Series (SIRS), which formerly selected articles from periodicals and published them in loose-leaf volumes, each dedicated to a specific topic, begin the entry with the original publication information, followed by the medium of publication. Then add the relevant information for the loose-leaf volume in which the article is reprinted, treating the volume like a book (see 6.6)—title (italicized), name of editor (if any), volume number (if any), city of publication, publisher, year of publication, and article number (preceded by the abbreviation *Art.*).

> Edmondson, Brad. "AIDS and Aging." *American Demographics* Mar.
> 1990: 28+. Print. *The AIDS Crisis*. Ed. Eleanor Goldstein. Vol. 2.
> Boca Raton: SIRS, 1991. Art. 24.

See 6.7.3–4 for articles on the Web.

6.8.17   A PUBLICATION ON CD-ROM OR DVD-ROM

Citations for publications on CD-ROM and DVD-ROM are similar to those for print sources, with the following important differences.

Vendor's Name. The persons or groups responsible for supplying the information in publications on CD-ROM and DVD-ROM are sometimes also the publishers of the works. But many information providers choose instead to lease the data to vendors (e.g., ProQuest) for distribution. It is important to state the vendor's name in your works-cited list, if it is given in your source, because the information provider may have leased versions of the data to more than one vendor and the versions may not be identical. Usually the vendor's name is recorded in the part of the entry reserved for supplementary information.

Publication Dates. Some databases published on CD-ROM or DVD-ROM are updated regularly (e.g., annually, quarterly). Updates add information and may also correct or otherwise alter information that previously appeared in the database. Therefore, a works-cited-list entry for material derived from such a database commonly contains the publication date of the document, as indicated in the source, as well as the publication date of the database (or the date of its most recent update [see 6.8.17b]).

The sections below contain recommendations for citing nonperiodical publications on CD-ROM or DVD-ROM (6.8.17a), materials from periodically published databases on CD-ROM or DVD-ROM (6.8.17b), and multidisc publications (6.8.17c).

a. A Nonperiodical Publication on CD-ROM or DVD-ROM

Many publications on CD-ROM or DVD-ROM are issued as books are — that is, without a plan to update or otherwise revise the work regularly. Cite a nonperiodical publication on CD-ROM or DVD-ROM as you would a book, but add a description of the medium of publication. When the information provider and the publisher are the same, no vendor's name appears, and only one publication date is given. The typical works-cited-list entry for the source consists of the following items:

1. Author's name (if given). If only an editor, a compiler, or a translator is identified, cite that person's name, followed by the appropriate abbreviation (*ed., comp., trans.*).

2. Title of the publication (italicized)
3. Name of the editor, compiler, or translator (if relevant)
4. Edition, release, or version (if relevant)
5. Place of publication
6. Name of the publisher
7. Date of publication
8. Medium of publication consulted
9. Supplementary information

If you cannot find some of this information, cite what is available.

> *Le Robert électronique.* Paris: Robert, 1992. CD-ROM.
>
> Shakespeare, William. *Macbeth.* Ed. A. R. Braunmuller. New York:
>   Voyager, 1994. CD-ROM.

If publication information for a printed source or printed analogue is indicated, begin the citation with that information. Give the publication data for the CD-ROM or DVD-ROM following the record of the medium of publication.

> Aristotle. *The Complete Works of Aristotle: The Revised Oxford*
>   *Translation.* Ed. Jonathan Barnes. 2 vols. Princeton: Princeton
>   UP, 1984. CD-ROM. Clayton: InteLex, 1994.

If the work you are citing is part of another work, state which part. If the work is of a type likely to be published on its own, such as a book, italicize the title; if not, enclose the title in quotation marks. If the source supplies page numbers, paragraph numbers, screen numbers, or some other kind of section numbers, state the range of the numbers in the part if a single numbering encompasses all the parts.

> "Albatross." *The Oxford English Dictionary.* 2nd ed. Oxford: Oxford
>   UP, 1992. CD-ROM.
>
> Coleridge, Samuel Taylor. "Dejection: An Ode." *The Complete Poetical*
>   *Works of Samuel Taylor Coleridge.* Ed. Ernest Hartley Coleridge.
>   Vol. 1. Oxford: Clarendon, 1912. 362-68. CD-ROM. *English Poetry*
>   *Full-Text Database.* Rel. 2. Cambridge: Chadwyck-Healey, 1993.
>
> "Parque." *Le Robert électronique.* Paris: Robert, 1992. CD-ROM.
>
> Rodes, David S. "The Language of Ambiguity and Equivocation."
>   *Macbeth.* By William Shakespeare. Ed. A. R. Braunmuller. New
>   York: Voyager, 1994. CD-ROM.

b. Material from a Periodically Published Database on CD-ROM or DVD-ROM

Some periodicals (journals, magazines, newspapers) and periodically published reference works, such as annual bibliographies and collections of abstracts, are published both in print and on CD-ROM or DVD-ROM as databases or as parts of databases. To cite such a work, begin with the publication data for the printed source or printed analogue, as identified in the disc publication. If the print version is a book or a pamphlet (see the entry for *Guidelines for Family Television Viewing*), follow the guidelines in 6.6; if the print version is an article in a periodical, follow 6.5. The typical works-cited-list entry consists of the following items:

1. Author's name (if given)
2. Publication information for the printed source or printed analogue (including title and date of print publication)
3. Medium of publication consulted
4. Title of the database (italicized)
5. Name of the vendor
6. Publication date of the database

If you cannot find some of this information, cite what is available.

> Brady, Philip. "Teaching Tu Fu on the Night Shift." *College English*
>   57.5 (1995): 562-69. Abstract. CD-ROM. *ERIC*. SilverPlatter. Sept.
>   1996.
>
> Coates, Steve. "Et Tu, Cybernetica Machina User?" *New York Times*
>   28 Oct. 1996, late ed.: D4. CD-ROM. *New York Times Ondisc*.
>   UMI-ProQuest. Dec. 1996.
>
> *Guidelines for Family Television Viewing*. Urbana: ERIC
>   Clearinghouse on Elementary and Early Childhood Educ., 1990.
>   CD-ROM. *ERIC*. SilverPlatter. June 1993.
>
> Rodríguez, Miguel Angel. "Teatro de los Puppets: Diversión y
>   educación." *Opinión* 6 Sept. 1993: 1D. CD-ROM. *Ethnic Newswatch*.
>   Dataware Technologies. 1995.
>
> Russo, Michelle Cash. "Recovering from Bibliographic Instruction
>   Blahs." *RQ: Reference Quarterly* 32 (1992): 178-83. CD-ROM.
>   *Infotrac: Magazine Index Plus*. Information Access. Dec. 1993.
>
> Stephenson, Denise R. "Blurred Distinctions: Emerging Forms of
>   Academic Writing." Diss. U of New Mexico, 1996. *DAI* 57.4 (1996):

item DA9626438. CD-ROM. *Dissertation Abstracts Ondisc.* UMI-
ProQuest. Dec. 1996.

United States. Cong. House. Committee on the Judiciary. *Report on
the Fair Use of Copyrighted Works.* 102nd Cong., 1st sess.
CD-ROM. *Congressional Masterfile 2.* Congressional Information
Service. Dec. 1996.

c. A Multidisc Publication

If you are citing a CD-ROM or DVD-ROM publication of more than
one disc, complete the entry either with the total number of discs or
with a specific disc number if you use material from only one.

The Complete New Yorker. New York: New Yorker, 2005. DVD-ROM.
8 discs.

United States. Dept. of State. *Patterns of Global Terrorism.* 1994.
CD-ROM. *National Trade Data Bank.* US Dept. of Commerce. Dec.
1996. Disc 2.

6.8.18   A DIGITAL FILE

Digital files can exist independently from the Web or a published disc.
Examples are a PDF file stored on your computer, a document created
by a colleague using a word processor, a scanned image you received as
an e-mail attachment, and a sound recording formatted for playing on
a digital audio player. In general, determine the kind of work you are
citing (e.g., a book, a manuscript, a photograph, a sound recording),
and follow the relevant guidelines in this manual for formatting the entry in the works-cited list. In the place reserved for the medium of publication, record the digital file format, followed by the word *file* — *PDF
file*, Microsoft Word *file*, *JPEG file*, *MP3 file*, *XML file*, and so on — neither
italicized (except for titles of software programs) nor enclosed in quotation marks. The file type is usually indicated by the extension at the
end of the file name, after a period: OurCulturalCommonwealth.pdf.
If you cannot identify the file type, use *Digital file.*

American Council of Learned Societies. Commission on
Cyberinfrastructure for the Humanities and Social Sciences. *Our
Cultural Commonwealth.* New York: ACLS, 2006. PDF file.

Cortez, Juan. "Border Crossing in Chicano Narrative." 2007. *Microsoft Word* file.

Delano, Jack. *At the Vermont State Fair.* 1941. Lib. of Cong., Washington. JPEG file.

Hudson, Jennifer, perf. "And I Am Telling You I'm Not Going." *Dreamgirls: Music from the Motion Picture.* Sony BMG, 2006. MP3 file.

Your research may require that you cite more facts about the file, such as its date or name. For example, you may encounter multiple versions of a document with the same author and title, such as a sequence of drafts an author made in developing a work. Record such facts in the place reserved for the version or edition of a work.

Cortez, Juan. "Border Crossing in Chicano Narrative." File last modified on 4 Apr. 2007. *Microsoft Word* file.

6.9

A WORK IN MORE THAN ONE PUBLICATION MEDIUM

If a work you used is published in more than one medium (e.g., a book with a CD-ROM), follow the format for the medium of the component you primarily consulted. In the place for the medium of publication, specify alphabetically all the media you consulted.

Bauman, H-Dirksen L., Jennifer L. Nelson, and Heidi M. Rose, eds. *Signing the Body Poetic: Essays on American Sign Language Literature.* Berkeley: U of California P, 2006. DVD, print.

Burnard, Lou, Katherine O'Brien O'Keeffe, and John Unsworth, eds. *Electronic Textual Editing.* New York: MLA, 2006. CD-ROM, print.

Or, if you consulted only one part:

Rahtz, Sebastian. "Storage, Retrieval, and Rendering." *Electronic Textual Editing.* Ed. Lou Burnard, Katherine O'Brien O'Keeffe, and John Unsworth. New York: MLA, 2006. 310-33. Print.

7

DOCUMENTATION: CITING SOURCES IN THE TEXT

7.1

PARENTHETICAL DOCUMENTATION AND THE LIST OF WORKS CITED

While the list of works cited plays an important role in the acknowledgment of sources (see ch. 6), it does not in itself provide sufficiently detailed and precise documentation. You must indicate to your readers not only what works you used but also what material you derived from each source and where in the work you found the material. The most practical way to supply this information is to insert a brief parenthetical acknowledgment in your writing wherever you incorporate another's words, facts, or ideas. Usually the author's last name and a page or other numbered reference are enough to identify the source and the specific location from which you borrowed material.

> Medieval Europe was a place both of "raids, pillages, slavery, and extortion" and of "traveling merchants, monetary exchange, towns if not cities, and active markets in grain" (Townsend 10).

The parenthetical reference "(Townsend 10)" indicates that the quotations come from page 10 of a work by Townsend. Given the author's last name, your readers can find complete publication information for the source in the alphabetically arranged list of works cited that follows the text of your work.

> Townsend, Robert M. *The Medieval Village Economy*. Princeton: Princeton UP, 1993. Print.

The sample references in 7.4 offer recommendations for documenting many other kinds of sources.

7.2
INFORMATION REQUIRED IN
PARENTHETICAL DOCUMENTATION

In determining the information needed to document sources accurately, keep the following guidelines in mind.

References in the text must clearly point to specific sources in the list of works cited. The information in your parenthetical references in the text must match the corresponding information in the entries in your list of works cited. For a typical works-cited-list entry, which begins with the name of the author (or editor, translator, or compiler), the parenthetical reference begins with the same name. When the list contains only one work by the author cited, you need give only the author's last name to identify the work: "(Patterson 183–85)." If your list contains more than one author with the same last name, you must add the first initial—"(A. Patterson 183–85)" and "(L. Patterson 230)"—or, if the initial is shared too, the full first name. If two or three names begin the entry, give the last name of each person listed: "(Rabkin, Greenberg, and Olander vii)." If the work has more than three authors, follow the form in the bibliographic entry: either give the first author's last name followed by *et al.*, without any intervening punctuation—"(Lauter et al. 2601–09)"—or give all the last names. If there is a corporate author, use its name, shortened or in full (see 7.4.5). If the work is listed by title, use the title, shortened or in full (see 7.4.4). If the list contains more than one work by the author, add the cited title, shortened or in full, after the author's last name (see 7.4.6).

Identify the location of the borrowed information as specifically as possible. Sources include a variety of reference markers to help users locate passages. For sources that use page numbering, give the relevant page number or numbers in the parenthetical reference (see esp. 7.4.2) or, if you cite from more than one volume of a multivolume work, the volume and page numbers (see 7.4.3). In a reference to a common work of literature, it is sometimes helpful to give information other than, or in addition to, the page number—for example, the chapter, book, or stanza number or the numbers of the act, scene, and line (see 7.4.8). You may omit page numbers when citing complete works (see 7.4.1). A page reference is similarly unnecessary if you use a passage from a one-page work. Electronic publications sometimes include paragraph numbers or other kinds of reference numbers (see 7.4.2). Of course, sources such as films, television broadcasts, performances, and electronic sources with no pagination or other type of reference markers cannot be cited by number. Such works are usually cited in their entirety (see 7.4.1) and often by title (see 7.4.4).

7.3
READABILITY

Keep parenthetical references as brief—and as few—as clarity and accuracy permit. Give only the information needed to identify a source, and do not add a parenthetical reference unnecessarily. Identify sources by author and, if necessary, title; do not use abbreviations such as *ed.*, *trans.*, and *comp.* after the name. If you are citing an entire work, for example, rather than a specific part of it, the author's name in the text may be the only documentation required. The statement "Booth has devoted an entire book to the subject" needs no parenthetical documentation if the list of works cited includes only one work by Booth. If, for the reader's convenience, you wish to name the book in your text, you can recast the sentence: "Booth has devoted an entire book, *The Rhetoric of Fiction*, to the subject."

Remember that there is a direct relation between what you integrate into your text and what you place in parentheses. If, for example, you include an author's name in a sentence, you need not repeat the name in the parenthetical page citation that follows, provided that the reference is clearly to the work of the author you mention. The paired sentences below illustrate alternative ways of identifying authors. Note that sometimes one version is more concise than the other.

AUTHOR'S NAME IN TEXT

Tannen has argued this point (178-85).

AUTHOR'S NAME IN REFERENCE

This point has already been argued (Tannen 178-85).

AUTHORS' NAMES IN TEXT

Others, like Jakobson and Waugh (210-15), hold the opposite point of view.

AUTHORS' NAMES IN REFERENCE

Others hold the opposite point of view (e.g., Jakobson and Waugh 210-15).

AUTHOR'S NAME IN TEXT

Only Daiches has seen this relation (2: 776-77).

AUTHOR'S NAME IN REFERENCE

Only one scholar has seen this relation (Daiches 2: 776-77).

AUTHOR'S NAME IN TEXT

It may be true, as Robertson maintains, that "in the appreciation of medieval art the attitude of the observer is of primary importance . . ." (136).

AUTHOR'S NAME IN REFERENCE

It may be true that "in the appreciation of medieval art the attitude of the observer is of primary importance . . ." (Robertson 136).

To avoid interrupting the flow of your writing, place the parenthetical reference where a pause would naturally occur (preferably at the end of a sentence), as near as possible to the material documented. The parenthetical reference precedes the punctuation mark that concludes the sentence, clause, or phrase containing the borrowed material.

> In his *Autobiography*, Benjamin Franklin states that he prepared a list of thirteen virtues (135-37).

A reference directly after a quotation follows the closing quotation mark.

> In the late Renaissance, Machiavelli contended that human beings were by nature "ungrateful" and "mutable" (1240), and Montaigne thought them "miserable and puny" (1343).

If the quotation, whether of poetry or prose, is set off from the text (see 3.9.2–4), type a space after the concluding punctuation mark of the quotation and insert the parenthetical reference.

> John K. Mahon adds a further insight to our understanding of the War of 1812:
>
>> Financing the war was very difficult at the time. Baring Brothers, a banking firm of the enemy country, handled routine accounts for the United States overseas, but the firm would take on no loans. The loans were in the end absorbed by wealthy Americans at great hazard—also, as it turned out, at great profit to them. (385)

> Elizabeth Bishop's "In the Waiting Room" is rich in evocative detail:
>
>> It was winter. It got dark
>> early. The waiting room
>> was full of grown-up people,
>> arctics and overcoats,
>> lamps and magazines. (6-10)

For guidelines on citing common works of literature, see 7.4.8. If you need to document several sources for a statement, you may cite them in a note to avoid unduly disrupting the text (see 7.5).

When you borrow from a source several times in succession, you may be able to make your citations more concise by using one of the following techniques. Always give your citations in full, however, if these techniques would create ambiguity about your sources.

If you quote more than once from the same source within a single paragraph and no quotation from another source intervenes, you may give a single parenthetical reference after the last quotation.

> *Romeo and Juliet* presents an opposition between two worlds: "the world of the everyday . . . and the world of romance." Although the two lovers are part of the world of romance, their language of love nevertheless becomes "fully responsive to the tang of actuality" (Zender 138, 141).

Here it is clear that the first page number in the parenthesis must apply to the first quotation and the second number to the second quotation.

But suppose you decide to break the first quotation into two parts. Then the parenthetical citation will be ambiguous, because three quotations will be followed by two numbers. It will not be clear how the page numbers should be matched to the borrowings. In that case, the citations should be separated. You can use another technique for making citations more economical — not repeating what is understood.

> *Romeo and Juliet* presents an opposition between two worlds: "the world of the everyday," associated with the adults in the play, and "the world of romance," associated with the two lovers (Zender 138). Romeo and Juliet's language of love nevertheless becomes "fully responsive to the tang of actuality" (141).

The second parenthetical citation, "(141)," omits the author's name. This omission is acceptable because the reader will conclude that the author must be Zender. No other understanding is possible. If you include material from a different source between the two borrowings, however, you must repeat this author's name in the second citation: "(Zender 141)."

A third technique is to define a source in the text at the start.

> According to Karl F. Zender, *Romeo and Juliet* presents an opposition between two worlds: "the world of the everyday," associated with the adults in the play, and "the world of romance," associated with the two lovers (138). Romeo and Juliet's language of love nevertheless becomes "fully responsive to the tang of actuality" (141).

This technique can be useful when an entire paragraph is based on material from a single source. When a source is stated in this way and followed by a sequence of borrowings, it is important to signal at the end of the borrowings that you are switching to another source or to your own ideas. For example:

> According to Karl F. Zender, *Romeo and Juliet* presents an opposition between two worlds: "the world of the everyday," associated with the adults in the play, and "the world of romance," associated with the two lovers (138). Romeo and Juliet's language of love nevertheless becomes "fully responsive to the tang of actuality" (141). I believe, in addition, that . . .

> Work Cited
>
> Zender, Karl F. "Loving Shakespeare's Lovers: Character Growth in *Romeo and Juliet*." *Approaches to Teaching Shakespeare's* Romeo and Juliet. Ed. Maurice Hunt. New York: MLA, 2000. 137-43. Print.

7.4
SAMPLE REFERENCES

Each of the following sections concludes with a list of the works cited in the examples. Note that the lists for the first five sections (7.4.1–5) do not include more than one work by the same author. On citing two or more works by an author, see 7.4.6.

7.4.1   CITING AN ENTIRE WORK, INCLUDING
A WORK WITH NO PAGE NUMBERS

If you wish to cite an entire work, it is often preferable to include in the text, rather than in a parenthetical reference, the name of the person (e.g., author, editor, director, performer) that begins the corresponding entry in the works-cited list. (See 7.4.4 for citing a work by title.)

> But Anthony Hunt has offered another view.

> Gilbert and Gubar broke new ground on the subject.

> The utilitarianism of the Victorians "attempted to reduce decision-making about human actions to a 'felicific calculus'" (Everett).

Chan considers the same topic in the context of Hong Kong cinema.

Kurosawa's *Rashomon* was one of the first Japanese films to attract a Western audience.

Diana Rigg gave a memorable interpretation of Medea.

Margaret Atwood's remarks drew an enthusiastic response.

Michael Joyce was among the first to write fiction in hypertext.

Works Cited

Atwood, Margaret. "Silencing the Scream." Boundaries of the Imagination Forum. MLA Annual Convention. Royal York Hotel, Toronto. 29 Dec. 1993. Address.

Chan, Evans. "Postmodernism and Hong Kong Cinema." *Postmodern Culture* 10.3 (2000): n. pag. *Project Muse*. Web. 20 May 2002.

Everett, Glenn. "Utilitarianism." *The Victorian Web*. Ed. George P. Landow. U Scholars Programme, Natl. U of Singapore, 11 Oct. 2002. Web. 18 May 2007.

Gilbert, Sandra M., and Susan Gubar. *The Madwoman in the Attic: The Woman Writer and the Nineteenth-Century Literary Imagination*. New Haven: Yale UP, 1979. Print.

Hunt, Anthony. "Singing the Dyads: The Chinese Landscape Scroll and Gary Snyder's *Mountains and Rivers without End*." *Journal of Modern Literature* 23.1 (1999): 7-34. Print.

Joyce, Michael. *Afternoon: A Story*. 1987. Watertown: Eastgate, 1999. CD-ROM.

Kurosawa, Akira, dir. *Rashomon*. Perf. Toshiro Mifune. Daiei, 1950. Film.

Rigg, Diana, perf. *Medea*. By Euripides. Trans. Alistair Elliot. Dir. Jonathan Kent. Longacre Theatre, New York. 7 Apr. 1994. Performance.

7.4.2   CITING PART OF A WORK

If you quote, paraphrase, or otherwise use a specific passage in a book, an article, or another work, give the relevant page or section (e.g., paragraph) number or numbers. When the author's name is in your text, give only the number reference in parentheses, but if the context does not clearly identify the author, add the author's last name before the reference. Leave a space between them, but do not insert punctuation or, for a page reference, the word *page* or *pages* or the abbreviation *p.* or *pp.* If you used only one volume of a multivolume work and included the volume number in the bibliographic entry, you need give only page numbers in the reference (see the Lauter et al. example), but if you used more than one volume of the work, you must cite both volume and page numbers (see 7.4.3).

If your source uses explicit paragraph numbers rather than page numbers—as, for example, some electronic publications do—give the relevant number or numbers preceded by the abbreviation *par.* or *pars.*; if the author's name begins such a citation, place a comma after the name. If another kind of section is numbered in the source (e.g., sections), either write out the word for the section or use a standard abbreviation (see ch. 8); if the author's name begins such a citation, place a comma after the name. When a source has no page numbers or any other kind of reference numbers, no number can be given in the parenthetical reference. The work must be cited in its entirety (see 7.4.1), though you may indicate in your text an approximate location of the cited passage (e.g., "in the final third of his article, Jones argues for a revisionist interpretation"). Do not count unnumbered paragraphs.

> The cluster on literacy in the anthology by Lauter and his coeditors is a resource for teaching the place of oral cultures in postbellum America (155-66).

> Winters's mumbling performs a "labor of disarticulation" (Litvak 167).

> Although writings describing utopia have always seemed to take place far from the everyday world, in fact "all utopian fiction whirls contemporary actors through a costume dance no place else but here" (Rabkin, Greenberg, and Olander vii).

> "The study of comparative literature," Bill Readings wrote, "takes off from the idea of humanity" (6).

> The Committee on Scholarly Editions provides an annotated bibliography on the theory of textual editing (sec. 4).

Works Cited

Committee on Scholarly Editions. "Guidelines for Editors of Scholarly Editions." *Modern Language Association.* MLA, 25 Sept. 2007. Web. 22 Jan. 2008.

Lauter, Paul, et al., eds. *The Heath Anthology of American Literature.*
5th ed. Vol. C. Boston: Houghton, 2006. Print.

Litvak, Joseph. "The Aesthetics of Jewishness: Shelley Winters."
Aesthetic Subjects. Ed. Pamela R. Matthews and David McWhirter.
Minneapolis: U of Minnesota P, 2003. 153-70. Print.

Rabkin, Eric S., Martin H. Greenberg, and Joseph D. Olander. Preface.
No Place Else: Explorations in Utopian and Dystopian Fiction. Ed.
Rabkin, Greenberg, and Olander. Carbondale: Southern Illinois
UP, 1983. vii-ix. Print.

Readings, Bill. "*Translatio* and Comparative Literature: The Terror
of European Humanism." *Surfaces* 1 (1991): 1-19. Web. 15 Mar.
2007.

7.4.3	CITING VOLUME AND PAGE NUMBERS OF A MULTIVOLUME WORK

When citing a volume number as well as a page reference for a multi-volume work, separate the two by a colon and a space: "(Wellek 2: 1–10)." Use neither the words *volume* and *page* nor their abbreviations. The functions of the numbers in such a citation are understood. If, however, you wish to refer parenthetically to an entire volume of a multivolume work, there is no need to cite pages. Place a comma after the author's name and include the abbreviation *vol.*: "(Wellek, vol. 2)." If you integrate such a reference into a sentence, spell out *volume*: "In volume 2, Wellek deals with. . . ."

The anthology by Lauter and his coeditors contains both Stowe's
"Sojourner Truth, the Libyan Sibyl" (B: 2601-09) and Gilman's
"The Yellow Wall-Paper" (C: 578-90).

Between 1945 and 1972, the political-party system in the United States
underwent profound changes (Schlesinger, vol. 4).

Wellek admits in the middle of his multivolume history of modern
literary criticism, "An evolutionary history of criticism must fail. I
have come to this resigned conclusion" (5: xxii).

Works Cited

Lauter, Paul, et al., eds. *The Heath Anthology of American Literature.*
5th ed. 5 vols. Boston: Houghton, 2006. Print.

> Schlesinger, Arthur M., Jr., gen. ed. *History of U.S. Political Parties.*
>   4 vols. New York: Chelsea, 1973. Print.
> Wellek, René. *A History of Modern Criticism, 1750-1950.* 8 vols. New
>   Haven: Yale UP, 1955-92. Print.

7.4.4   CITING A WORK LISTED BY TITLE

In a parenthetical reference to a work alphabetized by title in the list of works cited, the full title (if brief) or a shortened version precedes the page, paragraph, section, or reference number or numbers (if any; see 7.2), unless the title appears in your text. When abbreviating the title, begin with the word by which it is alphabetized. Do not, for example, shorten *Glossary of Terms Used in Heraldry* to *Heraldry*, since this abbreviation would lead your reader to look for the bibliographic entry under *h* rather than *g*. If you are citing two or more anonymous works that have the same title, find a publication fact that distinguishes the works in their works-cited-list entries, and add it to their parenthetical references (see the "Burlesque" example). This fact could be the date of publication or the title of the work that encompasses the cited work. If you wish to cite a specific definition in a dictionary entry, give the relevant designation (e.g., number, letter) after the abbreviation *def.* (see the "Noon" example).

> A *New York Times* editorial called Ralph Ellison "a writer of universal
> reach" ("Death").
>
> A presidential commission reported in 1970 that recent campus
> protests had focused on "racial injustice, war, and the university
> itself" (*Report* 3).
>
> Even *Sixty Minutes* launched an attack on modern art, in a segment
> entitled "Yes . . . but Is It Art?"
>
> *Perseus 1.0* revolutionized the way scholars conduct research on
> ancient civilizations.
>
> Milton's description of the moon at "her highest noon" signifies the
> "place of the moon at midnight" ("Noon," def. 4b).
>
> Though *burlesque* is broadly known as a comedic performance
> "that achieves its effects through distortion, exaggeration, and
> imitation" ("Burlesque," *Benét's Reader's Encyclopedia*), the term
> has a more specific referent in the United States, where since about

1860 it has referred to a variety show featuring striptease and including comedians and other performers ("Burlesque," *Harvard Dictionary*).

Works Cited

"Burlesque." *Benét's Reader's Encyclopedia*. Ed. Bruce Murphy. 4th ed. New York: Harper, 1996. Print.

"Burlesque." *The Harvard Dictionary of Music*. Ed. Don Michael Randel. 4th ed. Cambridge: Belknap-Harvard UP, 2003. Print.

"Death of a Writer." Editorial. *New York Times* 20 Apr. 1994, late ed.: A18. Print.

"Noon." *The Oxford English Dictionary*. 2nd ed. Oxford: Oxford UP, 1992. CD-ROM.

Perseus 1.0: Interactive Sources and Studies on Ancient Greece. New Haven: Yale UP, 1992. CD-ROM, laser disc.

Report of the President's Commission on Campus Unrest. New York: Arno, 1970. Print.

"Yes . . . but Is It Art?" Narr. Morley Safer. *Sixty Minutes*. CBS. WCBS, New York. 19 Sept. 1993. Television.

7.4.5   CITING A WORK BY A CORPORATE AUTHOR

To cite a work by a corporate author, you may use the author's name followed by a page reference: "(United Nations, Economic Commission for Africa 79–86)." It is better, however, to include a long name in the text, so that the reading is not interrupted with an extended parenthetical reference. When giving the name of a corporate author in parentheses, shorten terms that are commonly abbreviated (see 8.4): "(Natl. Research Council 15)."

According to a study sponsored by the National Research Council, the population of China around 1990 was increasing by more than fifteen million annually (15).

By 1992 it was apparent that the American health care system, though impressive in many ways, needed "to be fixed and perhaps radically modified" (Public Agenda Foundation 4).

A study prepared by the United States Department of State defined terrorism as "premeditated, politically motivated violence against noncombatant targets by subnational groups or clandestine agents, usually intended to influence an audience" (lines 14-16).

In 1963 the United Nations Economic Commission for Africa predicted that Africa would evolve into an advanced industrial economy within fifty years (1-2, 4-6).

Works Cited

National Research Council. *China and Global Change: Opportunities for Collaboration*. Washington: Natl. Acad., 1992. *National Academies Press*. Web. 15 Mar. 2007.

Public Agenda Foundation. *The Health Care Crisis: Containing Costs, Expanding Coverage*. New York: McGraw, 1992. Print.

United Nations. Economic Commission for Africa. *Industrial Growth in Africa*. New York: United Nations, 1963. Print.

United States. Dept. of State. *Patterns of Global Terrorism*. 1994. CD-ROM. *National Trade Data Bank*. US Dept. of Commerce. Dec. 1996. Disc 2.

7.4.6   CITING TWO OR MORE WORKS BY
                     THE SAME AUTHOR OR AUTHORS

In a parenthetical reference to one of two or more works by the same author, put a comma after the author's last name and add the title of the work (if brief) or a shortened version and the relevant page reference: "(Frye, *Double Vision* 85)," "(Durant and Durant, *Age* 214–48)." If you state the author's name in the text, give only the title and page reference in parentheses: "(*Double Vision* 85)," "(*Age* 214–48)." If you include both the author's name and the title in the text, indicate only the pertinent page number or numbers in parentheses: "(85)," "(214–48)."

In *The Age of Voltaire*, the Durants portray eighteenth-century England as a minor force in the world of music and art (214-48).

To Will and Ariel Durant, creative men and women make "history forgivable by enriching our heritage and our lives" (*Dual Autobiography* 406).

Shakespeare's *King Lear* has been called a "comedy of the grotesque" (Frye, *Anatomy* 237).

For Northrop Frye, one's death is not a unique experience, for "every moment we have lived through we have also died out of into another order" (*Double Vision* 85).

Moulthrop sees the act of reading hypertext as "struggle": "a chapter of chances, a chain of detours, a series of revealing figures in commitment out of which come the pleasures of the text" ("Traveling").

Hypertext, as one theorist puts it, is "all about connection, linkage, and affiliation" (Moulthrop, "You Say," par. 19).

Works Cited

Durant, Will, and Ariel Durant. *The Age of Voltaire*. New York: Simon, 1965. Print. Vol. 9 of *The Story of Civilization*. 11 vols. 1933-75.

---. *A Dual Autobiography*. New York: Simon, 1977. Print.

Frye, Northrop. *Anatomy of Criticism: Four Essays*. Princeton: Princeton UP, 1957. Print.

---. *The Double Vision: Language and Meaning in Religion*. Toronto: U of Toronto P, 1991. Print.

Moulthrop, Stuart. "Traveling in the Breakdown Lane: A Principle of Resistance for Hypertext." *Mosaic* 28.4 (1995): 55-77. *University of Baltimore*. Web. 15 Mar. 2007.

---. "You Say You Want a Revolution? Hypertext and the Laws of Media." *Postmodern Culture* 1.3 (1991): n. pag. *Project Muse*. Web. 3 Apr. 1997.

7.4.7   CITING INDIRECT SOURCES

Whenever you can, take material from the original source, not a secondhand one. Sometimes, however, only an indirect source is available — for example, someone's published account of another's spoken remarks. If what you quote or paraphrase is itself a quotation, put the abbreviation *qtd. in* ("quoted in") before the indirect source you cite in your parenthetical reference. (You may document the original source in a note; see 7.5.1.)

Samuel Johnson admitted that Edmund Burke was an "extraordinary man" (qtd. in Boswell 2: 450).

The commentary of the sixteenth-century literary scholars Bernardo Segni and Lionardo Salviati shows them to be less-than-faithful followers of Aristotle (qtd. in Weinberg 1: 405, 616-17).

Works Cited

Boswell, James. *The Life of Johnson*. Ed. George Birkbeck Hill and L. F. Powell. 6 vols. Oxford: Clarendon, 1934-50. Print.

Weinberg, Bernard. *A History of Literary Criticism in the Italian Renaissance*. 2 vols. Chicago: U of Chicago P, 1961. Print.

7.4.8   CITING COMMON LITERATURE

In a reference to a commonly studied prose work, such as a novel or play, that is available in several editions, it is helpful to provide more information than just a page number from the edition used; a chapter number, for example, would help readers locate a quotation in any copy of a novel. In such a reference, give the page number first, add a semicolon, and then give other identifying information, using appropriate abbreviations: "(130; ch. 9)," "(271; bk. 4, ch. 2)."

Raskolnikov first appears in *Crime and Punishment* as a man contemplating a terrible act but frightened of meeting his talkative landlady on the stairs (Dostoevsky 1; pt. 1, ch. 1).

In one version of the William Tell story, the son urges the reluctant father to shoot the arrow (Sastre 315; sc. 6).

In *A Vindication of the Rights of Woman*, Mary Wollstonecraft recollects many "women who, not led by degrees to proper studies, and not permitted to choose for themselves, have indeed been overgrown children" (185; ch. 13, sec. 2).

When you cite an unpaginated source, the chapter number or similar designation may be the only identifying information you can give.

Douglass notes that he had "no accurate knowledge" of his date of birth, "never having had any authentic record containing it" (ch. 1).

In citing commonly studied verse plays and poems, omit page numbers altogether and cite by division (act, scene, canto, book, part) and line, with periods separating the various numbers—for example, "*Iliad* 9.19" refers to book 9, line 19, of Homer's *Iliad*. If you are citing only line numbers, do not use the abbreviation *l.* or *ll.*, which can be confused with numerals. Instead, initially use the word *line* or *lines* and then, having established that the numbers designate lines, give the numbers alone.

In general, use arabic numerals rather than roman numerals for division and page numbers. Although you must use roman numerals when citing pages of a preface or other section that are so numbered, designate volumes, parts, books, and chapters with arabic numerals even if your source does not. Some editors prefer roman numerals, however, for citations of acts and scenes in plays (*King Lear* IV.i), but if your editor does not require this practice, use arabic numerals (*King Lear* 4.1). On numbers, see 3.10.

When citing scripture, provide an entry in the works-cited list for the edition you consulted. While general terms like Bible, Talmud, and Koran are not italicized, full and shortened titles of specific editions are italicized (see 3.8.5). The first time you borrow from a particular work of scripture in your manuscript, state in the text or in a parenthetical citation the element that begins the entry in the works-cited list (usually the title of the edition but sometimes an editor's or a translator's name). Identify the borrowing by divisions of the work—for the Bible, give the name of the book and the chapter and verse numbers—rather than by a page number. Subsequent citations of the same edition may provide the divisions alone (see the *New Jerusalem Bible* example).

When included in parenthetical references, the titles of the books of the Bible and of famous literary works are often abbreviated (1 Chron. 21.8, Rev. 21.3, *Oth.* 4.2.7–13, *FQ* 3.3.53.3). The most widely used and accepted abbreviations for such titles are listed in 8.6. Follow prevailing practices for other abbreviations (*Troilus* for Chaucer's *Troilus and Criseyde*, "Nightingale" for Keats's "Ode to a Nightingale," etc.).

> Chaucer's purpose is "The double sorwe of Troilus to tellen, / That was the kyng Priamus sone of Troye" (1.1-2).

> Like the bard who made the *Ballad of Sir Patrick Spence*, Coleridge sees the "New-moon winter-bright" with the "old Moon in her lap, foretelling / The coming-on of rain and squally blast" (1.9, 13-14).

> In "Marching Song," Nesbit declares, "Our arms and hearts are strong for all who suffer wrong . . ." (line 11).

> Shakespeare's Hamlet seems resolute when he asserts, "The play's the thing / Wherein I'll catch the conscience of the King" (2.2.633-34).

In one of the most vivid prophetic visions in the Bible, Ezekiel saw "what seemed to be four living creatures," each with the faces of a man, a lion, an ox, and an eagle (*New Jerusalem Bible*, Ezek. 1.5-10). John of Patmos echoes this passage when describing his vision (Rev. 4.6-8).

Works Cited

Chaucer, Geoffrey. *Troilus and Criseyde*. *The Works of Geoffrey Chaucer*. Ed. F. N. Robinson. 2nd ed. Boston: Houghton, 1957. 385-479. Print.

Coleridge, Samuel Taylor. "Dejection: An Ode." *The Samuel Taylor Coleridge Archive*. Ed. Marjorie A. Tiefert. Electronic Text Center, Alderman Lib., U of Virginia, 1999. Web. 15 Mar. 2007.

Dostoevsky, Feodor. *Crime and Punishment*. Trans. Jessie Coulson. Ed. George Gibian. New York: Norton, 1964. Print.

Douglass, Frederick. *Narrative of the Life of Frederick Douglass*. Boston, 1845. *Department of History, University of Rochester*. Web. 15 Mar. 2007.

Nesbit, E[dith]. "Marching Song." 1887. *Ballads and Lyrics of Socialism: 1883-1908*. London: Fabian Soc.; Fifield, 1908. 9. *Victorian Women Writers Project*. Web. 15 Mar. 2007.

The New Jerusalem Bible. Henry Wansbrough, gen. ed. New York: Doubleday, 1985. Print.

Sastre, Alfonso. *Sad Are the Eyes of William Tell*. Trans. Leonard Pronko. *The New Wave Spanish Drama*. Ed. George E. Wellwarth. New York: New York UP, 1970. 165-321. Print.

Shakespeare, William. *Hamlet*. Ed. Barbara A. Mowat and Paul Werstine. New York: Washington Square-Pocket, 1992. Print.

Wollstonecraft, Mary. *A Vindication of the Rights of Woman*. Ed. Carol H. Poston. New York: Norton, 1975. Print.

7.4.9   CITING MORE THAN ONE WORK IN A SINGLE
PARENTHETICAL REFERENCE

If you wish to include two or more works in a single parenthetical reference, cite each work as you normally would in a reference, and use semicolons to separate the citations.

(Kaku 42; Stafford)

(Natl. Research Council 25-35; "U.S.'s Paulson")

(Rabkin, Greenberg, and Olander vii; Boyle 96-125)

(Gilbert and Gubar, *Madwoman* 1-25; Murphy 39-52)

(Gilbert and Gubar, *Norton Anthology*; Manning)

(Lauter et al., vol. B; Crane)

Keep in mind, however, that a long parenthetical reference such as the following example may prove intrusive and disconcerting to your reader:

(Gilbert and Gubar, *Madwoman* 1-25; Gilbert and Gubar, *Norton Anthology*; Manning; Murphy 39-52)

To avoid an excessive disruption, cite multiple sources in a note rather than in parentheses in the text (see 7.5.2).

Works Cited

Boyle, Anthony T. "The Epistemological Evolution of Renaissance Utopian Literature, 1516-1657." Diss. New York U, 1983. Print.

Crane, Stephen. *The Red Badge of Courage: An Episode of the American Civil War*. 1895. Ed. Fredson Bowers. Charlottesville: UP of Virginia, 1975. Print.

Gilbert, Sandra M., and Susan Gubar. *The Madwoman in the Attic: The Woman Writer and the Nineteenth-Century Literary Imagination*. New Haven: Yale UP, 1979. Print.

---, eds. *The Norton Anthology of Literature by Women: The Tradition in English*. 2nd ed. New York: Norton, 1996. Print.

Kaku, Michio. *Hyperspace: A Scientific Odyssey through Parallel Universes, Time Warps, and the Tenth Dimension*. New York: Oxford UP, 1994. Print.

Lauter, Paul, et al., eds. *The Heath Anthology of American Literature*. 5th ed. 5 vols. Boston: Houghton, 2006. Print.

Manning, Anita. "Curriculum Battles from Left and Right." *USA Today* 2 Mar. 1994: 5D. Print.

Murphy, Cullen. "Women and the Bible." *Atlantic Monthly* Aug. 1993: 39-64. Print.

National Research Council. *China and Global Change: Opportunities for Collaboration*. Washington: Natl. Acad., 1992. *National Academies Press*. Web. 15 Mar. 2007.

Rabkin, Eric S., Martin H. Greenberg, and Joseph D. Olander. Preface. *No Place Else: Explorations in Utopian and Dystopian Fiction*. Ed. Rabkin, Greenberg, and Olander. Carbondale: Southern Illinois UP, 1983. vii-ix. Print.

Stafford, Barbara Maria. "The Combinatorial Aesthetics of Neurobiology." *Aesthetic Subjects*. Ed. Pamela R. Matthews and David McWhirter. Minneapolis: U of Minnesota P, 2003. 251-67. Print.

"U.S.'s Paulson Urges China to Open Financial Markets." *CNN.com*. Cable News Network, 7 Mar. 2007. Web. 15 Mar. 2007.

7.4.10 CITING A BOOK WITH SIGNATURES AND NO PAGE NUMBERS

Some books published before 1800 lack page numbers but include letters, numbers, or other symbols, called signatures, at regular intervals at the feet of the pages. These notations were intended to help the bookbinder assemble groups of pages into the proper order. The pages between signatures typically bear the preceding signature symbol with an added numeral (arabic or roman).

In citing books without page numbers but with signatures, indicate the signature symbol, the leaf number, and the abbreviation *r* ("recto") or *v* ("verso") in the parenthetical reference. If no leaf number is printed, supply one: the leaf on which a signature first appears should be considered 1, the next leaf 2, and so forth, until the following signature. The front of a leaf — the side appearing on the reader's right — is the recto; the back of a leaf — the side appearing on the reader's left — is the verso. Thus, A1r is followed by A1v, A2r, A2v, and so on. (On citing books published before 1900, see 6.6.23.)

John Udall, paraphrasing Satan's temptation of Christ, writes, "[T]hrow thy selfe downe" so that "the men of Jerusalem" will "receive thee with a common applause" (E7v).

Work Cited

Udall, John. *The Combate betweene Christ and the Devill: Four Sermones on the Temptations of Christ*. London, 1589. Print.

7.5

USING NOTES WITH PARENTHETICAL DOCUMENTATION

Two kinds of notes may be used with parenthetical documentation:

- Content notes offering the reader comment, explanation, or information that the text cannot accommodate
- Bibliographic notes containing either several sources or evaluative comments on sources

In providing this sort of supplementary information, place a superscript arabic numeral at the appropriate place in the text and write the note after a matching numeral either at the end of the text (as an endnote) or at the bottom of the page (as a footnote). See the examples in 7.5.1–2.

7.5.1   CONTENT NOTES

In your notes, avoid lengthy discussions that divert the reader's attention from the primary text. In general, comments that you cannot fit into the text should be omitted unless they provide essential justification or clarification of what you have written. You may use a note, for example, to give full publication facts for an original source for which you cite an indirect source.

> Brooks's "The Ballad of Chocolate Mabbie" is a poem about a series of proposed metonymic relations (Mabbie next to the grammar school gate, Mabbie next to Willie Boone) that concludes with the speaker's hopeful recognition that if Mabbie aligns herself with like figures (her "chocolate companions") she will achieve a positive sense of self-reliance ("Mabbie on Mabbie to be").[1]

> Note
> 1. In this essay, I follow the definition of *metonymy* as a figure of contiguity. For a helpful exposition of the term, see Martin.

> Works Cited
> Brooks, Gwendolyn. "The Ballad of Chocolate Mabbie." *Selected Poems*. New York: Perennial-Harper, 2006. 7. Print.

Martin, Wallace. "Metonymy." *The New Princeton Encyclopedia of Poetry and Poetics*. Ed. Alex Preminger and T. V. F. Brogan. Princeton: Princeton UP, 1993. *Literature Online*. Web. 26 Mar. 2008.

7.5.2   BIBLIOGRAPHIC NOTES

Use notes for evaluative comments on sources and for references containing numerous citations.

Many observers conclude that health care in the United States is inadequate.[1]

Technological advancements have brought advantages as well as unexpected problems.[2]

Notes

1. For strong points of view on different aspects of the issue, see Public Agenda Foundation 1-10 and Sakala 151-88.

2. For a sampling of materials that reflect the range of experiences related to recent technological changes, see Taylor A1; Moulthrop, pars. 39-53; Armstrong, Yang, and Cuneo 80-82; and Kaku 42.

Works Cited

Armstrong, Larry, Dori Jones Yang, and Alice Cuneo. "The Learning Revolution: Technology Is Reshaping Education—at Home and at School." *Business Week* 28 Feb. 1994: 80-88. Print.

Kaku, Michio. *Hyperspace: A Scientific Odyssey through Parallel Universes, Time Warps, and the Tenth Dimension*. New York: Oxford UP, 1994. Print.

Moulthrop, Stuart. "You Say You Want a Revolution? Hypertext and the Laws of Media." *Postmodern Culture* 1.3 (1991): n. pag. *Project Muse*. Web. 3 Apr. 1997.

Public Agenda Foundation. *The Health Care Crisis: Containing Costs, Expanding Coverage*. New York: McGraw, 1992. Print.

Sakala, Carol. "Maternity Care Policy in the United States: Toward a More Rational and Effective System." Diss. Boston U, 1993. Print.

Taylor, Paul. "Keyboard Grief: Coping with Computer-Caused Injuries." *Globe and Mail* [Toronto] 27 Dec. 1993: A1+. Print.

8

ABBREVIATIONS

8.1
INTRODUCTION

Abbreviations are used regularly in the list of works cited and in tables but rarely in the text of scholarly publications (except within parentheses). In choosing abbreviations, keep your audience in mind. While economy of space is important, clarity is more so. Spell out a term if the abbreviation may puzzle your readers.

When abbreviating, always use accepted forms. In appropriate contexts, you may abbreviate the names of days, months, and other measurements of time (see 8.2); the names of states, provinces, countries, and continents (see 8.3); terms and reference words common in scholarship (see 8.4); publishers' names (see 8.5); the titles of well-known works (see 8.6); and the names of languages (8.7).

The trend in abbreviation is to use neither periods after letters nor spaces between letters, especially for abbreviations made up of all capital letters.

BC	PhD	S
NJ	CD-ROM	US

The chief exception to this trend continues to be the initials used for personal names: a period and a space ordinarily follow each initial.

J. R. R. Tolkien

Most abbreviations that end in lowercase letters are followed by periods.

assn.	fig.	Mex.
Eng.	introd.	prod.

In most abbreviations made up of lowercase letters that each represent a word, a period follows each letter, but no space intervenes between letters.

a.m.	i.e.
e.g.	n.p.

But there are numerous exceptions.

mph	os
ns	rpm

8.2
TIME DESIGNATIONS

Spell out the names of months in the text but abbreviate them in the list of works cited, except for May, June, and July. Whereas words denoting units of time are also spelled out in the text (*second, minute, week, month, year, century*), some time designations are used only in abbreviated form (*a.m., p.m., AD, BC, BCE, CE*).

AD   after the birth of Christ (from Lat. *anno Domini* 'in the year of the Lord'; used before numerals ["AD 14"] and after references to centuries ["twelfth century AD"])

a.m.	before noon (from Lat. *ante meridiem*)
Apr.	April
Aug.	August
BC	before Christ (used after numerals ["19 BC"] and references to centuries ["fifth century BC"])
BCE	before the common era (used after numerals and references to centuries)
CE	common era (used after numerals and references to centuries)
cent.	century
Dec.	December
Feb.	February
Fri.	Friday
hr.	hour
Jan.	January
Mar.	March
min.	minute
mo.	month
Mon.	Monday
Nov.	November
Oct.	October
p.m.	after noon (from Lat. *post meridiem*)
Sat.	Saturday
sec.	second
Sept.	September
Sun.	Sunday
Thurs.	Thursday
Tues.	Tuesday
Wed.	Wednesday
wk.	week
yr.	year

8.3

GEOGRAPHIC NAMES

Spell out the names of states, territories, and possessions of the United States in the text, except usually in addresses and sometimes in parentheses. Likewise, spell out in the text the names of countries, with a few exceptions (e.g., USSR). In documentation, however, abbreviate the names of states, provinces, countries, and continents.

AB	Alberta
Afgh.	Afghanistan
Afr.	Africa
AK	Alaska
AL	Alabama
Alb.	Albania
Alg.	Algeria
Ant.	Antarctica
AR	Arkansas
Arg.	Argentina
Arm.	Armenia
AS	American Samoa
ASSR	Autonomous Soviet Socialist Republic
Aus.	Austria
Austral.	Australia
AZ	Arizona
Azer.	Azerbaijan
Bang.	Bangladesh
BC	British Columbia
Belg.	Belgium
Bol.	Bolivia
Bos.-Herz.	Bosnia-Herzegovina
Braz.	Brazil
Bulg.	Bulgaria
BWI	British West Indies

CA	California
Can.	Canada
CAR	Central African Republic
CO	Colorado
Col.	Colombia
CT	Connecticut
Czech Rep.	Czech Republic
DC	District of Columbia
DE	Delaware
Dem. Rep. Congo	Democratic Republic of Congo
Den.	Denmark
Dom. Rep.	Dominican Republic
Ecua.	Ecuador
Eng.	England
Equat. Guinea	Equatorial Guinea
Eth.	Ethiopia
Eur.	Europe
Fin.	Finland
FL	Florida
FM	Federated States of Micronesia
Fr.	France
Ga.	Georgia (republic)
GA	Georgia (US state)
Ger.	Germany
Gr.	Greece
Gt. Brit.	Great Britain
GU	Guam
Guat.	Guatemala
HI	Hawaii
Hond.	Honduras
Hung.	Hungary

IA	Iowa
ID	Idaho
IL	Illinois
IN	Indiana
Indon.	Indonesia
Ire.	Ireland
Isr.	Israel
It.	Italy
Jpn.	Japan
Kazakh.	Kazakhstan
KS	Kansas
KY	Kentucky
Kyrg.	Kyrgyzstan
LA	Louisiana
Lat. Amer.	Latin America
Leb.	Lebanon
Lith.	Lithuania
Lux.	Luxembourg
MA	Massachusetts
Madag.	Madagascar
MB	Manitoba
MD	Maryland
ME	Maine
Mex.	Mexico
MH	Marshall Islands
MI	Michigan
MN	Minnesota
MO	Missouri
Moz.	Mozambique
MP	Northern Mariana Islands
MS	Mississippi

MT	Montana
NB	New Brunswick
NC	North Carolina
ND	North Dakota
NE	Nebraska
Neth.	Netherlands
NH	New Hampshire
Nic.	Nicaragua
NJ	New Jersey
NL	Newfoundland and Labrador
NM	New Mexico
No. Amer.	North America
Norw.	Norway
NS	Nova Scotia
NT	Northwest Territories
NU	Nunavut
NV	Nevada
NY	New York
NZ	New Zealand
OH	Ohio
OK	Oklahoma
ON	Ontario
OR	Oregon
PA	Pennsylvania
Pak.	Pakistan
Pan.	Panama
Para.	Paraguay
PE	Prince Edward Island
Phil.	Philippines
PNG	Papua New Guinea
Pol.	Poland

Port.	Portugal
PR	Puerto Rico
PRC	People's Republic of China
PW	Palau
QC	Quebec, Québec
RI	Rhode Island
RSFSR	Russian Soviet Federalist Socialist Republic
Russ.	Russia
Russ. Fed.	Russian Federation
SC	South Carolina
Scot.	Scotland
SD	South Dakota
Serb. and Mont.	Serbia and Montenegro
Sing.	Singapore
SK	Saskatchewan
So. Afr.	South Africa
So. Amer.	South America
Sp.	Spain
Swed.	Sweden
Switz.	Switzerland
Tajik.	Tajikistan
Tanz.	Tanzania
Tas.	Tasmania
Thai.	Thailand
TN	Tennessee
Trin. and Tob.	Trinidad and Tobago
Turk.	Turkey
Turkm.	Turkmenistan
TX	Texas
UAE	United Arab Emirates
UK	United Kingdom

Ukr.	Ukraine
Uru.	Uruguay
US, USA	United States, United States of America
USSR	Union of Soviet Socialist Republics
UT	Utah
Uzbek.	Uzbekistan
VA	Virginia
Venez.	Venezuela
VI	Virgin Islands
VT	Vermont
WA	Washington
WI	Wisconsin
WV	West Virginia
WY	Wyoming
YT	Yukon Territory

----------------------- **8.4** -----------------------

COMMON SCHOLARLY ABBREVIATIONS
AND REFERENCE WORDS

The following list includes abbreviations and reference words commonly used in humanities scholarship. Terms within parentheses are alternative but not recommended forms. Terms within brackets are no longer recommended. The list provides some plurals of abbreviations (e.g., *nn, MSS*). Plurals of most other noun abbreviations not ending in *s* and longer than one letter can be formed through the addition of *s* (e.g., *adjs., bks., DVDs, figs., insts., pts.*). Most of the abbreviations listed would replace the spelled forms only in parentheses, tables, and documentation.

AAUP	American Association of University Professors; Association of American University Presses
AB	bachelor of arts (from Lat. *artium baccalaureus*)

abbr.	abbreviation, abbreviated
abl.	ablative
abr.	abridgment, abridged, abridged by
acad.	academy
acc.	accusative
act.	active
adapt.	adapter, adaptation, adapted by
add.	addendum
adj.	adjective
adv.	adverb
ALS	autograph letter signed
AM	master of arts (from Lat. *artium magister*)
Amer.	America, American
Anm.	Ger. *Anmerkung* 'note'
anon.	anonymous
ant.	antonym
app.	appendix
arch.	archaic
art.	article
ASCII	American Standard Code for Information Interchange
assn.	association
assoc.	associate, associated
attrib.	attributive; attributed to
aux.	auxiliary verb
b.	born
BA	bachelor of arts
Bd., Bde.	Ger. *Band, Bände* 'volume, volumes'
BEd	bachelor of education
BFA	bachelor of fine arts
bib.	biblical

bibliog.	bibliographer, bibliography, bibliographic
biog.	biographer, biography, biographical
BiP	*Books in Print*
bk.	book
BL	British Library, London
BM	British Museum, London (library transferred to British Library in 1973)
BN	Bibliothèque Nationale de France, Paris
BS	bachelor of science
bull.	bulletin
©, copr.	copyright ("© 2007")
c. (ca.)	circa, *or* around (used with approximate dates: "c. 1796")
cap.	capital, capitalize
CD	compact disc
CD-ROM	compact disc read-only memory
cf.	compare (not "see"; from Lat. *confer*)
ch. (chap.)	chapter
chor.	choreographer, choreographed by
cit.	citation, cited
cl.	clause
cog.	cognate
col.	column
coll.	college
colloq.	colloquial
com	commercial (used as a suffix in Internet domain names: "www.nytimes.com")
comp.	compiler, compiled by
compar.	comparative
cond.	conductor, conducted by
conf.	conference

cong.	congress
Cong. Rec.	*Congressional Record*
conj.	conjunction
cons.	consonant
const.	constitution
cont.	contents; continued
(contd.)	continued
contr.	contraction
copr., ©	copyright
CV	curriculum vitae
d.	died
DA	doctor of arts
DA, DAI	*Dissertation Abstracts, Dissertation Abstracts International*
DAB	*Dictionary of American Biography*
dat.	dative
def.	definition; definite
dept.	department
der.	derivative
dev.	development, developed by
DFA	doctor of fine arts
d.h.	Ger. *das heisst* 'that is'
dial.	dialect, dialectal
dict.	dictionary
dim.	diminutive
dir.	director, directed by
diss.	dissertation
dist.	district
distr.	distributor, distributed by
div.	division
DMCA	Digital Millennium Copyright Act
DNB	*Dictionary of National Biography*

doc.	document
DOI	digital object identifier
DTD	document type definition
DVD	originally *digital videodisc*, but now used to describe discs containing a wide range of data
DVD-ROM	digital videodisc read-only memory
ed.	editor, edition, edited by
EdD	doctor of education
edu	educational (used as a suffix in Internet domain names: "www.indiana.edu")
educ.	education, educational
e.g.	for example (from Lat. *exempli gratia*; rarely capitalized; set off by commas, unless preceded by a different punctuation mark)
e-mail	electronic mail
encyc.	encyclopedia
enl.	enlarged (as in "rev. and enl. ed.")
esp.	especially
et al.	and others (from Lat. *et alii, et aliae, et alia*)
etc.	and so forth (from Lat. *et cetera*; like most abbreviations, not appropriate in text)
ETD	electronic thesis or dissertation
[et seq., et seqq.]	and the following (from Lat. *et sequens, et sequentes* or *sequentia*)
ex.	example
[f., ff.]	and the following page(s) or line(s) (avoided in favor of specific page or line numbers)
fac.	faculty
facsim.	facsimile

fasc.	fascicle
fem.	feminine
fig.	figure
fl.	flourished, *or* reached greatest development or influence (from Lat. *floruit*; used before dates of historical figures when birth and death dates are not known: "fl. 1200")
[fn.]	footnote
[fol.]	folio
fr.	from
front.	frontispiece
FTP	file transfer protocol
fut.	future
fwd.	foreword, foreword by
geb.	Ger. *geboren* 'born'
gen.	general (as in "gen. ed.")
ger.	gerund
gest.	Ger. *gestorben* 'died'
gov	government (used as a suffix in Internet domain names: "www.census.gov")
govt.	government
GPO	Government Printing Office, Washington, DC
H. Doc.	House of Representatives Document
hist.	historian, history, historical
HMSO	Her (His) Majesty's Stationery Office, London
HR	House of Representatives
H. Rept.	House of Representatives Report
H. Res.	House of Representatives Resolution
HTML	hypertext markup language

http	hypertext transfer protocol (used at the beginning of an Internet address)
[ib., ibid.]	in the same place (from Lat. *ibidem*)
[id.]	the same (from Lat. *idem*)
i.e.	that is (from Lat. *id est*; rarely capitalized; set off by commas, unless preceded by a different punctuation mark)
illus.	illustrator, illustration, illustrated by
ILMP	*International Literary Market Place*
imp.	imperative
imperf.	imperfect
inc.	including; incorporated
indef.	indefinite
indic.	indicative
infin.	infinitive
[infra]	below
inst.	institute, institution
interjec.	interjective
interrog.	interrogative
intl.	international
intrans.	intransitive
introd.	introduction, introduced by
ips	inches per second (used in reference to tape recordings)
irreg.	irregular
ISP	Internet service provider
JD	doctor of law (from Lat. *juris doctor*)
jour.	journal
Jr.	Junior
KB	kilobyte
[l., ll.]	line, lines (avoided in favor of *line* and *lines* or, if clear, numbers only)

lang.	language
LC	Library of Congress
leg.	legal
legis.	legislator, legislation, legislature, legislative
LHD	doctor of humanities (from Lat. *litterarum humaniorum doctor*)
lib.	library
lit.	literally; literature, literary
LittB	bachelor of letters (from Lat. *litterarum baccalaureus*)
LittD	doctor of letters (from Lat. *litterarum doctor*)
LittM	master of letters (from Lat. *litterarum magister*)
LLB	bachelor of laws (from Lat. *legum baccalaureus*)
LLD	doctor of laws (from Lat. *legum doctor*)
LLM	master of laws (from Lat. *legum magister*)
LMP	*Literary Market Place*
[loc. cit.]	in the place (passage) cited (from Lat. *loco citato*)
LP	long-playing phonograph record
ltd.	limited
m.	Fr. *mort, morte*; It. *morto, morta*; Sp. *muerto, muerta* 'died'
MA	master of arts
mag.	magazine
masc.	masculine
MB	megabyte
MD	doctor of medicine (from Lat. *medicinae doctor*)
MEd	master of education
MFA	master of fine arts

misc.	miscellaneous
mod.	modern
MS	master of science
MS, MSS	manuscript, manuscripts (as in "Bodleian MS Tanner 43"; cf. *TS, TSS*)
n, nn	note, notes (used immediately after the number of the page containing the text of the note or notes: "56n," "56n3," "56nn3–5")
n.	noun; *also* Fr. *né, née*; It. *nato, nata*; Lat. *natus, nata*; Sp. *nacido, nacida* 'born'
narr.	narrator, narrated by
natl.	national
NB	take notice (from Lat. *nota bene*; always capitalized)
n.d.	no date of publication
NED	*A New English Dictionary* (cf. *OED*)
neut.	neuter
no.	number (cf. *numb.*)
nom.	nominative
nonstand.	nonstandard
n.p.	no place of publication; no publisher
n. pag.	no pagination
ns	new series
NS	New Style (calendar designation)
numb.	numbered (cf. *no.*)
ob.	he or she died (from Lat. *obiit*)
obj.	object, objective
obs.	obsolete
OCLC	Online Computer Library Center
OCR	optical character reader; optical character recognition

OED	*The Oxford English Dictionary* (formerly *A New English Dictionary* [*NED*])
o.J.	Ger. *ohne Jahr* 'without year'
o.O.	Ger. *ohne Ort* 'without place'
op.	opus (work)
[op. cit.]	in the work cited (from Lat. *opere citato*)
orch.	orchestra (also It. *orchestra*, Fr. *orchestre*, etc.), orchestrated by
org	organization (used as a suffix in Internet domain names: "www.mla.org")
orig.	original, originally
orn.	ornament, ornamented
os	old series; original series
OS	Old Style (calendar designation)
P	Press (also Fr. *Presse*, *Presses*; used in documentation; cf. *PU* and *UP*)
p., pp.	page, pages (omitted before page numbers unless necessary for clarity)
pág.	Sp. *página* 'page'
par.	paragraph
part.	participle
pass.	passive
[passim]	through the work, *or* here and there
PDF	portable document format
perf.	performer, performed by
pers.	person, personal
p. es.	It. *per esempio* 'for example'
p. ex.	Fr. *par exemple* 'for example'
PhD	doctor of philosophy (from Lat. *philosophiae doctor*)
philol.	philology, philological
philos.	philosophy, philosophical
pl.	plate; plural

por ej.	Sp. *por ejemplo* 'for example'
poss.	possessive
p.p.	past participle
pref.	preface, preface by
prep.	preposition
pres.	present
prob.	probably
proc.	proceedings
prod.	producer, produced by
pron.	pronoun
pronunc.	pronunciation
pr. p.	present participle
PS	postscript
pseud.	pseudonym
pt.	part
PU	Fr. *Presse de l'Université, Presses Universitaires* (used in documentation)
pub. (publ.)	publisher, publication, published by
Pub. L.	Public Law
qtd.	quoted
q.v.	which see (from Lat. *quod vide*)
r	righthand page (from Lat. *recto*)
r.	reigned
rec.	record, recorded
Ref.	Reference (used to indicate the reference section in a library)
refl.	reflexive
reg.	registered; regular
rel.	relative; release
rept.	report, reported by
res.	resolution
resp.	respectively

rev.	review, reviewed by; revision, revised, revised by (spell out *review* where *rev.* might be ambiguous)
RLIN	Research Libraries Information Network
rpm	revolutions per minute (used in reference to phonograph recordings)
rpt.	reprint, reprinted, reprinted by
S	Senate
s.	Ger. *siehe* 'see'
S.	Ger. *Seite* 'page'
sc.	scene (omitted for verse plays: "*King Lear* 4.1")
s.d.	Fr. *sans date*, It. *senza data*, Lat. *sine die* 'without date'
S. Doc.	Senate Document
sec. (sect.)	section
ser.	series
sess.	session
s.f.	Sp. *sin fecha* 'without date'
SGML	standard generalized markup language
sic	thus in the source (in square brackets as an editorial interpolation, otherwise in parentheses; not followed by an exclamation point)
sig.	signature
sing.	singular
s.l.	Fr. *sans lieu*, It. *senza luogo*, Lat. *sine loco*, Sp. *sin lugar* 'without place'
s.l.n.d.	Fr. *sans lieu ni date* 'without place or date'
soc.	society
spec.	special
Sr.	Senior
S. Rept.	Senate Report

S. Res.	Senate Resolution
st.	stanza
St., Sts. (S, SS)	Saint, Saints
Stat.	Statutes at Large
Ste, Stes	Fr. fem. *Sainte, Saintes* 'saint, saints'
subj.	subject, subjective; subjunctive
substand.	substandard
superl.	superlative
supp.	supplement
[supra]	above
s.v.	under the word, under the heading (from Lat. *sub verbo, sub voce*)
syn.	synonym
t.	Fr. *tome*, Sp. *tomo* 'volume'
TEI	Text Encoding Initiative
TLS	typed letter signed
trans. (tr.)	transitive; translator, translation, translated by
TS, TSS	typescript, typescripts (cf. *MS, MSS*)
U	University (also Fr. *Université*, Ger. *Universität*, It. *Università*, Sp. *Universidad*, etc.; used in documentation; cf. *PU* and *UP*)
univ.	university (used outside documentation— e.g., in parentheses and tables: "Montclair State Univ.")
UP	University Press (used in documentation: "Columbia UP")
URL	uniform resource locator
USC	United States Code
usu.	usually
usw.	Ger. *und so weiter* 'and so on'
v	lefthand page (from Lat. *verso*)

v.	see (from Lat. *vide*; cf. *vs. (v.)*)
v., vv. (vs., vss.)	verse, verses (cf. *vs. (v.)*)
var.	variant
vb.	verb
[v.d.]	various dates
vers.	version
vgl.	Ger. *vergleiche* 'compare'
VHS	video home system (the recording and playing standard for videocassette recorders)
v.i.	verb intransitive
[viz.]	namely (from Lat. *videlicet*)
voc.	vocative
vol.	volume
vs. (v.)	versus (*v.* preferred in titles of legal cases)
v.t.	verb transitive
writ.	writer, written by
www	World Wide Web (used in the names of servers, or computers, on the Web)
XML	extensible markup language
z.B.	Ger. *zum Beispiel* 'for example'

8.5
PUBLISHERS' NAMES

In the list of works cited, shortened forms of publishers' names immediately follow the cities of publication, enabling the reader to locate books or to acquire more information about them. Since publications like *Books in Print*, *Literary Market Place*, and *International Literary Market Place* list publishers' addresses, you need give only enough information so that your reader can look up the publishers in one of these sources. It is usually sufficient, for example, to give "Harcourt" as the publisher's name even if the title page shows "Harcourt Brace" or one of the earlier names of that firm (Harcourt, Brace; Harcourt, Brace, and World; Harcourt Brace Jovanovich). If you are preparing a bibliographic study, however, or if publication history is important to your work, give the publisher's name in full.

In shortening publishers' names, keep in mind the following points:

- Omit articles (*A*, *An*, *The*), business abbreviations (*Co.*, *Corp.*, *Inc.*, *Ltd.*), and descriptive words (*Books*, *House*, *Press*, *Publishers*, *Librairie*, *Verlag*). When citing a university press, however, always add the abbreviation *P* (Ohio State UP) because the university itself may publish independently of its press (Ohio State U).
- If the publisher's name includes the name of one person (Harry N. Abrams, W. W. Norton, John Wiley), cite the surname alone (Abrams, Norton, Wiley). If the publisher's name includes the names of more than one person, cite only the first of the surnames (Bobbs, Dodd, Faber, Farrar, Funk, Grosset, Harcourt, Harper, Houghton, McGraw, Prentice, Simon).
- Use standard abbreviations whenever possible (*Acad.*, *Assn.*, *Soc.*, *UP*; see 8.4).
- If the publisher's name is commonly abbreviated with capital initial letters and if the abbreviation is likely to be familiar to your audience, use the abbreviation as the publisher's name (GPO, MLA, UMI). If your readers are not likely to know the abbreviation, shorten the name according to the general guidelines given above (Mod. Lang. Assn.).

Following are examples of how various types of publishers' names are shortened:

Acad. for Educ. Dev.	Academy for Educational Development, Inc.
ACLS	American Council of Learned Societies
ALA	American Library Association
Basic	Basic Books
CAL	Center for Applied Linguistics
Cambridge UP	Cambridge University Press
Eastgate	Eastgate Systems
Einaudi	Giulio Einaudi Editore
ERIC	Educational Resources Information Center

Farrar	Farrar, Straus and Giroux, Inc.
Feminist	The Feminist Press at the City University of New York
Gale	Gale Research, Inc.
Gerig	Gerig Verlag
GPO	Government Printing Office
Harper	Harper and Row, Publishers, Inc.; HarperCollins Publishers, Inc.
Harvard Law Rev. Assn.	Harvard Law Review Association
HMSO	Her (His) Majesty's Stationery Office
Houghton	Houghton Mifflin Co.
Knopf	Alfred A. Knopf, Inc.
Larousse	Librairie Larousse
Little	Little, Brown and Company, Inc.
Macmillan	Macmillan Publishing Co., Inc.
McGraw	McGraw-Hill, Inc.
MIT P	The MIT Press
MLA	The Modern Language Association of America
NCTE	The National Council of Teachers of English
NEA	The National Education Association
Norton	W. W. Norton and Co., Inc.
Planeta	Editorial Planeta Mexicana
PUF	Presses Universitaires de France
Random	Random House, Inc.
Scribner's	Charles Scribner's Sons
Simon	Simon and Schuster, Inc.
SIRS	Social Issues Resources Series
State U of New York P	State University of New York Press
St. Martin's	St. Martin's Press, Inc.
UMI	University Microfilms International

| U of Chicago P | University of Chicago Press |
| UP of Mississippi | University Press of Mississippi |

8.6
TITLES OF WORKS

In documentation, you may abbreviate the titles of works and parts of works. It is usually best to introduce an abbreviation in parentheses immediately after the first use of the full title in the text: "In *All's Well That Ends Well (AWW)*, Shakespeare. . . ." Abbreviating titles is appropriate, for example, if you repeatedly cite a variety of works by the same author. In such a discussion, abbreviations make for more concise parenthetical documentation—"*(AWW* 3.2.100–29)," "*(MM* 4.3.93–101)"—than the usual shortened titles would: "*(All's Well* 3.2.100–29)," "*(Measure* 4.3.93–101)." For works not on the following lists, you may use the abbreviations you find in your sources, or you may devise simple, unambiguous abbreviations of your own.

8.6.1   BIBLE

The following abbreviations and spelled forms are commonly used for parts of the Bible (Bib.). While the Hebrew Bible and the Protestant Old Testament include the same parts in slightly different arrangements, Roman Catholic versions of the Old Testament also include works listed here as apocrypha.

HEBREW BIBLE OR OLD TESTAMENT (OT)

Amos	Amos
Cant. of Cant.	Canticle of Canticles (also called Song of Solomon and Song of Songs)
1 Chron.	1 Chronicles
2 Chron.	2 Chronicles
Dan.	Daniel
Deut.	Deuteronomy
Eccles.	Ecclesiastes (also called Qoheleth)

Esth.	Esther
Exod.	Exodus
Ezek.	Ezekiel
Ezra	Ezra
Gen.	Genesis
Hab.	Habakkuk
Hag.	Haggai
Hos.	Hosea
Isa.	Isaiah
Jer.	Jeremiah
Job	Job
Joel	Joel
Jon.	Jonah
Josh.	Joshua
Judg.	Judges
1 Kings	1 Kings
2 Kings	2 Kings
Lam.	Lamentations
Lev.	Leviticus
Mal.	Malachi
Mic.	Micah
Nah.	Nahum
Neh.	Nehemiah
Num.	Numbers
Obad.	Obadiah
Prov.	Proverbs
Ps.	Psalms
Qoh.	Qoheleth (also called Ecclesiastes)
Ruth	Ruth
1 Sam.	1 Samuel
2 Sam.	2 Samuel

Song of Sg.	Song of Songs (also called Canticle of Canticles and Song of Solomon)
Song of Sol.	Song of Solomon (also called Canticle of Canticles and Song of Songs)
Zech.	Zechariah
Zeph.	Zephaniah

NEW TESTAMENT (NT)

Acts	Acts
Apoc.	Apocalypse (also called Revelation)
Col.	Colossians
1 Cor.	1 Corinthians
2 Cor.	2 Corinthians
Eph.	Ephesians
Gal.	Galatians
Heb.	Hebrews
Jas.	James
John	John
1 John	1 John
2 John	2 John
3 John	3 John
Jude	Jude
Luke	Luke
Mark	Mark
Matt.	Matthew
1 Pet.	1 Peter
2 Pet.	2 Peter
Phil.	Philippians
Philem.	Philemon
Rev.	Revelation (also called Apocalypse)

Rom.	Romans
1 Thess.	1 Thessalonians
2 Thess.	2 Thessalonians
1 Tim.	1 Timothy
2 Tim.	2 Timothy
Tit.	Titus

SELECTED APOCRYPHA

Bar.	Baruch
Bel and Dr.	Bel and the Dragon
Ecclus.	Ecclesiasticus (also called Sirach)
1 Esd.	1 Esdras
2 Esd.	2 Esdras
Esth. (Apocr.)	Esther (Apocrypha)
Jth.	Judith
1 Macc.	1 Maccabees
2 Macc.	2 Maccabees
Pr. of Man.	Prayer of Manasseh
Sir.	Sirach (also called Ecclesiasticus)
Song of 3 Childr.	Song of Three Children
Sus.	Susanna
Tob.	Tobit
Wisd.	Wisdom (also called Wisdom of Solomon)
Wisd. of Sol.	Wisdom of Solomon (also called Wisdom)

8.6.2   WORKS BY SHAKESPEARE

Ado	*Much Ado about Nothing*
Ant.	*Antony and Cleopatra*
AWW	*All's Well That Ends Well*

AYL	*As You Like It*
Cor.	*Coriolanus*
Cym.	*Cymbeline*
Err.	*The Comedy of Errors*
F1	First Folio ed. (1623)
F2	Second Folio ed. (1632)
Ham.	*Hamlet*
1H4	*Henry IV, Part 1*
2H4	*Henry IV, Part 2*
H5	*Henry V*
1H6	*Henry VI, Part 1*
2H6	*Henry VI, Part 2*
3H6	*Henry VI, Part 3*
H8	*Henry VIII*
JC	*Julius Caesar*
Jn.	*King John*
LC	*A Lover's Complaint*
LLL	*Love's Labour's Lost*
Lr.	*King Lear*
Luc.	*The Rape of Lucrece*
Mac.	*Macbeth*
MM	*Measure for Measure*
MND	*A Midsummer Night's Dream*
MV	*The Merchant of Venice*
Oth.	*Othello*
Per.	*Pericles*
PhT	*The Phoenix and the Turtle*
PP	*The Passionate Pilgrim*
Q	Quarto ed.
R2	*Richard II*
R3	*Richard III*

Rom.	*Romeo and Juliet*
Shr.	*The Taming of the Shrew*
Son.	*Sonnets*
TGV	*The Two Gentlemen of Verona*
Tim.	*Timon of Athens*
Tit.	*Titus Andronicus*
Tmp.	*The Tempest*
TN	*Twelfth Night*
TNK	*The Two Noble Kinsmen*
Tro.	*Troilus and Cressida*
Ven.	*Venus and Adonis*
Wiv.	*The Merry Wives of Windsor*
WT	*The Winter's Tale*

8.6.3 WORKS BY CHAUCER

BD	*The Book of the Duchess*
CkT	The Cook's Tale
ClT	The Clerk's Tale
CT	*The Canterbury Tales*
CYT	The Canon's Yeoman's Tale
FranT	The Franklin's Tale
FrT	The Friar's Tale
GP	The General Prologue
HF	*The House of Fame*
KnT	The Knight's Tale
LGW	*The Legend of Good Women*
ManT	The Manciple's Tale
Mel	The Tale of Melibee
MerT	The Merchant's Tale
MilT	The Miller's Tale
MkT	The Monk's Tale

MLT	The Man of Law's Tale
NPT	The Nun's Priest's Tale
PardT	The Pardoner's Tale
ParsT	The Parson's Tale
PF	*The Parliament of Fowls*
PhyT	The Physician's Tale
PrT	The Prioress's Tale
Ret	Chaucer's Retraction
RvT	The Reeve's Tale
ShT	The Shipman's Tale
SNT	The Second Nun's Tale
SqT	The Squire's Tale
SumT	The Summoner's Tale
TC	*Troilus and Criseyde*
Th	The Tale of Sir Thopas
WBT	The Wife of Bath's Tale

8.6.4   OTHER WORKS

Aen.	Vergil, *Aeneid*
Ag.	Aeschylus, *Agamemnon*
Ant.	Sophocles, *Antigone*
Bac.	Euripides, *Bacchae*
Beo.	*Beowulf*
Can.	Voltaire, *Candide*
Dec.	Boccaccio, *Decameron*
DJ	Byron, *Don Juan*
DQ	Cervantes, *Don Quixote*
Eum.	Aeschylus, *Eumenides*
FQ	Spenser, *The Faerie Queene*
Gil.	*Epic of Gilgamesh*
GT	Swift, *Gulliver's Travels*

Hept.	Marguerite de Navarre, *Heptameron*
Hip.	Euripides, *Hippolytus*
Il.	Homer, *Iliad*
Inf.	Dante, *Inferno*
LB	Wordsworth, *Lyrical Ballads*
Lys.	Aristophanes, *Lysistrata*
MD	Melville, *Moby-Dick*
Med.	Euripides, *Medea*
Mis.	Molière, *Le misanthrope*
Nib.	*Nibelungenlied*
Od.	Homer, *Odyssey*
OR	Sophocles, *Oedipus Rex* (also called *Oedipus Tyrannus* [*OT*])
Or.	Aeschylus, *Oresteia*
OT	Sophocles, *Oedipus Tyrannus* (also called *Oedipus Rex* [*OR*])
Par.	Dante, *Paradiso*
PL	Milton, *Paradise Lost*
Prel.	Wordsworth, *The Prelude*
Purg.	Dante, *Purgatorio*
Rep.	Plato, *Republic*
SA	Milton, *Samson Agonistes*
SGGK	*Sir Gawain and the Green Knight*
Sym.	Plato, *Symposium*
Tar.	Molière, *Tartuffe*

8.7

NAMES OF LANGUAGES

Abbreviations for the names of languages are used not only in documentation but also in the text of linguistic studies where the context makes the abbreviations clear. Periods are not used in abbreviations containing all capital letters (*ME*), but a period follows an abbreviation ending in a lowercase letter (*Chin.*). An abbreviation that combines two abbreviations and ends in a lowercase letter contains only one period, by convention, at the end; no space is left between the two elements (*OFr., AmerInd.*).

AFr.	Anglo-French
Afrik.	Afrikaans
Alb.	Albanian
AmerFr.	American French
AmerInd.	American Indian
AmerSp.	American Spanish
AN	Anglo-Norman
Ar.	Arabic
Arab.	Arabian
Aram.	Aramaic
Arm.	Armenian
AS	Anglo-Saxon
Assyr.	Assyrian
Bab.	Babylonian
Beng.	Bengali
BrazPort.	Brazilian Portuguese
Bret.	Breton
Bulg.	Bulgarian
Bur.	Burmese
CanFr.	Canadian French
Cant.	Cantonese
Catal.	Catalan
Celt.	Celtic
Chin.	Chinese
Copt.	Coptic
Corn.	Cornish

Dan.	Danish
Dor.	Doric
Du.	Dutch
E, Eng.	English
EE	Early English
EGmc.	East Germanic
Egypt.	Egyptian
Esk.	Eskimo
Finn.	Finnish
Flem.	Flemish
Fr.	French
Fris.	Frisian
G, Ger.	German
Gael.	Gaelic
Gk.	Greek
Gmc.	Germanic
Goth.	Gothic
Heb.	Hebrew
HG	High German
Hitt.	Hittite
Hung.	Hungarian
Icel.	Icelandic
IE	Indo-European
Ind.	Indian
Ir.	Irish
It.	Italian
Jav.	Javanese
Jpn.	Japanese
Kor.	Korean
L	Late (e.g., *LGk.*, *LHeb.*, *LL*); Low (e.g., *LG*)
L, Lat.	Latin

LaFr.	Louisiana French
Lith.	Lithuanian
M	Medieval (e.g., *ML*); Middle (e.g., *ME*, *MFlem.*, *MHG*, *MLG*)
Maced.	Macedonian
Mal.	Malay
MexSp.	Mexican Spanish
Mod.	Modern (e.g., *ModE*)
Mong.	Mongolian
N	New (e.g., *NGk.*, *NHeb.*, *NL*); Norse
Norw.	Norwegian
O	Old (e.g., *OE*, *OFr.*, *OHG*, *ON*, *OProv.*, *OS*)
PaGer.	Pennsylvania German
Pek.	Pekingese
Per.	Persian
PhilSp.	Philippine Spanish
Pol.	Polish
Port.	Portuguese
Prov.	Provençal
Pruss.	Prussian
Rom.	Romanian
Russ.	Russian
S	Saxon
Scand.	Scandinavian
Scot.	Scottish
Sem.	Semitic
Serb.	Serbian
Skt.	Sanskrit
Slav.	Slavic
Sp.	Spanish
Swed.	Swedish

Syr.	Syriac
Tag.	Tagalog
Toch.	Tocharian
Turk.	Turkish
VL	Vulgar Latin
W	Welsh
WGmc.	West Germanic

────────────────── **8.8** ──────────────────

PROOFREADING SYMBOLS

Proofreading symbols with marginal corrections are used to correct proof. A list of proofreading symbols and a sample of their applications follow. The symbols are divided into two sections: those used in the text and those used in the margin. Every symbol used in the text requires a corresponding symbol or notation in the margin.

8.8.1   SYMBOLS USED IN THE TEXT

error|	Delete a character. The delete symbol is written in the margin.
errar	Replace a character. The correct character is written in the margin.
er ror	Close up a space. The symbol is repeated in the margin.
errｊor	Delete a character and close up. The delete-and-close-up symbol is written in the margin.
Love truth, but ~~but~~ pardon error.	Delete or replace more than one character. The delete symbol or the replacement copy is written in the margin.
Love truth~~uth~~, but pardon error.	Delete more than one character and close up. The delete-and-close-up symbol is written in the margin.

love truth, but pardon error.

> Capitalize or lowercase text. The abbreviation *cap* or *lc*, circled, is written in the margin.

Love truth, but pardon *error*.

> Italicize text or make it roman. The abbreviation *ital* or *rom*, circled, is written in the margin.

eror

> Insert text. The material to be inserted is written in the margin.

Love truth, but pardon error.

> Add a space. The space symbol is written in the margin.

error3/

> Set a letter or number as a superscript. The symbol is repeated in the margin.

Love truth, pardon but error.

> Transpose text. The abbreviation *tr*, circled, is written in the margin.

Love truth, but pardon error.

> Move a block of text. To indicate the new location, a line is drawn on the proof, or instructions are written in the margin.

2nd error

> Spell out a number or an abbreviation. The spelled form or the abbreviation *sp*, circled, is written in the margin.

8.8.2 SYMBOLS USED IN THE MARGIN

/
> separates corrections in the same line; indicates that a correction is to be made more than once

≡
> indicates that an addition is a capital letter (placed under letter)

=
> indicates that an addition is a small capital letter (placed under letter)

⎯
> indicates that an addition is italic (placed under characters)

Ø
> numeral 0, not capital letter O

⌢	close up
⌿	delete
⌿	delete and close up
(tr)	transpose
#	add a space
(more#)	add more space
(less #)	remove space
⊙	add a period
⌃	add a comma
:	add a colon
;	add a semicolon
∨	add an apostrophe or a single closing quotation mark
∨	add a single opening quotation mark
∜ ∜	add double quotation marks
( )	add parentheses
[ ]	add square brackets
/	add a slash
=	add a hyphen
⊥M	add a one-em dash
⊥N	add a one-en dash
(cap)	capitalize
(sc)	make into small capitals
(lc)	lowercase
(ital)	italicize
(rom)	make roman
(bf)	make boldface
(sp)	spell out
¶	begin a new paragraph
(no ¶)	remove a paragraph break, running sentences together
⌐	move to the left
⌐	move to the right

⌐‾‾¬	move up
∟__⌐	move down
‖	align vertically
(stet)	let stand as printed
(wf)	wrong font

8.8.3   SAMPLE MARKED PROOF

"Now, waht I want is Facts. Teach these boys and girls nothing but Facts. Facts alone are ard wanted in life. Plant nothing else, an'nd root out everything else. You can only form the minds reasoning of animals upon facts nothing else will ever be of any sevice to them. This is the principle on which I bring up my own up my own children, and this is the principle on which I bring up these children. Stick to the Facts, sir!

APPENDIX: SPECIALIZED STYLE MANUALS

Every scholarly field has its preferred style. MLA style, as presented in this manual, is widely accepted in humanities disciplines. The following manuals describe the styles of other disciplines.

BIBLICAL LITERATURE

Alexander, Patrick H., et al., eds. *The SBL Handbook of Style: For Ancient Near Eastern, Biblical, and Early Christian Studies.* Peabody: Hendrickson, 1999. Print.

CHEMISTRY

Coghill, Anne M., and Lorrin R. Garson, eds. *The ACS Style Guide: Effective Communication of Scientific Information.* 3rd ed. Washington: Amer. Chemical Soc., 2006. Print.

GEOLOGY

United States. Geological Survey. *Suggestions to Authors of the Reports of the United States Geological Survey.* 7th ed. Washington: GPO, 1991. Print, Web.

LAW

Association of Legal Writing Directors and Darby Dickerson. *ALWD Citation Manual: A Professional System of Citation.* 3rd ed. New York: Aspen, 2006. Print.

Harvard Law Review Association. *The Bluebook: A Uniform System of Citation.* 18th ed. Cambridge: Harvard Law Rev. Assn., 2005. Print.

LINGUISTICS

"Language Style Sheet." *Linguistic Society of America.* Linguistic Soc. of Amer., n.d. Web. 4 Apr. 2007.

MEDICINE

Iverson, Cheryl, et al. *AMA Manual of Style: A Guide for Authors and Editors.* 10th ed. New York: Oxford UP, 2007. Print.

PHYSICS

American Institute of Physics. *AIP Style Manual.* 4th ed. New York: Amer. Inst. of Physics, 1990. Print, Web.

POLITICAL SCIENCE

American Political Science Association. Committee on Publications. *Style Manual for Political Science.* 2nd rev. ed. Washington: Amer. Political Science Assn., 2006. Print.

PSYCHOLOGY

American Psychological Association. *Publication Manual of the American Psychological Association.* 5th ed. Washington: Amer. Psychological Assn., 2001. Print.

SCIENCE

Council of Science Editors. Style Manual Committee. *Scientific Style and Format: The CSE Manual for Authors, Editors, and Publishers.* 7th ed. Reston: Council of Science Eds., 2006. Print.

SOCIOLOGY

American Sociological Association. *ASA Style Guide.* 3rd ed. Washington: Amer. Sociological Assn., 2007. Print.

There are also style manuals that provide detailed guidance on procedures for preparing all kinds of manuscripts for publication.

The Chicago Manual of Style. 15th ed. Chicago: U of Chicago P, 2003. Print, Web.

Skillin, Marjorie E., et al. *Words into Type*. 3rd ed. Englewood Cliffs: Prentice, 1974. Print.

United States. Government Printing Office. *Style Manual*. 29th ed. Washington: GPO, 2000. CD-ROM, print, Web.

SOURCES OF
EXAMPLES IN 3.4–5

Page 86 — "Synonyms have": adapted from Frederic G. Cassidy, "Learning from Dictionaries" (*Language Variation in North American English: Research and Teaching*; ed. A. Wayne Glowka and Donald M. Lance; New York: MLA, 1993; 67; print).

Page 86 — "Inexpensive examples": Paula R. Feldman, "How Their Audiences Knew Them: Forgotten Media and the Circulation of Poetry by Women" (*Approaches to Teaching British Women Poets of the Romantic Period*; ed. Stephen C. Behrendt and Harriet Kramer Linkin; New York: MLA, 1997; 37; print; Approaches to Teaching World Lit. 60).

Page 86 — "Priests, conjurers": Thomas L. Clark, "Using Toponymic Onomastics in a Pedagogical Setting to Demonstrate Phonological Variation (An Essay on Names)" (*Language Variation in North American English: Research and Teaching*; ed. A. Wayne Glowka and Donald M. Lance; New York: MLA, 1993; 72; print).

Page 86 — "To some writers": adapted from William Costanzo, "Reading, Writing, and Thinking in an Age of Electronic Literacy" (*Literacy and Computers: The Complications of Teaching and Learning with Technology*; ed. Cynthia L. Selfe and Susan Hilligoss; New York: MLA, 1994; 16; print).

Page 86 — "Originally the plantations": adapted from Salikoko S. Mufwene, "Investigating Gullah: Difficulties in Ensuring 'Authenticity'" (*Language Variation in North American English: Research and Teaching*; ed. A. Wayne Glowka and Donald M. Lance; New York: MLA, 1993; 178; print).

Page 87 — "Perhaps the most ambitious": Jahan Ramazani, "The Wound of History: Walcott's *Omeros* and the Postcolonial Poetics of Affliction" (*PMLA* 112.3 [1997]: 406; print).

Page 87 — "For men": adapted from Karin A. Wurst, introduction (Adelheit von Rastenberg: *An English Translation*; by Eleonore Thon; trans. George F. Peters; New York: MLA, 1996; xxv; print; Texts and Trans. 4).

Page 87 — "The dialogue": Karin A. Wurst, introduction (Adelheit von Rastenberg: *An English Translation*; by Eleonore Thon; trans. George F. Peters; New York: MLA, 1996; vii; print; Texts and Trans. 4).

Page 87 — "A title": Lev Petrovich Yakubinsky, "On Dialogic Speech" (trans. Michael Eskin; *PMLA* 112.2 [1997]: 252; print).

Page 87 — "It is not": Angelika Bammer, letter (*PMLA* 111.5 [1996]: 1151; print).

Pages 87–88 — "Baron François-Pascal-Simon Gérard": Joan DeJean, introduction (Ourika: *An English Translation*; by Claire de Duras; trans. John Fowles; introd. DeJean and Margaret Waller; New York: MLA, 1994; viii–ix; print; Texts and Trans. 3).

Page 88 — "All these subjects": adapted from James Thorpe, introduction (*Relations of Literary Study: Essays on Interdisciplinary Contributions*; ed. Thorpe; New York: MLA, 1967; viii; print).

Page 88 — "A brief comparison": Karin A. Wurst, introduction (Adelheit von Rastenberg: *An English Translation*; by Eleonore Thon; trans. George F. Peters; New York: MLA, 1996; xvii; print; Texts and Trans. 4).

Page 88 — "After the separation": Joan DeJean, introduction (*Letters from a Peruvian Woman*; by Françoise de Graffigny; trans. David Kornacker; introd. DeJean and Nancy K. Miller; New York: MLA, 1993; x; print; Texts and Trans. 2).

Page 88 — "In this charged atmosphere": adapted from Philip Fisher, "American Literary and Cultural Studies since the Civil War" (*Redrawing the Boundaries: The Transformation of English and American Literary Studies*; ed. Stephen Greenblatt and Giles Gunn; New York: MLA, 1992; 233; print).

Page 89 — "When Zilia": Nancy K. Miller, introduction (*Letters from a Peruvian Woman*; by Françoise de Graffigny; trans. David Kornacker; introd. Joan DeJean and Miller; New York: MLA, 1993; xx; print; Texts and Trans. 2).

Page 89 — "Fin de siècle Spain": adapted from Joyce Tolliver, introduction (*"Torn Lace" and Other Stories*; by Emilia Pardo Bazán; trans. María Cristina Urruela; New York: MLA, 1996; xiv; print; Texts and Trans. 5).

Page 89 — "Sometimes this is where": Angelika Bammer, letter (*PMLA* 111.5 [1996]: 1151; print).

Page 89 — "Alexander Pope": adapted from John B. Vickery, "Literature and Myth" (*Interrelations of Literature*; ed. Jean-Pierre Barricelli and Joseph Gibaldi; New York: MLA, 1982; 69; print).

Page 89 — "What makes Sartre's theory": adapted from Matei Calinescu, "Literature and Politics" (*Interrelations of Literature*; ed. Jean-Pierre Barricelli and Joseph Gibaldi; New York: MLA, 1982; 135; print).

Page 89 — "In 1947": adapted from Harold B. Allen, "American English Enters Academe" (*Language Variation in North American English: Research and Teaching*; ed. A. Wayne Glowka and Donald M. Lance; New York: MLA, 1993; 6; print).

Page 89 — "Bakhtin's notion": adapted from Carrie Noland, "Poetry at Stake: Blaise Cendrars, Cultural Studies, and the Future of Poetry in the Literature Classroom" (*PMLA* 112.1 [1997]: 41; print).

Page 90 — "Miller has taken": adapted from Matthew C. Roudané, "Materials" (*Approaches to Teaching Miller's* Death of a Salesman; ed. Roudané; New York: MLA, 1995; 16; print; Approaches to Teaching World Lit. 52).

Page 90 — "In the afterlife": adapted from Paula Bennett, "Phillis Wheatley's Vocation and the Paradox of the 'Afric Muse'" (*PMLA* 113.1 [1998]: 71; print).

Page 90 — "From his darkness": adapted from Ann Paton, "*King Lear* in a Literature Survey Course" (*Approaches to Teaching Shakespeare's* King Lear; ed. Robert H. Ray; New York: MLA, 1986; 76; print; Approaches to Teaching World Lit. 12).

Page 90 — "The current political": adapted from Eric Gadzinski, "The Year of Living Dangerously; or, Not Just an Adventure, but a Job" (*ADE Bulletin* 117 [1997]: 35; print).

Page 91 — "Shelley remarks": adapted from Susan J. Wolfson, "Feminist Inquiry and *Frankenstein*" (*Approaches to Teaching Shelley's* Frankenstein; ed. Stephen C. Behrendt; New York: MLA, 1990; 59; print; Approaches to Teaching World Lit. 33).

Page 91 — "Thérèse, the washerwoman": adapted from Rosemarie Garland Thomson, "Speaking about the Unspeakable: The Representation of Disability as Stigma in Toni Morrison's Novels" (*Courage and Tools: The Florence Howe Award for Feminist Scholarship, 1974–1989*; ed. Joanne Glasgow and Angela Ingram; New York: MLA, 1990; 250; print).

Page 91 — "All five": adapted from Richard Pilgrim, "The *Tale of Genji* in a Religio-Aesthetic Perspective" (*Approaches to Teaching Murasaki Shikibu's* The Tale of Genji; ed. Edward Kamens; New York: MLA, 1993; 48; print; Approaches to Teaching World Lit. 47).

Page 91 — "As Emerson's friend": adapted from Joel Conarroe, introduction (*Introduction to Scholarship in Modern Languages and Literatures*; ed. Joseph Gibaldi; New York: MLA, 1981; xi; print).

Page 91 — "Most such standards": Paul Hernadi, "Literary Theory" (*Introduction to Scholarship in Modern Languages and Literatures*; ed. Joseph Gibaldi; New York: MLA, 1981; 110; print).

Page 92 — "Atwood's other visual art": Thomas B. Friedman and Shannon Hengen, "Materials" (*Approaches to Teaching Atwood's* The Handmaid's Tale and Other Works; ed. Sharon R. Wilson, Friedman, and Hengen; New York: MLA, 1996; 15; print; Approaches to Teaching World Lit. 56).

Page 92 — "The new art relation": adapted from Jon D. Green, "Determining Valid Interart Analogies" (*Teaching Literature and Other Arts*; ed. Jean-Pierre Barricelli, Joseph Gibaldi, and Estella Lauter; New York: MLA, 1990; 10; print).

Page 92 — "The human race": Linda Kauffman, "Special Delivery: Twenty-First-Century Epistolarity in *The Handmaid's Tale*" (*Courage and Tools: The Florence Howe Award for Feminist Scholarship, 1974–1989*; ed. Joanne Glasgow and Angela Ingram; New York: MLA, 1990; 234; print).

Page 93 — "Most newcomers": adapted from Thomas L. Clark, "Using Toponymic Onomastics in a Pedagogical Setting to Demonstrate Phonological Variation (An Essay on Names)" (*Language Variation in North American English: Research and Teaching*; ed. A. Wayne Glowka and Donald M. Lance; New York: MLA, 1993; 73; print).

Page 93 — "Whether we locate": adapted from Annette Kolodny, "Dancing through the Minefield: Some Observations on the Theory, Practice, and Politics of a Feminist Literary Criticism" (*Courage and Tools: The Florence Howe Award for Feminist Scholarship, 1974–1989*; ed. Joanne Glasgow and Angela Ingram; New York: MLA, 1990; 95; print).

Page 97 — "Teachers often": adapted from Teresa Vilardi, "Bard College: Freshman Workshop in Language and Thinking" (*New Methods in College Writing Programs: Theories in Practice*; ed. Paul Connolly and Vilardi; New York: MLA, 1986; 8; print).

Page 97 — "Baillie relies": Andrea Henderson, "Passion and Fashion in Jo-anna Baillie's 'Introductory Discourse'" (*PMLA* 112.2 [1997]: 208; print).

Page 97 — "One commentator": adapted from Neil ten Kortenaar, "Beyond Authenticity and Creolization: Reading Achebe Writing Culture" (*PMLA* 110.1 [1995]: 41; print).

Page 97 — "From its inception": adapted from Stephen Barker, "The Crisis of Authenticity: *Death of a Salesman* and the Tragic Muse" (*Approaches to Teaching Miller's* Death of a Salesman; ed. Matthew C. Roudané; New York: MLA, 1995; 82; print; Approaches to Teaching World Lit. 52).

Page 97 — "During the Meiji period": adapted from John Whittier Treat, "Beheaded Emperors and the Absent Figure in Contemporary Japanese Literature" (*PMLA* 109.1 [1994]: 106; print).

Page 97 — "In a 1917 letter": Richard Heinemann, "Kafka's Oath of Service: 'Der Bau' and the Dialectic of Bureaucratic Mind" (*PMLA* 111.2 [1996]: 257; print).

Page 98 — "The editor": adapted from Francis I. Andersen, "The Hebrew Bible (Old Testament)" (*Scholarly Editing: A Guide to Research*; ed. D. C. Greetham; New York: MLA, 1995; 47; print).

Page 98 — "The essay": adapted from Joseph A. Boone, "Vacation Cruises; or, The Homoerotics of Orientalism" (*PMLA* 110.1 [1995]: 103; print).

Page 98 — "The class": adapted from Wendy Steiner, "Literature and Paint-ing" (*Teaching Literature and Other Arts*; ed. Jean-Pierre Barricelli, Joseph Gibaldi, and Estella Lauter; New York: MLA, 1990; 42; print).

Page 100 — "The exercise": adapted from Mary Fuller and Donald A. Daiker, "Miami University: Freshman Composition Program" (*New Methods in College Writing Programs: Theories in Practice*; ed. Paul Connolly and Teresa Vilardi; New York: MLA, 1986; 80; print).

INDEX